New Worlds

A Course in Guided Composition, with Reading and Conversation

Florence Baskoff

New York University
The American Language Institute

HH Heinle & Heinle Publishers ■ Boston
A Division of Wadsworth, Inc.

CREDITS

The previous editions of this book were published under the title *Guided Composition*.

The authors and editors would like to thank the following authors and publishers for granting permission to use copyrighted material:

"Be a Clown," from *OffBeat Careers: 50 Ways to Avoid Being a Lawyer* by Al Sacharov (Word of Mouth Press, 1985) pp. 26–27. Copyright © Al Sacharov, 1985. Reprinted by permission of the author.

"War of the Worlds," from *The Panic Broadcast* by Howard Koch (Little Brown and Company, 1970). Copyright © Howard Koch, 1940. Reprinted by permission of the author.

"A Dry Martini and Double-Nut Mocha," by Gautam Adhikari, *New York Times* (January 15, 1988): p. A31. Copyright © 1988 by The New York Times Company. Reprinted by permission.

"Robo-Home," by Lori Nelson, *The West Side Spirit* (December 7, 1987): cover, page 5 +. Reprinted by permission of *The West Side Spirit*.

"How to Call a Waiter," from *The How-to Book* by John Malone. Copyright © 1985. Reprinted by permission of Facts On File, Inc., New York.

"A Day in the Life of an NYU Interpreter," by Candace Broecker, *Access* 3, No 1 (Fall/Winter 1987; published by the Henry and Lucy Moses Center for Students with Disabilities): p. 3. Reprinted by permission of the author.

Selections from *Guinness Book of World Records 1989*, David A. Boehm, ed. (New York: Sterling Publishing Co., Inc., 1989). Copyright © 1988 Guinness Publishing Limited. Reprinted by permission.

"Why I Love—and Hate Blind Dates," by Robert Masello, *Mademoiselle* (August 1982): p.122. Reprinted by permission of the author.

"How TV Americanizes Immigrants . . . for Better or Worse," by Susan Littwin, *TV Guide* (April 9, 1988): p. 4. Reprinted with permission from TV Guide® Magazine. Copyright © 1988 by News America Publications Inc., Radnor, Pennsylvania.

Selections from *In One Day* by Tom Parker. Copyright © 1984 by Tom Parker. Reprinted by permission of Houghton Mifflin Company.

Free To Be . . . a Family by Marlo Thomas & Friends, (Bantam Books, 1987). Copyright © 1987 by Free to Be Foundation, Inc. Reprinted by permission of Bantam Books, a division of Bantam, Doubleday, Dell Publishing Group, Inc.

Credits for other texts, and for photos, illustrations, and realia, may be found at the end of the book.

Cover Photograph By © Spencer Grant/Photo Researchers, Inc.

Heinle & Heinle Publishers is a division of Wadsworth, Inc.

Manufactured in the United States of America.

ISBN 0-8384-1702-7 (Instructor's Annotated Edition)
ISBN 0-8384-1670-5 (Student's Edition)

10 9 8 7

Contents

Preface

To the Student

The main purpose of this book is to teach you how to write English by giving you a lot of practice in this skill. In addition, the book will improve your listening, speaking, and reading skills. It also aims to help you learn how to communicate better in English by giving you a better knowledge of the structures of the language and by letting you apply this working knowledge through many listening, speaking, reading, and writing exercises.

Each lesson deals with a high-interest topic that you will learn to read about, talk about, and write about. Most of the exercises and activities in the lesson relate to this topic. You will be constantly interacting with your fellow students in oral and written activities, and you will soon find your vocabulary, and your listening, speaking, and writing abilities increasing even before you start writing your compositions.

The writing portion of each lesson is planned not only to help you learn the mechanics (the ability to spell, punctuate, and follow grammatical rules) but also to help you gain a degree of competence in your writing. The topic of each composition is always something that you would be familiar with through personal experience or knowledge. The model composition and an outline will show you how to organize it. In addition, the model composition and the previous exercises and activities in the lesson will help you learn the necessary words, phrases, and sentences.

By engaging in prewriting activities and by learning how to follow the models, you will keep your errors to a minimum and are less likely to become discouraged. You will soon find that you are learning how to write in an organized and understandable manner and gaining more confidence in your writing ability. The task of learning how to read, speak, and write is made as pleasant as possible.

The lessons in *New Worlds* are each divided into a number of parts, as explained in the following subsections.

Opener

The opener will give you a preview of what the lesson is about through one or two questions that you will discuss with your classmates. These will get you thinking about the topic.

Dialogues

Each lesson has at least two dialogue exercises to be practiced with a partner or in a small group. The first one is usually more guided and relates to the illustrations at the start of the lesson. Most of the elements in the dialogue are provided for you. The second dialogue gives you and your partner/partners the opportunity to be more creative and to express your own ideas. These dialogues will help you learn how to use the spoken language in everyday situations and conversations.

Reading

Every lesson has a short, interesting reading, usually taken from a newspaper or a magazine, with a glossed vocabulary, so that you won't have to stop and look up words. The topics have a cultural orientation and informational value. Not only will you find the reading entertaining and informative, but you will also be increasing your vocabulary and cultural understanding. These short readings will prepare you for longer, more advanced readings.

The discussion questions that follow each reading are not a quiz to find out whether you understood the reading. Instead, they are "think" questions, which require you to express your own ideas, thoughts, opinions, and knowledge of the reading theme. Working with your fellow classmates, you will come to better understand different cultures and personal values and learn to organize your thoughts and speak more freely.

The prewriting task may in part be oral, but it will also include some sort of writing activity—listing, outlining, and so on. This activity will help you go from the reading selection to the composition activity smoothly.

Model Composition

Each model composition shows how to use some particular structure or structures in the English language. The model compositions in the early lessons are simple, and then gradually, they become more complex as you learn how to write. Read and study each model composition carefully. You can use it as a guide in organizing your own composition, and it will give you many of the vocabulary words and phrases that you may need to write your composition. Try to read the model composition aloud so that you can hear the rhythm and intonation of the words, phrases, and sentences in a connected discourse.

The Elements of Style, a section that appears in some lessons, calls attention to the writing style used in the model composition for those lessons.

Structure

Each lesson closes with a "structure box," which consists of a short explanation of a particular grammatical structure or structures and examples. These structures either appear in the model composition or in the exercises that follow to give you practice in using them.

Exercises

All of the lessons contain exercises to be done with a partner or in groups. These will help you practice expressing your ideas in a group of your fellow classmates as preparation for writing your own individual composition.

Dictation/Dicto-Comp

The dictations and dicto-comps will improve your listening skills at the same time as they give you additional practice in writing in a connected-discourse style. In addition, the dicto-comps will give you practice in taking notes and in reconstructing a paragraph based on your listening comprehension and note-taking ability.

Outline and Composition Writing

The outline near the end of the lesson is the outline of the model composition. It gives you the skeleton organization for the composition you are going to write. You *must* follow this outline and the model when you write your own composition. The outline will organize your own writing, and the model composition will give you necessary words, phrases, and structures. You will write about your own ideas, facts, and experience, but you *must* stay within the framework of the outline. In some lessons, you will be asked to write your own outline. As you progress, you will be able to write more freely, but always following the outline.

Handbook

In the back of the book, you will find a short Handbook that will give you additional help in understanding the structure of English and in learning how to write compositions and letters. Furthermore, the Handbook will help you improve your ability to write in different rhetorical styles.

Quizzes

In the back of the book, you will also find quizzes based on the model composition. These quizzes will help you check yourself to see whether you have really learned the prepositions and verb forms used in the model composition.

If you follow the model composition and outline and complete the exercises in each lesson, you should have very few errors in your compositions. Before long, if you use the book correctly and follow the instructions, you will find that you can communicate better.

Remember, learning how to read, speak and write in a second language takes constant practice. You can do it!

To the Instructor

New Worlds is a textbook for students of English as a Second or Foreign Language at the advanced-beginning through intermediate levels. It is written in the belief that a holistic approach to learning a second language will greatly enhance a student's ability to read, speak, and write in that language. Since the book is interactively student-centered throughout, there will be a constant exchange of cultural values and understanding as students work together to complete the exercises. Through the use of dialogues, readings, and discussions as prewriting activities, you will find that what was once only internalized or passive knowledge will soon start to appear in the students' speaking and writing.

The text reflects the belief that students can start writing in coherent and connected paragraphs at an early stage of second-language learning if proper sequencing is followed and if the writing activity is combined with prewriting activities involving listening, speaking, and reading so that all four skills are reinforced.

Acknowledgments

The author and publisher would like to thank the following people for their comments and recommendations on the previous edition of this text *(Guided Composition)* and on manuscript for this new edition.

Roberta Alexander, Centre City Continuing Education Center, California.   Richard Applebaum, Broward Community College, Florida.   Donna M. Brinton, University of California, Los Angeles.   Mary Christie, Pine Manor College, Massachusetts.   Ramón Díaz, Community College of Philadelphia, Pennsylvania. Davene El-Khayyat, Arizona Western College, Arizona.   Miriam Jupp, Palomar Community College, California.   Jewel Keusder, Cypress College, California. Paula Kroonen, College of the Desert, California.   Alfred McDowell, Bergen Community College, New Jersey.   Richard Nuzzo, Clark County Community College, Nevada.   Linda Righi, Walsh College, Ohio.   Marcia Sola, University of Dubuque, Iowa.   Barbara Schwarte, Iowa State University, Iowa.   Glenn Tracy, Phillips University, Oklahoma.   William C. VanderWerf, City College of San Francisco, California.   Nancy Whichard, George Washington University, Washington D.C.   Martha Yaeger García, Cerritos Community College, California.

The author would like to thank her colleagues at The American Language Institute and especially Helen Harper, Helen Mintz, and Neil Williams for their support and encouragement. She would also like to thank Elana Mintz for her composition "On Being the Youngest."

PRELIMINARY
LESSON

Writing Paragraphs

Paragraph Form

A paragraph is a group of sentences that talks about only one idea. We call this idea the *topic* of the paragraph. It is necessary to understand the organization of a paragraph in English in order to write in a meaningful way.

It sometimes helps to think of a paragraph as a sandwich. The top and bottom layers (the first and last sentences) are general statements about the topic, and the filling (the middle sentences) has statements of facts and examples. The top and bottom layers tie the paragraph together.

The first line of every paragraph is indented, as in this section on paragraph form. This means that the first line begins a little farther to the right than the other lines of the paragraph.

Writing Mechanics

1. Put a title at the top center of the page.
2. Indent each paragraph.
3. Capitalize the first word of every sentence.
4. Put a period, question mark, or exclamation point at the end of every sentence.
5. Write on the lines.

Note how the following paragraph has been written according to the rules listed in "Writing Mechanics."

Foreign Language Study in the U.S.

Students in the United States usually study a foreign language both in high school and in college. The six leading languages studied are Spanish, French, German, Italian, Russian and Latin. Recently, there has been a big increase in the number of students studying Japanese and Chinese. In addition to these eight languages, schools offer over a hundred other languages.

Parallel Paragraphs

In this section, you will learn to write short descriptive paragraphs in English following a model. These similar paragraphs are what is meant by parallel paragraphs.

A.   Read the following description of Michael Brown:

Michael Brown is a student at Stanford University. He is 5 feet 6 inches tall, and he weighs 160 pounds. He has straight black hair and dark eyes. He is studying economics because he hopes to become an economist.

Now write a similar description of (1) Robert Jones, (2) Mary Carlson, (3) Tom O'Neill, (4) Elizabeth Day, and (5) yourself. Use the pronoun *I* in your description of yourself. Use *he* to refer to Robert Jones and Tom O'Neill and *she* to refer to Mary Carlson and Elizabeth Day.

1.   Robert Jones—the University of Virginia—6 feet—180 pounds—short brown hair—hazel eyes—medicine—doctor

_____

_____

_____

_____

2.   Mary Carlson—Colorado State University—5 feet 6 inches—120 pounds—long blonde hair—blue eyes—engineering—engineer

_____

_____

_____

_____

3.   Tom O'Neill—the University of Wisconsin—5 feet 10 inches—175 pounds—curly red hair—light blue eyes—law—lawyer

_____

_____

_____

_____

4.   Elizabeth Day—Radcliffe College—5 feet 2 inches—110 pounds—dark brown hair—green eyes—chemistry—chemist

_____

_____

_____

_____

5. (yourself)

_____

_____

_____

_____

B. Write a sentence following the examples for each of the fields of study and professions listed below. Be sure to change the pronoun to *she* for females.

He is studying education because he hopes to become a teacher.

She is studying law because she hopes to become a lawyer.

Field of study	*Profession*
business administration	businessman/businesswoman
computer programming	computer programmer
fashion design	fashion designer
art	artist
physics	physicist
psychology	psychologist

C. Look at the accompanying chart and familiarize yourself with the information about José Muñoz. Note: *(M)* = "male," *(F)* = "female."

Name	José Muñoz (M)	Silvia Pizano (F)	Mariko Yamada (F)	Classmate	Yourself
Country	Mexico	Italy	Japan		
Language	Spanish	Italian	Japanese		
Brothers	three	two	none (0)		
Sisters	none (0)	two	none (0)		
Hobby	collecting post cards	painting with oils	photography		
Sport	baseball	swimming	skiing		
Music	Latin music	jazz	classical music		
Weekends	go to movies	watch TV	go to concerts		

Now read the following description of José Muñoz and note how the information from the chart was used in the paragraph.

José Muñoz was born in Mexico, so his native language is Spanish. He has three brothers and no sisters. His favorite hobby is collecting post cards, and his favorite sport is baseball. He also enjoys listening to Latin music. On weekends, he likes to go to the movies.

Write a similar paragraph about Silvia Pizano and Mariko Yamada using information from the chart. Be sure to change the pronoun to *she* for females.

1. _____

_____

_____

_____

_____

_____

2. _____

_____

_____

_____

_____

D. Pair off with another student in your class and ask him/her the following questions. Fill in the answers on the chart accompanying the preceding exercise and let your instructor check the answers.

1. Where were you born?
2. What is your native language?
3. How many brothers do you have?
4. How many sisters do you have?
5. What is your favorite hobby?
6. What is your favorite sport?
7. What kind of music do you enjoy listening to?
8. What do you like to do on weekends?

E. Write a paragraph about your classmate using the answers from the chart accompanying Exercise C and following the model paragraph on José Muñoz. Use the pronoun *she* for females.

_____(classmate's name)

_____

_____

_____

_____

_____

F. Fill in the chart with information about yourself, and then write a paragraph about yourself. Use the pronoun *I*.

_____(*your name*)

_____

_____

_____

_____

_____

G. Write a sentence following the example for each of the countries and native languages listed below. Be sure to change the pronoun to *she* for females.

He/She was born in France, so his/her native language is French.

Country	Native language
Colombia	Spanish
Brazil	Portuguese
England	English
Saudi Arabia	Arabic
Germany	German
Korea	Korean
Taiwan	Chinese

1. _____

2. _____

3. _____

4. _____

5. _____

6. _____

The Weather

United States Cities

Following are the highest and lowest temperatures for the 15 hours ended 3 P.M. (E.S.T.) yesterday and expected conditions for today and tomorrow.

Weather conditions: C–cloudy, F–fog, H–haze, I–ice, PC–partly cloudy, R–rain, Sr–showers, S–sunny, Sn–snow, T–thunderstorms.

Cities	Yesterday	Today		Tomorrow	
Albany	28/3	45/20	S	46/33	PC
Anchorage	16/9	24/16	Sn	25/18	C
Atlanta	48/27	52/41	Sr	61/45	R
Chicago	43/32	41/36	R	38/34	C
Denver	44/26	46/15	PC	37/16	PC
Detroit	46/27	42/35	R	42/35	PC
Honolulu	74/69	83/67	S	82/67	S
Houston	61/48	71/60	T	71/51	C
Kansas City	54/41	40/32	C	43/28	C
Las Vegas	53/37	54/30	Sr	54/36	PC
Los Angeles	59/48	58/50	R	58/46	C
Miami	72/56	72/56	PC	80/66	PC
New Orleans	62/41	67/57	C	70/56	T
Oklahoma City	60/41	50/34	C	56/36	S
Portland, Ore.	41/37	42/34	Sr	43/32	Sr
St. Louis	52/35	48/40	R	45/33	C

Data compiled by WSI, from National Weather Service Observations and Forecast.

---

*I*n many parts of the United States, people listen closely to news reports. They want to find out what the weather will be for the day. They want to know what to wear, what outdoor activities they can do, what trips they can take. People often place weather thermometers outside a window. In this way, they can always be sure about the daily temperature.

A.   Imagine that today is January 17. Work with a partner and choose five U.S. cities listed in the weather chart. First, write the names of these cities and their highest and lowest temperatures today and yesterday. Then, alternate asking each other questions about temperatures in these cities.

| | Temperature today | | Temperature yesterday | |
U.S. cities	Highest	Lowest	Highest	Lowest
1. _____	_____	_____	_____	_____
2. _____	_____	_____	_____	_____
3. _____	_____	_____	_____	_____
4. _____	_____	_____	_____	_____
5. _____	_____	_____	_____	_____

S1: What's the *lowest* temperature in *Chicago* today?
S2: It's *36°*.
S1: What was the *highest* temperature in *Chicago* yesterday?
S2: It was *43°*.

B. Find a partner and role-play the following situation:

You have just picked up a friend at the airport. The friend is returning from one of the cities listed in the weather chart. Ask about weather conditions there for today and for tomorrow.

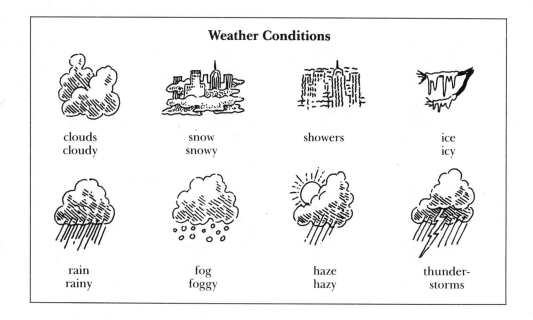

Weather Conditions

clouds / cloudy   snow / snowy   showers   ice / icy

rain / rainy   fog / foggy   haze / hazy   thunder-storms

S1: How's the weather in Los Angeles today?
S2: It's raining.
S1: What's the weather forecast for tomorrow?
S2: There will be clouds tomorrow. / It will be cloudy.

C. Sentence Combining   Combining sentences or parts of sentences will improve your style. Look at the weather chart and write a report about the weather today and tomorrow in the following cities. If the weather today and tomorrow is the same, combine the information using *and.* If the weather is different, use *but.*

> It is cloudy in Kansas City today, and it will be the same tomorrow.
>
> It is cloudy in New Orleans today, but there will be thunderstorms tomorrow.

1. Chicago _____

2. Los Angeles _____

3. Honolulu _____

4. Denver _____

5. Albany _____

READING

The Weather and You

Do you become unhappy when clouds appear? Are you more cheerful on a sunny day than on a rainy day? Does the weather really affect° your moods?

Most of us feel that stormy weather makes us sad, and many psychologists would agree: rain or snow *can* bring on sadness and depression° in some people. This feeling may be caused by having to stay indoors for too long during bad weather. But there are some people who are unusually sensitive° to weather. Rather than just feeling blue on a cold, dreary° day, for example, they actually find it difficult to carry out their daily routine. Even going to work or to school becomes a big job for these people. Some people also become very depressed during the dark days of winter. They suffer from a sickness called "seasonal affective disorder," or SAD. Doctors think this condition is due to lack° of sunlight.

In contrast, a sunny day, particularly during the winter in colder northern regions, can make people feel happy and optimistic.° When the weather is pleasant, people are friendlier and more willing to help each other. For example, it has been found that customers give waitresses bigger tips° on sunny days. But when the weather is too hot and humid, people tend to° become more aggressive.°

It shouldn't surprise you to learn that most people prefer moderate temperatures somewhere in the seventies, perhaps with a slight breeze.° People generally don't like too much wind, nor do they like it when the temperature changes more than fifteen degrees in a short period of time. Naturally, every-

cause some result or change

great sadness

feeling the effect of something strongly / sad, dull

absence

feeling hopeful or happy about life

small amounts of money paid for a service / usually

always ready to quarrel or fight

light wind

one enjoys sunny days, but after too many bright, cheerful days in a row,° even   **one after the other**
sunshine can lose its appeal. People look forward to a change of weather from
time to time.

The weather's powerful effect on us can be seen in the many weather-
related expressions found in our language. In English, you can be hot-blooded,°   **easily angered**
have a stormy° relationship, give someone a cold shoulder,° or have a sunny   **very changeable / act in an
disposition.°   unfriendly way toward
                                                                                     someone / happy
                                                                                     personality**

D.   Be prepared to answer the following questions.

  1. Are you sensitive to the weather? If so, why do you think so?
  2. How do you feel during cold weather?
  3. How do you feel during hot weather?
  4. What kind of weather do you like best?
  5. Do people in your country behave in different ways according to the
       weather? How do they behave?
  6. How do you think a country's economic or social conditions are
       affected by the weather?

E.   In English, *It's raining cats and dogs* means that it is raining very heavily.
         Work with a partner and discuss the following questions about weather
         expressions.

  1. Do you have an expression in your country for a heavy rain?
  2. Do you have a special expression for any other kind of weather?
  3. Do you know any other English expressions about weather?

MODEL COMPOSITION

The Weather in Boston

There are four seasons in Boston: winter, spring, summer, and autumn. In
the winter it is often very cold and windy, and in the summer it is sometimes
very hot and humid. The weather in the spring and autumn, however, is usually
very pleasant. For many people, these are the two best seasons of the year
because they are the only times the climate is comfortable. Boston is a city where
the weather often changes every few hours during the whole year. People like
to say, "If you don't like the weather now, wait a while." There is one thing that
is certain about Boston weather. It seldom stays the same.

F.   Write five sentences describing the weather in the country you come from. Use as many of the following adverbs of frequency as possible in your sentences.

always	often	occasionally	hardly ever
generally	frequently	seldom	never
usually	sometimes	rarely	

1. _____

2. _____

3. _____

4. _____

5. _____

G.   ***Dictation / Dicto-Comp***   Listen to your instructor dictate the following paragraph. Then follow his/her directions.

   San Francisco is a naturally air-conditioned city. There is fresh air all year round. The summers are cool and the winters are mild. The sun shines most of the time, but it sometimes rains between November and March. It is often foggy in the morning from May to August, but it clears up in the afternoon. The evenings are cool and comfortable. Flowers bloom throughout the year. The wonderful climate is one reason why San Francisco is the tourist's favorite city.

H.   Prepare an *oral composition* about the weather in the city you come from. Follow the sentence patterns in the model composition, and answer the following questions about your city.

Oral Composition: The Weather in _____

1. How many seasons are there in your city?
2. What are the names of the seasons?
3. How is the weather in each season?
4. What is the best season of the year? Why?
5. Is there anything certain about the weather in your city? What is it?

COMPOSITION   WRITING

I.   Write a paragraph about "The Weather in My City" following the model composition and your answers to the questions in Exercise H. Be sure to use correct paragraph form and to indent the first sentence.

S T R U C T U R E

There is / There are

In English, the usual word order for a statement sentence is *subject + verb*. The subject and verb must agree.

> The sun is bright. The people are happy. It is a fine day.
> S + V   S + V   S + V

An exception to this rule of word order is the use of *there is* and *there are* at the beginning of a sentence followed by a *noun* and a *place*.

> There is ice on the road. There are many accidents on the road.
> V + S   V + S

In these sentences, the subject follows the verb and must agree with the verb. The word *there* has no meaning in these sentences. It is used to introduce the verb and is called an *expletive*.

Adverbs of Frequency

Adverbs of frequency tell you how often something happens. Adverbs of frequency usually go before the main verb in a sentence, except for the verb *to be*. They go after the verb *to be*. The following scale shows the approximate frequency indicated by some common adverbs.

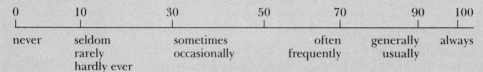

0	10	30	50	70	90	100
never	seldom rarely hardly ever	sometimes occasionally		often frequently	generally usually	always

> It *often* rains in summer. It is *seldom* sunny.

LESSON 2

We Are What We Do: Working

Pizza parlor

Shoe store

Restaurant

Diner

*I*n the United States, when you meet someone for the first time, he or she will probably ask you, "What do you do?" What a person does for a living is more important than his or her family or background. Americans like to talk about their jobs. As you read this lesson, think about workers and professionals that you know. What do they do on their jobs? Do they like what they do? Why or why not?

13

A.   Find a partner and role-play the following situation:

You work in one of the four places shown in the drawings at the start of this lesson. Your boss doesn't like the way you do your job. You tell a friend about your problem, and he/she suggests a solution.

Start by practicing the model dialogue. Then create your own dialogue, based on the drawings, using phrases from the lists that follow. Be sure to alternate roles.

S1: How's your job at *the pizza parlor?*
S2: *Not so hot. My boss is complaining.*
S1: How come?
S2: *Every time I toss the pizza up, it falls on the floor.*
S1: That's too bad. *I guess you ought to get glasses.*

Expression of dissatisfaction
My boss is dissatisfied.
My boss is angry with me.
My boss is upset.

Problem
Every time a customer tries on shoes, I put them on the wrong foot.
Every time I serve coffee, I spill it on someone.
Every time I make toast, I burn it.

Advice
I guess you'd better look for another job.
I guess you should change jobs.
Why don't you change jobs?

B.   In the United States, every state has a free State Employment Agency where an unemployed person can go to look for a job. Work with a partner and role-play the following situation. After your interview, exchange roles.

You are at the agency and are looking for a part-time job. You don't know what kind of job you want. The interviewer asks about your education, work experience, training, special abilities, language ability, immigration status, and so on. The interviewer ends the interview by suggesting a job for you.

Useful expressions	*Possible jobs*
Do you know how . . .	Waiter/Waitress
How much experience / training . . .	Typist
Can you / Are you able to . . .	Security guard
I think you could . . .	Messenger
	Salesperson
	Taxicab driver

READING

*C. **Prereading***   In this lesson, you will read about the professional training of a clown. First, look at the illustrations that show some things that a clown does in his/her job. Work with a partner and alternate asking about and describing what a clown does when he/she juggles, walks on stilts, and so forth. Begin your questions with *What does a clown do when he/she . . . ?*

to walk on stilts   to do slapstick   to juggle   to slide on a banana peel   to ride a unicycle   to walk the wire

Be a Clown

Almost every class has at least one class clown, and many teachers would like to send their class clown to a class for clowns. For teachers who feel this way, there is hope. They can send their clown to school at the winter home in Florida of the Ringling Brothers Circus.

Admission to the school, however, takes more than just sliding on a banana peel.° It is not necessary to have prior° clown experience, but an applicant to Clown College must be at least seventeen years old and send in a creative admission application. The application must answer questions like, "List five movies you would like to see again," and "When was the last time you cried and for what reason?" The college wants to find out about a person's soul as well as his brain. The Dean° of Clown College says that the most important asset° an applicant can have is the desire to be a good clown and a willingness to devote° oneself to the profession. It helps if you know how to juggle, but that is not necessary.

Every year the college admits sixty students for a course that takes ten and a half weeks. There is no tuition,° but the students must pay for their own room and board° during the training period. More than two dozen professional performers teach classes and give the students a thorough° knowledge of how to be a clown.

the outside skin of a banana / earlier, previous

person in charge of a college / something that has value / spend a great deal of time

money paid for a course

housing and food

complete in every way

Students-in-training help create their own routines and experiment in the makeup room to find out their best greasepaint° personality. During this time the clowns-in-training study juggling, wire walking, unicycling, slapstick, mime,° stiltwalking, and improvisation.° The students must pay attention to their comic timing° and to their safety techniques.

paint used by entertainers on their faces

(short for *pantomime*) using actions silently to show meaning / making up an act as one is playing a role /sense of when to say or do something for a comic effect

Graduation is a big event with all new clowns performing their acts. However, only about twenty of the students are actually hired to become part of the Ringling Brothers Circus, called "The Greatest Show on Earth." Those clowns who are hired have to go through three more years of training before they are considered master clowns. Those who are not hired can become performers at children's parties and on television shows.

A clown's life with the Ringling Brothers Circus is not easy. The circus travels to different cities for eleven months of the year and during this time the performers sleep on the circus train. The circus clowns must pay for their own meals and also a monthly charge to stay on the train.

If you don't mind constant traveling, you will love the work of a clown. The Dean of Clown College says, "Money can't buy the satisfaction you get. If you're good, you can spend a lifetime making people happy."

How many other professions can say that?

Adapted from Al Sacharov, *OffBeat Careers: 50 Ways to Avoid Being a Lawyer* (Yonkers, N.Y.: Word of Mouth Press, 1985), pp. 26–27.

D. Be prepared to discuss the following questions based on the reading.

1. Would you like to be a clown? Why or why not?
2. What three movies would you like to see again? Why?
3. When was the last time you cried and for what reason?
4. What did you want to be when you were a child? What do boys and girls in your country today want to be when they grow up?
5. How would you answer the last sentence in the reading?
6. Who is our class clown?

E. Work with a partner and answer the following questions. Take notes on your partner's answers. Then compare notes to make sure you understand correctly. Be prepared to give a class report on your partner's answer to question 5.

1. How does a person choose a career in your country? (school counseling, parent advice, government decision, other ways)

   _____

2. How does a person get a job in your country? (advertisement, family connections, through a friend, other ways)

   _____

3. How often do people change jobs or careers in your country? (never, once or twice, often)

   _____

4. How do people get a promotion in their jobs? (seniority, merit, family connections, other ways)

_____

5. What things are most important to you in a job? (good pay, opportunity to meet people, exciting work, other reasons)

_____

MODEL COMPOSITION

What Am I?

I usually go to work by limousine or taxi. I start work at different times, and I sometimes have to work nights, holidays, and weekends. I never start and finish my work in the same place unless I am on a shuttle run. Before I go to work, I put on my uniform. If I go overseas, I usually take a small bag with me because I have a twenty-four- to thirty-hour layover before my return flight. Then I am off for a few days.

My work is usually pleasant and sometimes exciting because it takes me all over the world. I meet all kinds of people and talk to everyone. I try to make everyone comfortable and give special attention to elderly and handicapped passengers and to children traveling alone. I know how to give first aid and what to do in case of a hijacking, bomb threat, or forced landing. I also show people what to do in case of an emergency. During mealtimes, I serve the passengers food, and I always ask, "Coffee or tea?" When the plane lands, I assist passengers as they leave the plane.

F. Work with a partner and write the sentences below, substituting the word *unless* for the words *if . . . not.*

1. A doctor can't practice if he doesn't have a license.

_____

2. The dentist won't pull your tooth if it isn't necessary.

_____

3. You can't get a good job if you don't have training or experience.

_____

4. The teacher is always on time if the weather isn't bad.

_____

5. You shouldn't be a veterinarian if you don't like animals.

_____

G. *Describing What Someone Does for Work*   Complete the following description with the correct form of the verb in parentheses. Use the simple present tense.

Ms. X _____ (get up) at 7:00 every morning.

It _____ (take) her about half an hour to get ready.

She _____ (leave) home at 7:30 and

_____ (drive) to work. She _____

(arrive) at her office at about 8:00 A.M. and _____

(start) to work. At 1:00 P.M., she usually_____ (eat)

lunch, and she sometimes _____ (take) a fifteen-

minute break in the afternoon. She usually _____

(leave) for home at 5:00 P.M.

Ms. X _____ (enjoy) her job very much because

she _____ (help) people with their problems and

_____ (advise) them. She _____ (try) to

be helpful to everyone. She _____ always

_____ (work—*negative*) in her office because she often

_____ (have to) be in court to defend somebody. Ms. X

_____ (have) a good reputation, and people

_____ (respect) her. Her purpose in life

_____ (be) to serve justice and to defend everyone's

rights. Ms. X is a lawyer.

H. *Dictation / Dicto-Comp*   Listen to your instructor dictate the following and then follow his/her directions.

I usually go to work by subway and get to work by 8:00 A.M. Before I start my job, I put on my uniform and look at myself in the mirror to make sure that I look neat. At 8:30 in the morning, I go on duty. I usually eat lunch from 12:00 to 1:00 and generally take a fifteen-minute break in the morning and in the afternoon. At 4:30 in the afternoon, I go off duty.

I enjoy my job very much because I meet all kinds of people. Many people ask me questions, and I give them the necessary information. I try to be very helpful, and I always call out floors very clearly. I never stay in one place long. On the contrary, I am constantly on the move. A few men still take off their hats in my car. Sometimes I tell passengers to put out their cigarettes. Some people smile at me, and others ignore me. My life is a series of "ups" and "downs." What am I?

COMPOSITION WRITING

I.   Write a composition in the third person singular describing someone's job. Use *Ms. X* or *Mr. Y* as the name of the person. Follow the model composition for organization, and use the following questions as a guide.

What Is She/He? (Ms. X or Mr. Y)

I. First paragraph
   A. What time does she/he start to work?
   B. What does she/he do before starting her/his job?
   C. What time does she/he finish work?
II. Second paragraph
   A. Does she/he enjoy her/his job?
   B. What kind of people does she/he meet?
   C. What does she/he do on the job?
   D. Does she/he stay in one place, or does she/he move around on the job?
   E. Closing sentence: final sentence about Ms. X or Mr. Y and the job.

STRUCTURE

> ### *Unless* and *if . . . not*
>
> The conjunction *unless* means *if . . . not.*
>
>   I never start and finish my work in the same place *unless* I am on a shuttle run.
>   I never start and finish my work in the same place *if* I am *not* on a shuttle run.
>
>   You can't pass the test *unless* you study.
>   You can't pass the test *if* you *don't* study.

3

Describing What Is Happening Around Us

*T*he human being is a very curious animal. We all like to observe our surroundings and learn what is happening around us. This is especially true if we are in a new or unusual situation. In this lesson, you will hear people talk or write about what is going on at a party, during an imaginary Martian invasion of the Earth, at a university library just before exams, and at a coffee house. Watch carefully how each person describes his/her surroundings and what is happening there.

A.   Two students at the party shown in the illustration are talking to each other about the other guests. Work with a partner and talk about what the people at the party are doing. Alternate asking each other questions and answering. Try to use adjective phrases, if possible.

> *S1:*   What's the woman *in the doorway* doing?
> *S2:*   She's. . . .
>
> *S2:*   What's the man *sitting on the couch* doing?
> *S1:*   He's. . . .

B.   Work with a partner. Both of you look at the picture for a minute; then, one of you looks away while the other one asks a question about what someone at the party is doing. Take turns asking and answering questions. See who can get the most correct answers.

> *S1:*   What's the woman *sitting next to the plant* doing?
> *S2:*   She's laughing.
> *S1:*   No, she isn't. She's eating.

READING

The Night the Martians Invaded the Earth

On October 30, 1938, at 8:00 P.M. Eastern Standard Time, there was an unforgettable radio broadcast in the United States. On that night, Orson Welles, an actor-writer, presented a dramatization of the H. G. Wells classic science-fiction novel, *The War of the Worlds*. In the play the announcer reported a Martian invasion of the Earth. Many radio listeners had not listened to the introduction at the beginning of the broadcast and they thought it was really happening. They didn't realize it was only a play. Here are some excerpts° of what they heard that night:

pieces taken from a complete work

"It was reported that at 8:50 P.M. a huge,° flaming object, believed to be a meteorite, fell on a farm in . . . New Jersey. . . .

very big

"Curious spectators now are pressing close to the object . . . the police are pushing the crowd back. . . . But it's no use. They're breaking right through. . . . One man wants to touch the thing. . . .

"Just a minute! Something's happening! . . . This end of the thing is beginning to flake off°! The top is beginning to rotate like a screw! . . . Someone's crawling out of the hollow top. . . . Good heavens, something's wriggling° out of the shadow like a grey snake. . . . The monster or whatever it is can hardly move. . . . This is the most extraordinary experience. I can't find words. . . .

come off in pieces
twisting from side to side

"We are bringing you an eyewitness account° of what's happening . . . in New Jersey. . . .

on-the-scene report

"Wait! . . . A humped shape is rising out of the pit. . . . There's a jet of flame . . . and it leaps right at the advancing men. It strikes them head on! Good Lord, they're turning into flame! . . . Now the whole field's caught fire. (Explosion) The woods . . . the barns . . . it's spreading everywhere. It's coming this way. About twenty yards to my right . . . (Crash of microphone . . . Then dead silence°. . .)"

complete silence

The dramatization continued with frequent news bulletins describing the invasion from Mars. Many listeners believed that the end of the world had come and a nationwide panic° occurred.

sudden, overwhelming fear

The police had to go to the broadcast station and order Orson Welles to announce that it was only a play. The station kept announcing this until midnight, but many people continued to believe it was really happening.

Adapted from Howard Koch, *"The Radio Play," The Panic Broadcast* (Boston: Little, Brown and Co., 1970, p. 33.)

C.   Be prepared to discuss the following questions based on the reading.

1. Why did many radio listeners believe that this was really happening?
2. Do you believe that a Martian invasion of the Earth could actually occur? Why or why not?
3. Do you think there is intelligent life on other planets? Is this life like us? How can we communicate with this life?
4. Would a radio audience react in the same way today if a similar program were broadcast? Why or why not?
5. Which do you think is more believable, a radio or a television version of a horror story? Why?

D.   Imagine that you are a reporter doing a live broadcast from the Boston Marathon. You are reporting on the large crowds at the marathon. Work with a partner and describe orally what the people in the crowd are doing. Then work with your partner and write a short paragraph of at least five sentences describing what some of the people in the crowd are doing. Begin with the following:

This is (*your name*) reporting live from the Boston Marathon today. Huge crowds are waiting impatiently for the runners.

MODEL COMPOSITION

A Letter to a Friend

May 10, 19___

Dear Carla,

It is three o'clock in the afternoon now, and I am sitting in the library and writing you this letter. It is a lovely spring day outside, but it is almost time for final exams, so there are a lot of students studying in the library today. The library is open until 2:00 A.M., and you can find many students studying here until very late. Right now, there are three students sitting opposite me. One is reading a philosophy book, another is studying mathematics, and the other is looking at art pictures. On one side of the room, there are five students working out problems on computers. On the other side of the room, there are two students who are wearing earphones and listening to music while they are studying. I wish I could listen to music and study at the same time. Most of the students are American, but there are lots of foreign students here, too. Some of the American students are leaning back in their chairs, with their feet up on the table. (This isn't usual in our country, but it isn't unusual here.) There are lots of good-looking fellows in the library today, and I am very busy people-watching. This is one of my favorite pastimes. It is more interesting than doing homework.

Well, I really must say "Good-by" now and get back to my work. Wish me luck on my exams! I hope all is going well with you. I miss you, so please write soon.

Fondly,
María

Elements of Style: Writing Descriptions

The model composition uses a descriptive style of composition writing. The situation is described, including the time and the setting. You can't describe everything that is going on, but you can give your readers an idea of what the scene is like, who the people there are, and what is happening. Remember, your readers are not present and have only your words to help them visualize the scene.

E.   *Sentence Combining*   Combine the two sentences by making the second sentence an adjective phrase. Remember that the adjective phrase directly follows the noun described.

The tall man is from Sweden. The man is talking to Lisa.
*The tall man **talking to Lisa** is from Sweden.*

The guest is bored. The guest has a beard.
*The guest **with a beard** is bored.*

1.   The girl is sitting near the window. The girl is wearing jeans.

2. I like the party sandwiches. The sandwiches were made by George.

_____

3. I am going to the party. The party is at John's house.

_____

4. The girl is very pretty. The girl is from Brazil.

_____

5. The man is talking with a friend. The man has a mustache.

_____

F. Rewrite the following sentences, using (a) *a lot of* and (b) *lots of.*

There are *many* students in the library today.
*There are **a lot of** students in the library today.*
*There are **lots of** students in the library today.*

1. Are there *many* students from your country in this class?

_____

_____

2. Do you have *much* free time from your studies?

_____

_____

3. Do you watch *much* TV?

_____

_____

4. There are *many* foreign students in this school.

_____

_____

5. María has *many* American friends.

_____

_____

G. Work with a partner and complete the following letter with the correct form of the verbs in parentheses.

April 12, 19___

Dear Peter,

It _____ (be) eleven o'clock in the morning, and I

_____ (sit) in the classroom and _____

(think) about the outdoors. It _____ (be) a warm spring

day outside, but inside the temperature is hot. My classmates

_____ (be) all very busy. There _____

(be) two students from Greece. One _____ (read), while the other _____ (talk) to a classmate. There _____ (be) three students from the Far East. One _____ (be) from Korea, another _____ (be) from Taiwan, and the third _____ (be) from Malaysia. The student from Korea _____ (look) at the blackboard, while the other two _____ (write) in their notebooks. There _____ (be) six Spanish-speaking students in the class. Most of them _____ (be) from Latin America, but one _____ (be) from Spain. The student from Spain_____ (look up) a word in his dictionary, while the Latin American students _____ (listen to) the teacher. I _____ (be) the only student in the class from France.

    It _____ (be) almost time for lunch, so I must stop writing now and get back to my English lessons.

Your friend,
Nicole

H. *Dictation / Dicto-Comp* Listen to your instructor dictate the following friendly letter written in a coffee house. Then follow his/her directions.

February 22, 19__

Dear Hiro,

    It is one o'clock in the afternoon, and I am sitting in the coffee house and writing you this letter. It is a cold, snowy day, but I can't see outside because this place is below street level, so it is windowless. On such a cold day, I like to sit here and people-watch. I try to imagine what the people I see here are doing. Three fellows are having lunch at a table next to me, and I think they are talking about the political situation. (I wish I could understand them.) Two young men with beards are sitting in a corner of the room and playing chess. I imagine they really are writers. At another table, there are four people who look like students. I suppose they are doing their homework. I can also see a food counter near the door of the coffee house and three young women standing in front of the counter. They all seem to be career women. Two are buying sandwiches, and the third is paying for her lunch. The coffee house is very crowded and noisy today. I'd like to write more, but I must say "So long" for now and get back to my lunch.

    Hope to see you very soon!

Sincerely yours,
Junchi

COMPOSITION WRITING

I.   Write a letter to a friend. Imagine that you are sitting in the lobby of a hotel or the airport, or the school cafeteria, or a café in your country, or waiting to see the doctor in the infirmary, or wherever you choose. Follow the outline, and use letter form.

A Letter to a Friend

    I.   Opening (generalization)
       A. Time of day (What time is it?)
       B. Setting (Where are you sitting?)
       C. Weather (What kind of day is it?)
   II. Specific description of scene
       A. Groups of people (Who is there?)
       B. Activities (What are they doing?)
       C. Opinion or reaction to some of the people or an activity there
  III. Closing (generalization)

S T R U C T U R E

*Use of **many** / **much** / **a lot of** / **lots of***

> *many / a lot of / lots of + countable nouns* (plural)

Are there *many* students in the class?
Are there *a lot of* students in the class?
Are there *lots of* students in the class?

> *much / a lot of / lots of + uncountable nouns* (singular)

Is there *much* noise in the room?
Is there *a lot of* noise in the room?
Is there *lots of* noise in the room?

> *Note: Much* is not usually used in affirmative statements. *A lot of*
> and *lots of* are not usually used in negative statements.

There is a lot of noise in the street.
There isn't much noise in this room.

Adjective Phrases

An adjective phrase is a group of words starting with a preposition or a participle (*-ing* form or *past participle* form of the verb). The adjective phrase tells you about a noun and immediately follows the noun.

the man *with a mustache*	the play *written by Shakespeare*
the book *lying on the table*	the book *without a cover*
the papers *on the desk*	the man *sitting near Mary*

Expressions of Location

at the top / bottom	in a room
to the right / left of the table	around a table
in the center	on the ceiling
over the bed	by / near the window
above the table	opposite the windows
below the ceiling	in the corner / middle of the room
across the street	on the right / left side of the room
behind the chair	

4

In the United States

*I*t is impossible to describe everything in the United States in one lesson. We can only talk about a few important topics: the people (total population, where they come from, why they come to the United States); the geography (size of the country, rivers, mountains, deserts); a few famous cities and places. Watch carefully to learn how to present these topics. You will then be able to briefly discuss your own country in a similar way.

A. Have you traveled to any of the places shown in the map of the United States? Work with a partner and find out what places he/she has visited in the United States as he/she locates them on the map.

    S1: Have you traveled anywhere in the United States?

    S2: Yes, I've been to . . . and. . . .
          or
          No, I haven't traveled anywhere yet, but I'd like / I hope / I plan to go to. . . . How about you?

    S1: Well, I've been to . . . and. . . .
          or
          No, I haven't traveled anywhere yet, but I intend / expect to visit . . . soon.

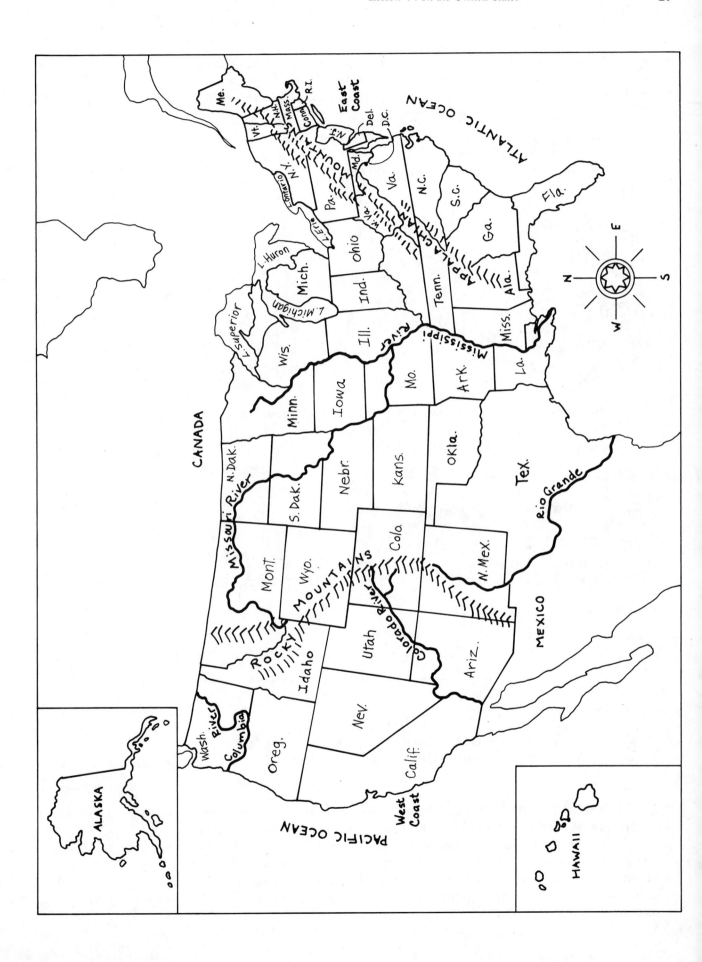

B. Work with a partner and discuss which of the places shown you would like to go to for your vacation in the United States and why. Alternate asking questions.

> S1: Where would you like to go for your vacation?
> S2: I'd like to go to New Orleans in Louisiana.
> S1: Why New Orleans?
> S2: Because I want to hear some good jazz.

New Orleans, Louisiana   Louisville, Kentucky   Kennedy Space Center, Florida

Hollywood, California   Waikiki Beach, Hawaii   Washington, D.C.

READING

The Story of Immigration

> Give me your tired, your poor,
> Your huddled° masses° yearning° to breathe free. . . .
>
> —From Emma Lazarus, *The New Colossus* (1883)

crowded together / large crowds of people / wanting, longing tenderly

These words, inscribed on the pedestal° of the Statue of Liberty, welcomed the millions of immigrants coming to the United States from European countries during the years of heaviest influx°—from 1890 to 1930, when 20 million new Americans entered the country. The United States has been known as a nation of immigrants throughout its history, and the incoming waves of people from abroad have helped develop this country and make it the vibrant,° wealthy, and powerful nation it is today.

foot or base of a statue

flowing in

full of energy, forceful

The nation's first immigrants looked upon the United States as the land of opportunity and came here seeking° political and religious freedom, economic opportunity, and a promise of equality. Today, people still immigrate to this country for the same reasons.

looking for, searching for

In the early years of America's development, most of the immigrants crossed the Atlantic from Europe. From 1840 to 1890, large numbers of immigrants came from Ireland, Germany, England, and the Scandinavian countries. From 1890 to 1930, the immigration pattern changed, and most of the immigrants came from the southern and eastern part of Europe, from countries such as Italy, Austria-Hungary, and Russia.

In the beginning, the United States encouraged immigration, but as the population grew, the country started to pass laws restricting° who could come in.

limiting, making available only to some

Today, the United States admits more than half a million immigrants a year, and almost 90 percent of them come from Latin America or Asia. Current law gives preferential treatment° to people who want to enter the country for the purpose of reuniting family. This means that if a member of your family—sibling,° parent, child, or spouse°—is a naturalized citizen,° you have priority° to enter. This system has worked to the detriment° of would-be immigrants from European countries who do not have the necessary family ties. As a result, there is an ongoing debate° in Congress aimed at changing the immigration laws once again.

gives first choice, favors one person over another

sister or brother / husband or wife / person who is granted citizenship rather than receiving it by birth / first choice / harm to someone's interests / formal argument

In 1986, the United States passed an amnesty° law that allowed illegal aliens who had entered the country before 1982 to apply for citizenship. It is expected that over 1 million people will become eligible for citizenship under the provisions of this act and will then be able to bring in their extended families.

pardon granted by a government

The question of immigration policy, always an emotional issue, is once again facing the United States. Many positions are being argued today in Congress. Some people feel that America's economic requirements should come first, and that preference should therefore be given to immigrants with skills that the country needs; others feel that immigrants with family ties of any sort should receive priority; and still others believe that preference should be given only to members of a naturalized citizen's immediate family—spouse, unmarried children, and parents. While nearly everyone agrees that the United States should keep its doors open to at least some new immigrants, the difficult dilemma° is to decide whom to let in.

problem, predicament

C. Be prepared to discuss the following questions based on the reading.

1. Before 1890, where did most immigrants to the United States come from?
2. What is the pattern of immigration today?
3. Do you think family ties should be more important than job skills for granting visas? Why?
4. Are there any groups that immigrate to your country today? If so, where do they come from?
5. Is there a debate about immigration policy in your country? Explain.
6. What do you think would be a fair and humane immigration policy for the United States? Explain.

D.   Work with a partner. Look at the graphs and be prepared to discuss the following.

   1. When did the majority of the immigrant population change from northern and western European to southern and eastern European?

   2. Where did most immigrants come from between 1981 and 1985?

   3. The United States has a large African-American population. Why is Africa not shown in the graphs?

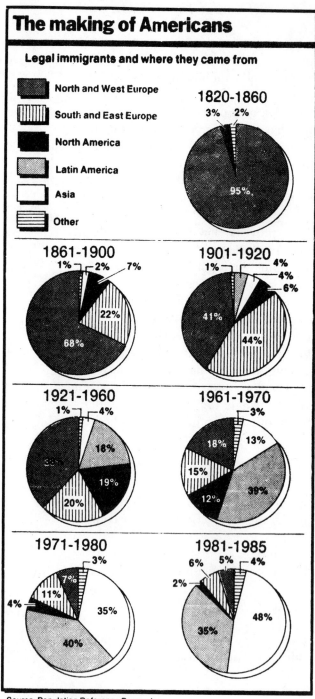

The making of Americans

Legal immigrants and where they came from

- North and West Europe
- South and East Europe
- North America
- Latin America
- Asia
- Other

1820-1860
3% 2%
95%

1861-1900
1% 2% 7%
68% 22%

1901-1920
1% 4% 4% 6%
41% 44%

1921-1960
1% 4%
18% 19% 20%

1961-1970
3%
18% 13%
15% 12% 39%

1971-1980
3%
7% 11% 35%
4% 40%

1981-1985
6% 5% 4%
2% 35% 48%

Source: Population Reference Bureau Inc.

E. Add a sentence that describes the immigrant population in the United States shown in the graphs from 1981 to 1985. Begin *During 1981 to 1985, there was the following pattern of immigration. . . .*

MODEL COMPOSITION

The United States

The United States is a very large country. From the Atlantic Ocean on the East Coast to the Pacific Ocean on the West Coast, it is about three thousand miles wide. Canada is the country to the north of the United States, and Mexico is the country to the south. The Rio Grande is the boundary between Mexico and the United States. The country is a composite of different geographic formations—high mountains and deep canyons, great river systems and land-locked lakes, rolling plains, forests and rocky coasts, sandy beaches, and even deserts. The major mountain ranges are the Appalachian Mountains in the East and the Rocky Mountains in the West. The most important rivers are the Mississippi and the Missouri rivers in the central part of the country and the Colorado and the Columbia rivers in the West. There are fifty states in the Union today. The two newest states, Hawaii and Alaska, are geographically separated from the other forty-eight states.

The United States has a heterogeneous population. The American people are of almost every creed and every ethnic background. This mix of many kinds of people is the result of the great immigration from abroad throughout American history. The population is now over 240 million people, including 1.5 million Native Americans. English is the common language.

F. Completion   You have seen use of the definite article with geographic place names in the model composition. Now complete the following descriptions of places with the definite article *the*, if necessary. If no article is necessary, put an *X* in the blank space.

1. _____ France is in _____ Europe.

2. _____ Andes Mountains are in _____ South America.

3. _____ Tokyo is the capital of _____ Japan.

4. _____ St. Lawrence River is between _____ United States and

_____ Canada.

5. _____ Sahara Desert in _____ Africa extends from _____ Atlantic Ocean to _____ Nile River.

6. _____ Lake Superior is the largest of _____ Great Lakes.

7. _____ Mount Everest in _____ Nepal is the highest mountain in the world.

8. _____ Black Forest is in _____ Germany.

9. _____ Bay of Biscay is between _____ Spain and _____ France.

10. _____ Caracas is the capital of _____ Venezuela.

G. Complete the following description of the State of Alaska with the definite article *the*, if necessary. If no article is necessary, put an *X* in the blank space.

_____ Alaska, the forty-ninth state, entered the Union in 1959. The capital of _____ Alaska is _____ Juneau. _____ Alaska is bounded on the north by _____ Arctic Ocean, on the east by _____ Canada, on the south by _____ Pacific Ocean, and on the west by _____ Bering Sea. The major rivers are _____ Yukon, _____ Tanana, and _____ Kuskokwim. The highest mountain in _____ North America, _____ Mount McKinley, is in _____ Alaska. _____ Alaska is the largest state in the Union. _____ State of _____ Alaska is commonly called _____ Last Frontier.

H. Read the following paragraph describing the State of California.

The State of California is located in the far western part of the United States. It is bordered on the north by Oregon, on the east by Nevada and Arizona, on the southeast by the Colorado River, on the south by Mexico, and on the west by the Pacific Ocean. The capital city is Sacramento. California entered the Union on September 9, 1850, as the thirty-first state. Its nickname is *The Golden State*.

Now look at the following chart and write the same kind of paragraph for Texas, Kansas, and Florida.

State	Location	Boundaries	Capital	Entered Union	Nickname
Kansas	Midwest	N: Nebraska E: Missouri River; Missouri S: Oklahoma W: Colorado	Topeka	1/29/1861; 34th state	The Sunflower State
Texas	Southwest	N: Oklahoma; Red River NE: Arkansas E: Louisiana; Sabine River S: Gulf of Mexico; Rio Grande; Mexico W: New Mexico	Austin	12/29/1845; 28th state	The Lone Star State
Florida	Extreme Southeastern	N: Alabama; Chatta-hoochee River; Georgia; St. Mary's River E: Atlantic Ocean S: Straits of Florida W: Gulf of Mexico	Tallahassee	3/3/1845; 27th state	The Sunshine State

I.   *Dictation / Dicto-Comp*   Listen to your instructor dictate the following paragraph. Then follow his/her directions.

The United States is sometimes called a salad bowl of nationalities. According to the 1980 census, more than 118 million people traced their ancestry back to one foreign country, while nearly 70 million listed more than one country as their ethnic homeland. The report stated that 26.34 percent of Americans listed England as their country of ethnic origin. Germany was second with 26.14 percent. The Irish were the third-largest ethnic group; the African Americans were the fourth with 11.13 percent; and the French were the fifth with 6.85 percent. This is why many people say that if you scratch an American, you will find the world.

Largest Ancestry Groups Reported Ranked in Descending Order*

English	*49,598,035*	*Italian*	*12,183,692*
German	*49,224,146*	*Scottish*	*10,048,816*
Irish	*40,165,702*	*Polish*	*8,228,037*
Afro-American	*20,964,729*	*Mexican*	*7,692,619*
French	*12,892,246*		

*Reported by 100,000 or more Americans according to U.S. Bureau of the Census "Ancestry of the Population by State." *1980 Census of the Population,* Supplement PC 80–S1–10. Washington, D.C., GPO, April 1983.

J. In the United States, you might be asked to give a presentation on your country before a community organization. Prepare an *oral composition,* for presentation to the class, about your country by answering the following questions.

  1. Where is your native country located?
  2. How large is it?
  3. What are its boundaries? (What lies to the east, the west, the north, the south?)
  4. What are the major mountain ranges, if any?
  5. What are the most important rivers, if any?
  6. What is the general topography of the country?
  7. What ethnic group(s) and creed(s) are represented among the population of your country?
  8. How large is the population?
  9. What is the common language?

COMPOSITION WRITING

K. Write a two-paragraph composition following the model composition and the outline. (See the "Paragraphs" section in the Handbook.)

My Country: _____

  I. Physical characteristics (first paragraph)
     A. Size
        1. Large or small
        2. Area in square miles
     B. Boundaries (north, south, east, and west)
        1. Natural: oceans, rivers, mountain ranges
        2. Political: national frontiers
     C. Principal geographic features
        1. Mountain ranges
        2. Rivers, lakes
        3. Deserts or jungles
     D. Subdivisions of the country
        1. Number of divisions (states, districts, and so forth)
        2. Geographically separated divisions (if any)
  II. The people (second paragraph)
     A. Background
        1. Origin
        2. Diversity
     B. Population size
     C. Common language

STRUCTURE

Use of the Definite Article Before Geographic Place Names

1. Use the definite article with the names of all bodies of water except individual lakes.

the Pacific Ocean	the Red Sea
the Atlantic Ocean	the Black Sea
the Mississippi River	the English Channel
the Suez Canal	the Persian Gulf

2. Use the definite article before the names of deserts and forests.

the Black Forest	the Sahara Desert

3. Use the definite article before all plural names.

the British Isles	the Great Lakes
the Philippines	the Rocky Mountains
the Netherlands	the Andes Mountains

4. Use the definite article before all names that end in an *of* phrase.

the Bay of Biscay	the People's Republic of China
the Gulf of Mexico	the University of New Mexico

5. Use the definite article before all names that designate a political union.

the British *Commonwealth*	the *United* States
the Dominican *Republic*	the *Union* of Soviet Socialist Republics

6. Use the definite article before the names of geographic areas.

the Near East	the Far East	the Orient
the Middle East	the West	the Occident

7. Don't use the definite article before the names of individual mountains.

Mount Blanc	*but*: the Matterhorn
Mount Everest	
Mount Whitney	

8. Don't use the definite article before the names of individual lakes.

Lake Erie	*but*: the Great Lakes
Lake Lucerne	the Finger Lakes
Lake Placid	

9. Don't use the definite article before the names of cities or continents.

Paris	Asia	*but*: The Hague
Istanbul	Europe	
Caracas	Australia	

10. Don't use the definite article before the name of a country unless the name includes a word for a political union.

Peru	Korea	Mexico
France	India	Canada

11. Don't use the definite article before the names of states.

New Jersey	*but*: the State of New Jersey
Illinois	the State of Illinois
California	the State of Florida
Ohio	

See the "Capitalization" section in the Handbook.

You Are What You Eat

Breakfast

Juices and Fruits

	Sm.	Lg.		
Orange juice ..	1.75	1.95	Half Melon	1.50
Apple juice ...	.95	1.15	Half Florida	
Grapefruit			Grapefruit	1.25
juice	.95	1.15	Fresh Fruit Salad ...	2.15

Breads and Pastries

Buttery Croissants
**Plain, Chocolate,
Almond** 1.25

Bagels
*Plain, Poppyseed, Sesame,
Garlic, Onion, Egg, Raisin*

Fresh Baked Muffins
Blueberry 1.00
Corn .... .90
Bran .... .90
Apple 1.10
Raisin .... .90

With or Without
Butter .... .70
With Cream Cheese.. 1.25
**With Cream Cheese
and Nova Scotia
Lox** 2.95

Eggs

2 any style with toast and home fries 2.50
2 any style with toast and bacon 3.80
2 any style with toast and ham 3.80
**2 any style with toast, home fries, and ham or
bacon** 4.20

Omelettes

Served with toast and home fries

OASIS SPECIAL, **mushrooms, onions, bacon,
tomatoes, cheddar cheese** 5.75
NACHO, **chopped pimento, sour cream, American
cheese** 4.90
CHEESE, **choice of one: American, Swiss, Muenster,
Cheddar, Monterey Jack** 4.50

Oasis /CAFÉ
31 Michigan Ave., Chicago, Il.
674-5525

Lunch

Burgers

Regular Burger 3.25
Burger Deluxe, with french fries, lettuce and
tomato 5.00
Cheeseburger 3.75
Cheeseburger Deluxe 5.65

Basic Sandwiches

Served on your choice of White, Rye, Whole Wheat, Roll

Turkey, all white meat 4.95
Turkey Club 5.95
Roast Beef 4.95
Baked Virginia Ham 3.95
Hot Pastrami 4.95
Tuna fish 3.65

Side Orders

French Fries	1.95	Onion Rings	2.15
Cole Slaw	1.95	Cottage Cheese	1.50

Beverages

Cold	Sm.	Lg.	Hot	
Sodas	.95	1.15	Coffee	.65
Iced Tea	.95	1.15	Decaf	.95
Iced Coffee ...	1.05	1.25	Tea	.60
Milk	.95	1.15	Hot Chocolate	.90

*I*n the United States, many people plan their daily menu, but others do not seem to care about what they eat. How about you? What are your food habits? Do you carefully select the kind of food that you eat every day? What kind of food, for example, would you select from the menu in this typical American restaurant?

A. Work with two other classmates and role-play the following dialogue. You are ordering lunch at The Oasis Café. One student will role-play the waiter/waitress, and the other two students will be the customers. Use the model as a guide and select from the menu shown.

> *Waiter:* Would you like to order now?
> *S1:* Yes, please. I'd like a hamburger deluxe.
> *Waiter:* How would you like your hamburger?
> *S1:* Medium well done.
> *Waiter:* Anything to drink?
> *S1:* . . .
> *S2:* I'd like a roast beef sandwich.
> *Waiter:* On white, rye, or whole wheat?
> *S2:* On rye. And . . . , please.

Food Notes

If you order certain foods, you must tell the waiter or waitress how you want them.

Hamburger and steak

rare / medium rare   medium   medium well done / well done

Coffee

light—with lots of milk or cream in it
regular—with some milk or cream in it
dark—with very little milk or cream in it
black—with no milk or cream in it

Eggs

scrambled	omelet
sunny-side up	soft-boiled
sunny-side down (over)	hard-boiled

B. Work with a partner and match each food expression to the appropriate illustration. Then, role-play the dialogue that follows.

1. _____

     _____

2. _____

     _____

3. _____

     _____

4. _____

_____

5. _____

_____

6. _____

_____

a couch potato	a habitual lounger, especially a person who spends a lot of time watching television
fish story	a series of lies or exaggerations; a false or improbable situation
to spill the beans	to reveal a secret or a surprise by accident
to be chicken	to be afraid or cowardly
to go bananas	to go crazy or become silly
to be in a pickle	to be in a predicament, a dilemma

> *S1:* Next week is Mary's birthday. Let's give her a party.
> *S2:* What kind of party are you thinking of?
> *S1:* How about a surprise party at my house?
> *S2:* That's a good idea. Whom should we invite?
> *S1:* Let's invite everyone in the class.
> *S2:* Terrific. But we've got to make sure that no one spills the beans.

Now work with a partner and write a dialogue or a short story in one paragraph using one of the other food expressions. Then, present it to the class.

READING

The following article describes one foreigner's feeling of confusion about the American diet.

A Dry Martini and Double-Nut Mocha

Ten years ago, if you were told in India that an American was about to visit you and you didn't know what he looked like, you would probably conjure up an image of° a large man—"beefy"°—who wore a baseball cap and ate most of the time. When he was not eating hamburgers, he would chew sugar-coated gum. But then the Great American Dietary Revolution came along. . . .

imagine / heavy and powerfully built

A couple of years ago, when I came to this country a few times on short visits, the food habits struck me as noteworthy.° . . .   **worthy of attention**

On the one hand, fast-food outlets tried to entice° you at every corner, and you could, in the major cities, find the widest variety of international cuisine available anywhere in the world. Restaurants overflowed.° . . . Eating out seemed to be the national pastime.° . . .   **persuade someone to do something**   **were crowded**   **activity that pleasantly occupies one's spare time**

On the other hand, whenever I actually went to a restaurant with friends, I would be made to feel vaguely° guilty all the time about my archaic° eating and drinking preferences. Not that my companions were openly disparaging°; they would simply ask for food that was less fatty, less sugary, less fried, less everything than I would. . . .   **in a way that is not clear in shape or form /antiquated, no longer current / disapproving**

Therefore, when I came to live in this country a couple of months ago, I came prepared. . . . I began to plan my lunch and dinner menus carefully. So much red meat and eggs and no more; plenty of lettuce, carrots and cabbage; very little alcohol and virtually° no sweets, especially no more of my beloved chocolates. As a result, I rapidly lost a lot of weight and a bit° of my sanity. . . .   **almost**   **small piece or quantity**

Soon, however, I noticed strange things. Most people around me were reaching into chocolate bins° and popping° handfuls into shopping carts. Ice cream shops were always crowded. . . .   **large wide-mouthed containers / throwing**

Now *The New York Times* has explained it all. "Most Americans, regardless of age, have not responded in a significant fashion to calls° for decreasing fat in the diet, reducing sodium, taking in fewer calories or otherwise eating more healthfully. . . . They still like french fries more than baked potatoes, red meat more than chicken or fish and soft drinks more than fruit juice. Snacking is a national pastime."   **demands**

Exactly what I had always suspected.

I am happy to announce that I have begun to regain a few lost pounds and a lot of that general sense of well-being° that you have when you eat chocolates regularly.   **state of being healthy and happy**

Adapted from Gautam Adhikari, "A Dry Martini and Double-Nut Mocha," *The New York Times* (January 15, 1988): p. A31.

C.   Be prepared to discuss the following questions based on the reading.

1. What do people in your country think Americans eat?
2. Has your country had a "dietary revolution" during your lifetime? How have your eating habits changed from your parents' eating habits?
3. What kind of fast-food outlets do you have in your country? Who eats there?
4. Are many people in your country on diets? What kind of diets?
5. Do people in your country snack? What kinds of snacks do they eat?
6. Have you changed your diet since you came here? What do you eat now that you didn't eat before?

D. Working in groups of four to five people, answer the following questions about your food habits in the United States. Be sure to note what all members of your group say. Then, select a person to be your recorder while the group writes a paragraph about its eating habits in the United States to present to the class.

   1. What foods are you eating less of now than when you were in your country? What foods are you eating more of?
   2. What foods do you try to avoid eating in the United States? Why?
   3. What is your favorite snack in the United States? How often do you eat between meals here?
   4. What is your favorite lunch or dinner in the United States? And dessert?

MODEL COMPOSITION

You Are What You Eat

John Smith, Mr. Average American, is a family man with two school-age children and a wife who works part-time. Let's look at his eating habits during a typical week.

Mr. Smith has either a small breakfast of juice, toast, and coffee or a big breakfast like ham or bacon and eggs, toast, and coffee. On weekends, Mrs. Smith tries to find time to make him waffles, pancakes, or french toast with both butter and maple syrup.

Mr. Smith works in a large office from 9:00 to 5:00. At 10:30 every morning, he has a doughnut or a Danish and coffee during the fifteen-minute "coffee break." He usually takes an hour for lunch at noon or 1:00 P.M. For lunch, he goes to a coffee shop and has soup and a ham and cheese or roast beef sandwich with lettuce and tomatoes, and some coffee. Sometimes, he has a hamburger and french fries and a soda.

Mr. Smith tries to be home by 6:00 or 6:30 every evening so that he can have dinner with his wife and children. His wife serves not only a full meal of chicken, meat, or fish, a salad, and vegetables but also a dessert of pie or cake. The parents have coffee, and the children drink milk. At about ten o'clock, while watching television, Mr. Smith has a snack of either some ice cream or another piece of pie.

Once a week, Mr. Smith goes out with his wife to a restaurant for dinner. They usually go to a Chinese, Italian, or Mexican restaurant because they like to try different international cuisine. On Saturday or Sunday afternoon, the whole family eats out at a fast-food place because that is what the children prefer.

Mr. Smith is gaining too much weight, and Mrs. Smith is very worried about him. She often says to him, "You should go on a diet." He usually answers, "I know. I'll start tomorrow—or the day after."

E.   Work with a partner. Ask each other and then answer the following questions about eating habits in your country. Take notes on your partner's answers in order to give a short report to the class on what you have learned.

  1. What was your favorite snack in your country?
  2. At which meals did all the people in your household sit down to eat together? How long did it usually take to eat a meal?
  3. If there is any food left over after a meal in your country, what is done with it?
  4. How often do people in your country eat in restaurants? What do they like to eat there?

F.   *Sentence Combining*   Work with a partner and connect the following pairs of sentences with the correlative conjunctions *either . . . or, neither . . . nor, both . . . and, not only . . . but (also)*.

   According to a health report, the American diet contains *both* too much fat *and* too much salt.

   Many Americans are *not only* well fed *but* are often overfed.

   Many Americans *neither* watch their diet *nor* get enough exercise.

   Most Americans eat lunch *either* at noon *or* at 1:00 P.M.

  1. Two out of three Americans don't smoke excessively. Two out of three Americans don't drink excessively. (neither . . . nor)

   _____

   _____

  2. Americans eat too many hamburgers. Americans eat too many hot dogs. (both . . . and)

   _____

   _____

  3. Diet plays a part in death from heart disease. Diet plays a part in death from cancer. (not only . . . but)

   _____

   _____

  4. Hamburgers aren't American. Hot dogs aren't American. (neither . . . nor)

   _____

   _____

  5. Hamburgers originally came from Germany. Hot dogs originally came from Germany. (both . . . and)

   _____

   _____

6. At any given time, many Americans are going on a diet. At any given time, many Americans are going off a diet. (either . . . or)

   _____

   _____

7. Most Americans eat breakfast in a hurry. Most Americans eat lunch in a hurry. (both . . . and)

   _____

   _____

8. Generally speaking, American food is rather bland. Generally speaking, American food is rather unspicy. (both . . . and)

   _____

   _____

9. Salads are popular in the summer. Salads are popular all year round. (not only . . . but)

   _____

   _____

10. Many Americans have a snack in midmorning. Many Americans have a snack in the afternoon. (either . . . or)

    _____

    _____

G. Complete the following sentences with the correct intensifier, *too* or *very*.

1. That child eats _____ much candy.

2. I don't eat a _____ large breakfast.

3. He smokes _____ much.

4. Green vegetables are _____ healthy.

5. Many Americans eat _____ much.

6. Some people think American food isn't _____ tasty.

7. That dessert is _____ delicious to pass up.

8. Salads are _____ popular all year round.

9. I am never _____ tired to eat.

10. _____ much food and _____ little exercise are bad for your health.

11. Are you a moderate drinker, or do you drink _____ much?

12. All kinds of snacks are _____ popular in this country.

H. ***Dictation / Dicto-Comp***   Listen to your instructor read the following paragraph. Then follow his/her directions.

Choice of food reveals a great deal about a country's culture, and American cooking is no exception. Except for the turkey at Thanksgiving, there is no other national dish. However, each region of the United States has its own special foods. New England is famous for its seafood, baked beans, brown bread, and Boston cream pie. The South is famous for its fried chicken, smoked ham, corn bread, and fritters. New Orleans is well known for its jambalaya—a spicy Creole dish of rice, ham, shrimp, and tomatoes. In the Southwest, barbecued food and good steaks are a specialty. Mexican dishes such as tamales, tacos, and chili are also very popular there. In addition to regional foods, the American diet also includes many international dishes. Each ethnic group in the United States has influenced the national cuisine.

COMPOSITION WRITING

I. Write a composition of six paragraphs that describes the eating habits of a typical person in your country. You can write about yourself or any man, woman, or child in your country. Follow the model composition and the outline.

You Are What You Eat: (country)

I. Introductory paragraph
   A. What kind of person are you writing about?
   B. What is his/her name?
II. Breakfast
   A. What is this person's typical breakfast?
   B. Where and with whom does he/she eat it?
   C. Does he/she eat a different breakfast on Sundays? What is it?
III. Lunch
   A. What time is lunch, and how long does it last?
   B. What is the typical lunch?
   C. Where does this person eat it?
IV. Dinner
   A. What time is dinner?
   B. Where does this person eat it and with whom?
   C. What is the typical dinner?
   D. What, if anything, does he/she eat after dinner?
 V. Weekend eating
   A. Does this person eat differently on weekends?
   B. How often does this person eat out on weekends and with whom?
   C. Where do they go to eat out?
VI. Closing
   What kind of general statement can you make about the diet in your country?

S T R U C T U R E

Correlative Conjunctions

Some conjunctions are used in pairs and are called correlative conjunctions. They are used to contrast the similarities and differences between people, places, things, and events.

both . . . and   neither . . . nor
either . . . or   not only . . but (also)

Men in the United States watch their diets.
Women in the United States watch their diets.
Both men *and* women in the United States watch their diets.

Men don't like to be overweight.
Women don't like to be overweight.
Neither men *nor* women like to be overweight.

People gain weight because they eat too much.
People gain weight because they don't get enough exercise.
People gain weight because they *either* eat too much *or* don't get
  enough exercise.

Mr. Smith eats too much.
Mr. Smith doesn't get enough exercise.
Not only does Mr. Smith eat too much, *but* he *also* doesn't get enough
  exercise.

> *Note:* Notice how the correlative conjunction *not only . . . but (also)*
> takes the question word order in the *not only* clause in the previous
> example.

*The Adverbs **very** and **too***

Very is an intensifier that strengthens the degree of the adjective or adverb that follows it.

The coffee was *very* hot, but I drank it.
The cake was *very* fattening, but I ate it.

Too is often used as an intensifier that indicates a high degree that is not acceptable to the speaker.

The coffee was *too* hot. (I couldn't drink it.)
The cake was *too* fattening for me to eat. (I couldn't eat it.)

6

LESSON

Life in the Twenty-first Century

*M*ost people in the United States feel that their lives will change in some way as the years go by. They know that they will have to adjust to these changes in their lives in order to succeed. Imagine that you are living in the year 2001. How will you be living then? In what ways will you have to adjust? Do you think you will like living in the year 2001?

A. Work with a partner and talk about what you think you'll be doing in the year 2001. Ask your partner three or four questions about the future. When he/she has answered your questions, exchange roles.

> *S1:* Where do you think you'll be living in the year 2001?
> *S2:* Well. . . .
> *S1:* How about a job?
> *S2:* . . .
> *S1:* Do you think you'll be married?
> *S2:* . . .

B. Think about your country's future. What is going to be different in your country in the year 2001? Work with a partner and ask each other questions. Consider changes in education, work opportunities, transportation, living conditions, food habits, government, and so on.

> *S1:* What kind of government is your country going to have in the year 2001?
> *S2:* . . .
> *S1:* What kind of changes are there going to be in the educational system?
> *S2:* . . .

READING

Robo-Home

Even before the year 2001, many of us will live in apartments or houses that today seem like space-age fantasies. Home will be a place where almost every practical need will be met. Technology is about to enter your life in ways you never dreamed possible.

According to Bob Mundt, manager of industrial design at General Electric, "It used to be that we could conceive° of things that couldn't be done, but now, for the first time in history, technology makes it possible for us to do things we can't even conceive of." — *imagine*

"Good morning, John," says the pleasant female voice of the alarm clock. "It's time to get up."

"Hmph," he mutters,° promptly falling back to sleep. — *speaks in a low, angry voice*

Activated by his voice, however, the clock will now send signals throughout the house. In the kitchen, the coffeemaker will go on, the microwave will adjust its time to toast the bagels° when the coffee is ready, and since it is Friday, the scanner° in the refrigerator and pantry° will begin taking the food inventory° and printing out a grocery list. — *hard rolls shaped like a doughnut / machine that checks a condition, a process, or the price of something / closet for food / list of all the items in a place*

Thermostats in every room will switch the heat, humidity, and purification systems to their daytime settings, curtains will open, and lights will turn off or turn on. In the bathroom, the tub will fill and the sauna will heat up, while, in

the living room, the TV will turn on to the morning news. Meanwhile, the dishwasher and washing machine will compute their hot water needs.

"Get up, John," says the alarm clock, in no uncertain terms,° "Breakfast is ready."

very firmly, in a commanding tone

As he eats, John will call his office and observe, through the video monitor on his phone, his colleagues° already at work. Then he will order a first-run film for the evening, which will be transmitted° to his television screen through the telephone line. Using this modem,° he will order groceries from the super-market, balance his bank account on his computer, and transfer a file of special data for the research project he is working on. After instructing his answering machine to relay° certain calls to specific numbers, he will program the security system to video-record messages from callers, and then he will leave for work.

fellow workers

sent

device that sends computer data over phone lines

send out

While there are no limits to imagining the home of the future, there are limits to how much technology people will accept. The technology of the future has been available for some time, but people aren't ready for it.

The teenagers of today, however, are the consumers° of tomorrow and their generation is free of the computer fears their parents and grandparents have. These young people have been raised on digital technology. "We might be taking some pretty big steps now toward the future," says Mundt, "but can you imagine the kinds of ideas these kids are going to come up with?"

persons who buy and use goods and services

Excerpts adapted from Lori Nelson, "Robo-Home," *The West Side Spirit* (December 7, 1987): cover and pp. 5, 28.

C.   Be prepared to answer the following questions based on the reading.

1. How would you like the alarm clock to wake you in the future? (With what words and in whose voice?)
2. Are you afraid of the rapid advances in modern technology? Why or why not?
3. What improvement would you most like to see in the home of the future?
4. What diseases do you think scientists will be able to cure by the year 2001?
5. What kinds of food do you think you will eat in the year 2001?

D.   Genetic engineers study ways to improve or prevent defects in living things. Imagine that you and two other classmates live in the year 2001 and work for a genetic-engineering company. Your job as a group is to redesign and improve the human form. Decide what changes you will make and draw a picture of your "new man/woman." Then, as a group, write five sentences about the changes you will make and explain why you want to make them. Use your imagination!

MODEL COMPOSITION

My Life in the Year 2001

In the year 2001, I will be thirty-one years old, and I think my life will be very different then from my life today. I plan to be a famous photographer, and I hope to have a good job and make enough money to live comfortably. I want to live in a small, quiet suburb near a big city, with a loving wife and two or three children. I would like to have two sons and a daughter. My family and I will live in a house made of a tough new plastic material. A new form of strong zippers and Velcro will hold the house together, so it will be very easy to change the design and add new rooms and parts whenever we want to. A few days each week, I will commute to the city in my autoplane with my personal robot, EZ. This car will be crashproof and will run on a computer, so I won't have to drive it. I will be able to watch television, read the paper, or do other things in my car while I ride to work. If there is too much traffic on the road, my autoplane will just fly over the other cars and continue on its way. At work, I will program my robot to take all my photos at the right speed, distance, and light when I push its buttons from a remote control. I expect to earn good money at my job, but I won't use money. Instead, everyone will use credit cards to buy everything. I think my life is going to be much easier in the year 2001. I can't wait.

E. Work with a partner and ask each other the following questions about the future. Write down your partner's answers in complete sentences. Then, check your partner's sentences to be sure they are correct.

1. What do you plan to study after this course?

    _____

2. What do you want to be in the future?

    _____

3. Where do you intend to live in the future?

    _____

4. How many children would you like to have?

    _____

5. How much money do you hope to have in the future?

    _____

F. Work with a partner and answer the following questions orally. Then, write your own answers in complete sentences, including the time clauses.

1. Where will you go after you leave school today?

    _____

2. What will you do while you are on the bus or subway, or walking home?

    _____

3. What will you do as soon as you get home?

    _____

4. What will you have to do before you can graduate?

    _____

5. What kind of job will you look for when you finish school?

    _____

G. Work together in groups of three to five students. Your group is going to form a new country. Decide on the name of the country and then discuss five new laws (such as the one described in the example below) that you will enact to make this a perfect country and a brave new world. Choose one person as recorder, but the entire group must agree on the laws. Use future time. When your group has finished, choose one person to report to the class.

The government will pay for all its citizens' medical and dental expenses.

H. Work with a group of three to five students. Put the following events in the order in which you think they will happen in the future. You may want to predict a date. Are there any that you think will never happen? When you have finished, compare your group's order of events with those of other groups in the class.

a cure for cancer	people will live on the moon
peace in the Middle East	robots will do most of our work
no more apartheid	humans will live to two hundred years
you will learn English well	no more wars

I.   ***Dictation / Dicto-Comp***   Listen to your instructor read the following paragraph and then follow his/her directions.

Futurists predict a world with many improvements in our daily lives. Here are some of their predictions: Did you forget where you put your keys? Don't worry. There will be a nasal spray that will help you remember. This spray will also improve older people's memories until the age of 120. Do you have an emotional problem? A computer will help you by performing psychotherapy. Would you like a wonderful dream tonight? A psychiatrist will design the special dream you want to have that night. Do you have a toothache? Not in the future. There will be a vaccine that prevents tooth decay. Is there too much air pollution from automobiles? In the future, we will all be driving electric cars. Do you need some information from a library? You will be able to read any book, magazine, or newspaper from any library on your own home computer. These are just some of the things that are coming in the brave new world of tomorrow!

COMPOSITION WRITING

J.   Write a composition about what you think your life will be like in the year 2001. Follow the model composition and use the questions here as an outline.

My Life in the Year 2001

1. How old will you be?
2. Will your life be very different?
3. What kind of job will you have?
4. Where will you live?
5. Whom will you marry?
6. How many children will you have?
7. What kind of house will you live in?
8. What will you do on a typical day?
9. How will technological advances change your life? What kind of life will you have?

S T R U C T U R E

Future Time

1. *Going to + simple verb* is usually used when expressing a planned or intended action.

   I am going to see a movie tonight.

2. *Will + simple verb* usually expresses a promise or a statement of simple futurity.

   I will see you tomorrow.

Future Time Expressions

tomorrow, the day after tomorrow, in two days
next week, next month, next year
the week after next, in two weeks, two weeks from now
soon
in a little while
in a few minutes
until next week, month, and so forth
in the coming days, weeks, and so forth
today, this afternoon, this evening (*when referring to the future*)

Adverbial Clauses of Time

If the main clause is in the future, the time clause is usually in the present.

   main clause + time clause

I will be able to read *while I am on my way to work.*
It will be easy to change *whenever we want to.*
I am going to wait here *until you arrive.*
My robot will take pictures *when I push its buttons.*
I will call you *before I leave my office.*
He is going to do his homework *as soon as he gets home.*
Where will you go *after you finish your work?*

Use of the Infinitive After Certain Verbs

I *plan to be* a photographer.
I *hope to have* three children.
I *want to live* in the suburbs.
I *expect to make* good money.
I *intend to program* the robot.
I *would like to work* as a photographer.

L E S S O N 7

Giving and Following Directions

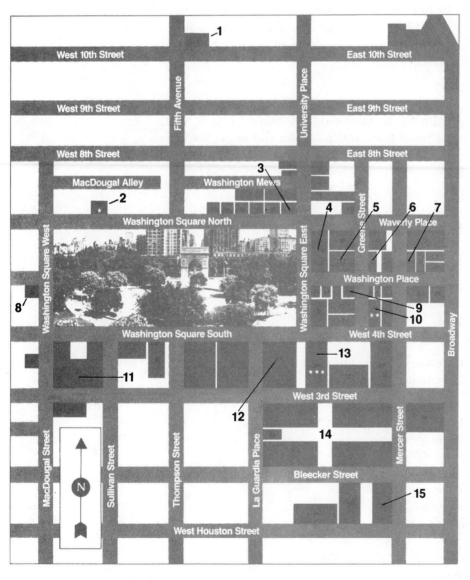

KEY TO LOCATIONS

1 Rubin Residence Hall, 35 Fifth Avenue.

2 Office of Undergraduate Admissions, 22 Washington Square North

3 The American Language Institute, 1 Washington Square North / 2 University Place

4 Main Building, Grey Art Gallery and Study Center, 100 Washington Square East

5 Brown Building, 29 Washington Place / 245 Greene Street

6 Student Activities Annex, 21 Washington Place

7 NYU Post Office, 5 Washington Place

8 Hayden Residence Hall, 33 Washington Square West

9 The Book Center, 18 Washington Place

10 Office of Financial Aid, 23–25 West Fourth Street

11 Vanderbilt Hall, School of Law, 40 Washington Square South

12 Elmer Holmes Bobst Library, 70 Washington Square South

13 University Information Center, Shimkin Hall, 50 West Fourth Street

14 Washington Square Village

15 Coles Sports and Recreation Center, 181 Mercer Street

*H*ow many times this week have you had to give or follow instructions? Perhaps you told someone how to use a copy machine. Or perhaps you had to listen carefully as someone explained how to get somewhere. In this lesson, you will learn how to give and follow instructions. Good luck!

A.   Follow the route on the map as your instructor or a classmate reads the directions for how to get to the Whitney Museum. Start at location number 3, the American Language Institute.

To get to the Whitney Museum from here, turn to your left after leaving this building. Cross to the east side of University Place and walk one and a half blocks north until you come to the bus shelter between East Ninth Street and East Tenth Street. Wait there until a number 2 or a number 3 bus comes along. Remember, you will need the exact change or a token for the fare. Get on the bus and tell the driver to let you off at Madison Avenue and East Seventy-fifth Street. When you get to East Seventy-fifth Street, get off the bus. You will see a very unusual modern building in front of you. This is the Whitney Museum.

B.   Assume that you are a new student at the university. Work with a partner and take turns asking for and giving directions to the following places. The student receiving directions should trace the route on the map. Start at location number 3, the American Language Institute. Then, alternate by starting from the library.

S1:   Could you tell me how I can get to the Bobst Library? (12)
S2:   Walk two blocks south to the end of the park. Cross West Fourth Street. The first building to your right is the library.

1. Vanderbilt Hall (11)
2. Brown Building (5)
3. Main Building (4)
4. Coles Sports Center (15)
5. Rubin Residence Hall (1)

C.   Imagine that you are having a party at your home on Friday. Find a partner and ask him/her if he/she is coming to the party. Explain where you live and how he/she can get there by bus / subway / car.

S1:   Are you coming to my party this Friday night?
S2:   Yes, but where do you live?
S1:   I live at. . . . (*complete address*)
S2:   How do I get there?
S1:   Where will you be coming from?
S2:   I'll be coming from school.
S1:   Will you be driving, or will you be coming by bus / subway?
S2:   . . .
S1:   O.K. Here's what you do. . . . (*Give directions.*)
S2:   . . . (*Close the conversation.*)

READING

How to Call a Waiter

You have practiced understanding and giving directions to places. Now you will read some instructions on social etiquette.

Calling a waiter is an art that differs from country to country. In a restaurant or cafe in the United States with first-rate service, there should never be a problem about attracting the attention of a waiter or waitress. A good waiter or waitress will regularly cast a quick glance° in the direction of any table he or she is serving. Unfortunately, many restaurants are understaffed,° and a lot of waiters seem to suffer from temporary° blindness at times. According to the books of etiquette,° the correct way to attract a waiter's attention in the United States is to raise a hand above one's head and motion the waiter to your table. Don't turn your hand palm outward and flap° it about; that is gauche.° Instead, hold your upraised hand, palm inward, with the index and middle finger raised, and the last two fingers bent inward over the palm. If you want the check, once you have attracted the waiter's attention, turn your hand over and make a writing gesture° in the air. This is a gesture that is understood in many countries.

In the United States, don't whistle, snap your fingers, clap your hands, or tap a spoon against a glass to get the waiter's attention. He will become offended° and probably act as though you don't exist. If you are in a restaurant and don't know how to catch the waiter's eye,° observe your fellow diners, and do as they do. But do it with authority. After all, you are paying the bill.°

Adapted from John Malone, *The How-To Book* (New York: Facts on File, 1985), p. 212.

take a quick look

not having enough employees / for a short time only
rules for polite behavior

move something up and down or from side to side / lacking social grace or experience

movement used to illustrate an idea

displeased, annoyed, having hurt feelings / get the waiter's attention
check, statement of charges for food and drink

D. Be prepared to answer the following questions related to the reading topic.

  1. How do you call a waiter/waitress in your country?
  2. How do you ask for the check in your country?
  3. How much do you tip a waiter/waitress in your country? How much do you think you should tip a waiter/waitress in the United States?
  4. Whom do you pay in your country, the waiter/waitress or a cashier?

E. Make a list of three or four things that are different about the service in restaurants in your country and in the United States.

MODEL COMPOSITION

The Heimlich Maneuver

You are in the cafeteria with three friends when a student at the table next to yours begins to choke, apparently on a piece of food. It becomes obvious that she cannot breathe or speak, and then her face starts to turn slightly blue. Something must be done quickly! What should you do to help?

Fortunately, there *is* something you can do, and it doesn't require a lot of first-aid training. On the contrary, the technique for helping a choking victim is easy both to learn and to perform, and is very often effective. This technique, called the Heimlich maneuver, has been approved by the American Heart Association. Here is how to perform the Heimlich maneuver.

With the victim standing in front of you, start by putting your arms around his or her waist from behind. Make a fist with one hand and grasp the fist with the other hand. Then, place the fist on the victim's abdomen. The thumb side of your fist must be facing the victim's abdomen, and the fist should be positioned just above his or her waist or navel and below his or her ribs. Next, compress the victim's abdomen by using your other hand to pull your fist in and up in one rapid motion. (Be sure your fist is positioned low enough so that you do not compress the victim's rib cage when you do the Heimlich maneuver, because such pressure may break some of the victim's ribs.) If the victim is still choking after you have compressed his or her abdomen, then repeat the abdominal-compression step, pulling your fist rapidly in and up. It may take several repetitions of this step before you can dislodge whatever the victim is choking on.

You can also perform the Heimlich maneuver as described above on a victim who is sitting down as long as the back of the victim's chair is not thick enough to prevent you from grasping him or her around the waist when you stand behind the chair.

F. ***A Magic Trick: Linking Paper Clips***   Work with a partner and complete the following instructions by using the verbs listed in the correct places. Use each verb only once. Then do the magic trick while your partner reads the instructions.

pull   place   get   practice   need

place   drop   perform   fold   link

To _____ a magic trick linking paper clips together,

you will _____ two paper clips and a paper money bill.

First, _____ the paper money bill in thirds as shown in

the diagram. Then, _____ one clip around the first and

second folds. Next, _____ the other clip around the sec-

ond and third folds. Finally, _____ the upper corners

away from you in a quick motion. The paper clips will

_____ together and _____ to the table.

_____ this at home until you _____ the

knack.

Elements of Style: Writing a Process Composition

Exposition is often used to give directions or to tell someone how to do
something. This type of composition is called a process composition.

There are certain basic requirements for writing process compositions:

1. Be very clear.
2. Choose a process that you are familiar with and that you have
   actually done yourself.
3. Give complete details and assume that the reader has not performed
   the process before.
4. Include directions that tell the reader what to avoid doing.
5. If necessary, include a sketch or a map to make the instructions
   easier to understand.

6. Use chronological order.
7. Think of the process as a list of steps: first, second, third, and so on.
8. Then, use the steps as an outline. Write the procedures the reader needs to follow simply and clearly in paragraph form.

Now reread the model composition. Which of the requirements do you think were followed in writing that process composition?

G. ***How to Make an Airplane*** Read carefully and then follow the instructions to make your airplane. To make an airplane from a post card, you will need the following materials: one post card, a ruler, Scotch tape, a pencil or ballpoint pen, and scissors.

The first step is to draw three lines lengthwise across the post card. The lines should divide the card into four equal parts (*see A*). Then, cut along the lines. One of the parts will be a body. On this part, draw three lengthwise lines that divide it into four equal parts (*see B*). Then, fold down the sides and tape them to form a body (*see C*). Next, another part of *A* will be a weight. Wind this second part of *A* around the top of the body and tape it there (*see D*). Next, another part of *A* will be the front wing. Draw a line down the center of this third part of *A* and tape it behind the weight on the body (*see E*). The last part of *A* will be the tail wing. First, cut this last part in half and then draw a line down the center of one of the halves and tape the tail wing to the body (*see F*). Then, turn down the center of the other half and tape the tail fin to the body (*see F*).

After that, try to fly the plane and try to control its flight well. Good luck!

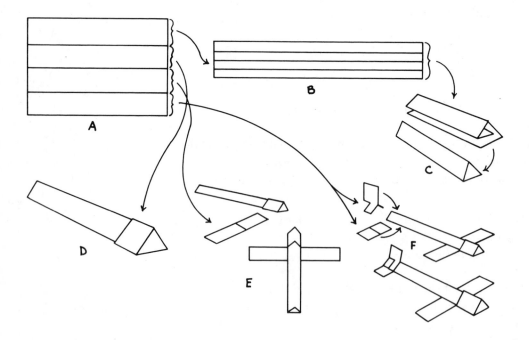

H. *Dictation / Dicto-Comp* Working with a classmate, arrange the sentences in correct order. Pay special attention to the words and phrases that indicate sequence of events. Then, listen as your instructor dictates the correctly ordered composition. Follow his/her directions.

How to Build a Sand Castle

When you have finished the towers, build a moat and a bridge for your castle.
First, get a pail and shovel.
When you have the water, build a little hill of sand so you have the material for your castle.
The last step is to put a beautiful flag on the top of the highest tower.
Then, choose a flat place on the beach.
Now start building towers from the sand hill.
After you have chosen a spot for your castle, go to the sea and fill the pail with water.
Wet the sand with the seawater to help you form walls and windows in the towers.
Remember: Build sand castles on the beach, not in your everyday life.

COMPOSITION WRITING

I. *Explaining a Process* Write a process composition following the model composition and the suggestions in the "Elements of Style" section. Use one of the topics listed here or some other topic of your choice. Be careful to choose a topic that is simple and not too broad.

how to cook your favorite
   food
how to bathe a dog
how to prepare for a test
how to use a washing machine
how to call long-distance

how to eat pizza
how to play a game or sport
how to use a copy machine
how to use a pay phone
how to take a book out of the library

J. *Giving Directions* Write a composition explaining to a friend how to get by car from one place to another. Choose a route that involves turns. Be sure to identify landmarks so that your reader will be able to follow your directions. Be guided by the following suggestions when giving directions and refer back to the paragraph in Exercise A.

   1. Choose the easiest route.
   2. Give the directions in the order in which they should be followed.
   3. If possible, name something that is easily seen near the place to be reached.
   4. Be very clear in your directions.

S T R U C T U R E

Linking Sentences in Exposition

When writing an expository paragraph explaining how to make or do something, linking expressions such as these help the reader follow the steps of the process smoothly:

> You begin by. . . . Then. . . . Next. . . . After you have. . . .
> First. . . . Next. . . . After that. . . . Finally. . . .
> After (adding the lemon). . . . Before (turning on the oven). . . . The
>   last step is to. . . .

Modal Auxiliaries

Modal auxiliary	Meaning	Example
can	ability	First aid can save a life.
		Can you catch his eye?
		He can't breathe.
may	permission	You may type your homework.
		May I erase the board?
	possibility	He may need help.
		It may rain tonight.
		She may not understand your instructions.
should	duty or obligation	You should go home early.
		We should know first aid.
		He shouldn't smoke.
must	necessity	You must help the man.
		I must get to work on time.

Note that the above modals are followed by the simple verb form.

8

L E S S O N

A Typical Day

A princess   A rock musician   A homeless person

*M*any Americans like to plan their schedule of daily activities and to follow it closely. They usually enjoy doing some of these activities very much and look forward to that part of their daily routine. Unfortunately, some people say they are bored by their daily routine and hate it. How about you? Do you plan your typical day? What do you enjoy doing the most in your typical day?

A. Imagine that the people shown in the illustrations are people in the news. Work with a partner and find out what he/she thinks each person does on a typical day. When you have finished, exchange roles and ask about another of the persons shown or about a famous person.

> *S1:* How do you think . . . spends his/her days?
> *S2:* What do you mean?
> *S1:* You know; what does he/she do all day long?
> *S2:* Oh, well, he/she probably. . . .
> *S1:* Would you like to be in his/her shoes?
> *S2:* . . .
> *S1:* Why? / Why not?
> *S2:* . . .

B. You are talking with a friend about your life before coming to the United States. You are comparing what he/she used to do often, always, and sometimes on a typical day with what you used to do. Work with a partner and role-play the situation. Then, reverse roles.

> *S1:* My life has changed so much since I came to the United States.
> *S2:* Mine has, too. I miss a lot of things from my country.
> *S1:* I do, too. I miss. . . . What was your typical day like in your country?
> *S2:* Well, I used to. . . . How about you?
> *S1:* Oh, I used to. . . .

R E A D I N G

New York University (NYU) provides interpreters for deaf students. The interpreters sit in the classroom and interpret what the instructor is saying using American sign language (ASL) or voicing° and lip movements.

the interpreter's using his / her voice to communicate what the deaf students want to say to the instructor

A Day in the Life of an NYU Interpreter

The alarm sounds. Oh please, just ten minutes more to sleep . . . mmmmm . . . I jump out of the cocoon,° shake off° the dream, pause in the kitchen to start the water and stumble° into the bathroom to take a quick warm shower where I slowly wake up. After the shower I turn on the radio to hear the weather report. Sunny? Good! Back in the kitchen I make my cup of coffee and take it into the bedroom and decide my "interpreter clothes" today will have to be suitable for cycling. Grabbing my backpack and sunglasses I hit Columbus Avenue on wheels. Riding down Ninth Avenue to West 4th feels good in the warmth of the sun. I lock up my bike° and go to my first class. I sit near the teacher and we exchange friendly looks. It is time for the class to begin. My fingers fly. This guy loves to talk as fast as humanly possible, I think to myself. Each student is different and I'm careful to include clear lip movements to aid in speechreading. Bing! The class is over. One down, three to go.° The next

a protective case / get rid of, free oneself from / walk unsteadily

bicycle

One class is finished. I have three more classes.

class includes one student who uses ASL as a preferred method of communication. It's a nice contrast and I relax into the topic at hand. This professor also must have taken a speed talking course. I begin to wonder if teachers share a common philosophy about imparting° knowledge as fast as they can? After class I head over° to the Center for Students with Disabilities.

giving

go

NYU employs over twenty-five interpreters and I never see them. Well, that's not quite true. Every other Wednesday when the timesheets° are due, I usually see three or four of my colleagues. We crowd around noisily catching up° on the latest events in our lives. We compare and complain: will we ever get membership to the Coles gymnasium, employment benefits or an increase in our pay rates. . . .

sheets on which hours worked are recorded

getting up to date

Returning to work, I wait for the elevator, enter the classroom, sit next to the teacher and wonder if I'll get a break this time before my arm falls off. Class ends and I rush out only to join the crowd of students at the elevator. Why are the elevators always so slow? The final class of the day includes a lively discussion with presentations, and I'm voicing for several deaf students. Yet another skill an interpreter brings into the classroom is the ability to capture the individual personalities of students and put that into the voicing of their signs. It is a relaxed informal class and one that I enjoy. The class ends and my arm is aching.° What a day!

hurting, painful

Riding through Washington Square Park on my bike, I stop and watch young teens practicing jumps on their skateboards and a guitar player with puppets° who attracts quite a crowd. Before moving on past some NYU film students setting up their next movie shot and babies in swings getting admiring smiles from their mothers, it occurs to me one reason I work here at NYU is that I enjoy its setting° in Greenwich Village. It's time to ride on, the day is done . . . ahhhh, but the night is young.

marionettes—figures made to move by someone pulling the strings

a place and its surroundings

Adapted from Candace Broecker, "A Day in the Life of an NYU Interpreter," *Access* 3, no. 1 (Fall/Winter 1987; published by the Henry and Lucy Moses Center for Students with Disabilities): p. 3.

C. Be prepared to discuss the following questions on the reading.

1. What items of clothing do you think the interpreter wears to work?
2. Have you ever tried to communicate with a deaf person? How did you do it?
3. How do some people speak to you when you don't understand their English?
4. List five activities that this interpreter does during the day.
5. List some activities that the interpreter does that you do, too. (Use *and I do, too* or *and so do I.*)
6. List three activities that the interpreter does that you don't do. (Use *but I don't.*)
7. Name three activities that neither the interpreter nor you do every day. (Use *and I don't either* or *and neither do I.*)

D. Work with three or four classmates. List three or four activities that you think the interpreter does at night. Be prepared to report back to the class what your group listed for activities.

MODEL COMPOSITION

A Typical Day in My Life

My alarm clock rings at seven o'clock every morning, and I usually get up at once. I jump out of bed and do physical exercises for ten minutes. Then, I am ready either to get back into bed or to take a quick cold shower. After my shower, I plug in my electric razor and shave. Then, I plug in my electric toothbrush and brush my teeth. Next, I comb my hair, wash my face again, and put on after-shave lotion. After that, I pick out my clothes for the day and get dressed. I prepare my own breakfast, which is usually grapefruit juice, scrambled eggs, toast, and coffee. I always listen to the news and weather report on the radio while I eat breakfast. By 8:00 A.M., I am ready to put on my coat and leave for school.

I generally go to school by subway, but the subway is always crowded, so I don't often get a seat. In the subway, on my way to school, I look at the signs on the walls of the car, watch the faces of other passengers, and read the newspaper headlines over someone's shoulder. It takes me about half an hour to get to school. When I get to school, I usually have time to talk to my classmates for a few minutes before class starts. My first class begins at nine o'clock, and my last class ends at three. After school hours, I sometimes go to the Student Center or to a coffee house with my friends for an hour or so. Afterwards, I go home.

As soon as I get home from school, I do my homework and study my lessons for the next day. At seven o'clock, I eat dinner with my brother. After dinner, I relax. Some nights, my brother and I watch television for an hour or two together. I really enjoy some of the sports programs because they are easy to understand. Other nights, I listen to my jazz records, work on my stamp collection, or write letters. My favorite nights are when I take a walk in the evening, visit a friend, or go out on a date. I try to get home by midnight, because by twelve o'clock I am generally rather tired. I take off my clothes, get into bed, and fall asleep immediately. I sleep until the alarm goes off again the next morning.

Elements of Style: Writing a Narrative

The model composition "A Typical Day in My Life" is in the narrative style of writing. A narrative tells a story. It is important in narrative writing to show the reader or listener the time relationship between sentences. In this way, the reader or listener can more easily follow the sequence of events. The order of the model composition is chronological. The first paragraph talks about the morning; the second paragraph discusses the afternoon; and the third paragraph describes the evening. To show the sequence of time, the following adverbials of time are used to link the sentences together.

> then . . . after my shower . . . next . . . after that . . . by 8:00 A.M. . . . when I get to school . . . after school hours . . . afterward (after that) . . . as soon as I get home from school . . . at seven o'clock . . . some nights . . . other nights

E. Look at the following paragraph. Complete the paragraph by putting adverbial expressions of time in the blank spaces to tie the sentences together. Use the following adverbial expressions of time:

first   next
after breakfast   after that
then

I get up at eight o'clock. _____I wash my

face and brush my teeth. _____I put on

my clothes. _____I eat breakfast.

_____I read the newspaper.

_____I leave my house and go to work.

F. Here is the daily schedule for Mr. Hill, an English teacher. Work with a group of classmates and write about Mr. Hill's morning, afternoon, or evening activities. (Follow your teacher's instructions as to the three groups that will be formed in the class.) After you have written your group composition, select a person to write it on the board. Correct each group's composition as it is written on the board. Try to show Mr. Hill as a real person with likes and dislikes and add details to his daily activities.

morning	6:00–7:00	wake up, jog, shower, get dressed
	7:00–7:45	eat breakfast, read the newspaper, leave for work
	9:00–12:00	teach English grammar
afternoon	12:00–1:00	Lunch
	1:00–3:00	teach English conversation
	3:00–5:00	correct papers, prepare lessons for next day
evening	5:00–7:00	go to computer class, leave for home
	7:00–11:00	drive home, eat dinner, relax with family, watch TV
	11:00	go to bed

G. Events in a narrative can also be tied together by indicating how much time it takes to do something. For example, in the model composition, it takes the narrator half an hour to get to school. Work with a partner and alternate asking and answering the following questions. Be sure to write your partner's answers and check with him/her to see that you wrote them correctly.

1. How long does it take you to get dressed in the morning?
2. How long does it take you to get to class?
3. How long does it take you to do your English assignments?
4. How long does it take a letter to get from the United States to your hometown?
5. How long does it take to fly from your country to the United States?

H. Work with a partner and alternate asking and answering the following questions about your daily schedule. Take notes on your partner's answers. Then, compare your answers. What things do you do the same way or at the same time? What things are different?

1. What time does your alarm clock go off in the morning?
2. Do you jump out of bed immediately?
3. What do you do as soon as you get up in the morning?
4. What do you eat for breakfast?
5. What time do you leave for school / work?
6. How do you go to school / work?
7. What interesting things do you see on the way?
8. What time do you get home from school / work?
9. When do you do your homework?
10. What do you usually do for an hour or two in the evening?
11. What things do you do for fun?
12. What time do you get ready for bed?

I. **Dictation / Dicto-Comp** Listen to your instructor dictate the following paragraphs. Then, follow his/her directions.

Julia Jones usually gets up at seven o'clock in the morning. She puts on her robe and slippers and goes to the bathroom to take a five-minute, warm shower. After her shower, she picks out her clothes for that day and gets dressed. Then, she has breakfast with her husband. After breakfast, she washes her face again and puts on her make-up and combs her hair. At eight o'clock, she kisses her husband good-by and leaves for work. Julia works as a dental hygienist in a dentist's office. At work, she cleans patients' teeth and gives them instructions on how to take care of their teeth. She works from nine o'clock to five o'clock.

As soon as she gets home from work, she takes a long bubble bath to relax. It makes her feel good. After her bath, she has dinner with her husband. On Thursday nights, she always goes to her oil-painting class, which she enjoys very much. She generally gets to bed by twelve o'clock feeling very tired, but happy.

COMPOSITION WRITING

J. Write a composition about "A Typical Day in My Life." First, work with a partner and make a three-paragraph outline following the organization of the model composition. Then, write your composition following that outline as closely as possible. Include details of your typical day so that your reader can get an idea of the kinds of things that make your life interesting in the United States.

STRUCTURE

Prepositions **by** *and* **until** *in Time Expressions*

1. The preposition *by* is used to show that something may happen before but not later than a certain time.

> I usually get home *by* midnight. (maybe before but not later than midnight)
> I generally get to school *by* nine o'clock. (not later than nine o'clock)
> He usually finishes his homework *by* ten o'clock. (not later than ten o'clock)

2. The preposition *until* indicates the end point of time of an activity or event.

> I sleep *until* my alarm goes off again the next morning. (Then, I wake up.)
> He goes to school from nine o'clock *until* three o'clock. (Then, he goes home.)
> He is going to wait for you *until* four o'clock. (Then, he is going to leave.)

It takes *in Time Expressions*

> *It takes + object pronoun + amount of time to do something.*

> It takes me about half an hour to get to school.
> It takes hims about two hours to do his homework.
> It takes me a long time to fall asleep.
> It takes them an hour to get to work.
> It takes us eight hours to fly from Europe to the United States.

Two-Word Verbs

Some verbs combine with other words, mainly prepositions, to form two-word verbs. These new verbs often have a meaning that is different from the meanings of the original two words. The preposition used with the verbs is sometimes called an adverb or a *particle*. Two-word verbs are common in the English language and should be memorized as a unit of meaning.

to catch up	to head over	to shake off
to crowd around	to jump out (of)	to sit down
to fall off	to leave for	to take off
to get back (into)	to listen to	to turn on
to get into	to lock up	to wait for
to get up	to pick out	to wake up
to go off	to put on	to work on
to go out	to rush out	

9

L E S S O N

Comparing and Contrasting
People and Places

Meadow Brook

Charming 2 bedroom

Spacious, 1200 sq. feet townhouses

High, 12-foot ceilings

Locked-door intercom system

4 large closets

Large eat-in kitchen

Private patio and garden

Very sunny and quiet

Gorgeous river view

45 minutes to downtown

$800 a month

Lexington Towers

Luxurious 2 bedroom, 10th floor

Galley kitchen

9-foot ceilings

24-hour doorman

Laundry on premises

Health club on premises

Garage on premises

Large 908 sq. feet

20 minutes to downtown

$1,000 a month

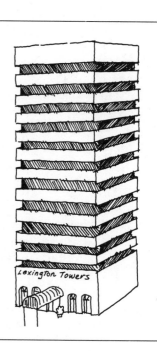

There is a well-known saying that nothing is good or bad, except by comparison. It is true that we are constantly making choices and decisions based on comparing similarities and contrasting differences. Where would you like to live? Which car should you buy? Is it better to go to Hawaii or to Colorado on vacation? Whom should you marry? Even your decision to study here was made after you compared several colleges and universities. By the way, how *did* you decide to study English at this school?

A. You want to rent an apartment near where you now live and have gone to talk with a friend about it. You need to decide between the two places shown in the illustrations. Complete the following dialogue and role-play the situation with a partner. When you are finished, exchange roles.

> *S1:* What do you think of the apartment in . . . ? I like it.
> *S2:* Why do you want to live there?
> *S1:* Well, because that apartment is / has. . . .
> *S2:* That's true, but that apartment is / has. . . . I like the other apartment because. . . .

B. By now, you must be an expert on how much it costs to live in this area. Work with a partner and compare the cost of things like food, clothing, gas, and housing.

> *S1:* Everything is so expensive around here!
> *S2:* Do you think so? You know, some things are cheaper here than in my country.
> *S1:* Really? What things?
> *S2:* Well. . . .
> *S1:* Don't you find anything more expensive here?
> *S2:* Yes. . . .

C. Work with a partner and ask your partner to compare herself/himself today and five years ago. How is she/he different today? How is she/he the same? Use some of the following vocabulary in your comparisons. Then, exchange roles.

Vocabulary of similarities	*Vocabulary of differences*
the same as	to be different from
to be the same	while
to be similar (to)	on the other hand
both	but
alike	however
as . . . as	whereas
like	unlike
	although

READING

World Records

The *Guinness Book of World Records* is the best-selling copyrighted° book of all time. In this book you can find old and new world records in hundreds of

having the legal right to distribute, publish, or sell a book or other creative work

categories°—from the most important inventions and discoveries to the most curious feats° of individuals.

> **divisions into groups**
>
> **clever actions showing strength or skill**

Here are some of the world records:

- The two longest rivers are the Amazon River, flowing into the Atlantic Ocean, and the Nile River, flowing into the Mediterranean Sea.
- The largest and heaviest mammal,° and the largest animal ever recorded, is the blue whale.

> **an animal whose young feed on their mother's milk**

- The largest living land animal is the African bush elephant.
- The fastest land animal over a short distance is the cheetah or hunting leopard.
- The richest cat in the world is "Charlie Chan," an alley cat° in Missouri, whose owner left the cat her entire estate of $250,000 when she died.

> **common cat with no known ancestry**

- The largest apple ever recorded weighed three pounds one ounce.
- The longest peanut was 3½ inches, grown in Georgia in 1987.
- The biggest tomato was grown in 1986 in Oklahoma. It weighed 7 pounds 12 ounces.
- The largest ocean is the Pacific Ocean.
- The largest gulf in the world is the Gulf of Mexico.
- The oldest written language with the longest continuous history is Chinese.
- The most commonly spoken language in the world is Mandarin Chinese.
- The second most commonly spoken language in the world is English.
- In written English, the most frequently used words, in order of frequency, are *the, of, and, to, a, in, that, is, I, it, for,* and *as.* The most used word in conversation is *I.*
- The singers with the greatest sales of records of any group have been the Beatles.
- The tallest office building in the world is the Sears Tower in Chicago with 110 stories.
- The largest amusement resort is Disney World in Central Florida.
- The country with the greatest area is the Soviet Union.
- The smallest independent country is the State of the Vatican City within the city of Rome.
- The longest speech made in the United Nations was one of 4 hours and 29 minutes by Fidel Castro, the president of Cuba, on September 26, 1960.
- The easiest test for a driver's license is in Egypt. You just have to have the ability to drive 19.7 feet forward and in reverse.
- The nearest planet to the earth is Venus.
- The largest of the major planets is Jupiter.
- The fastest barber on record is Gerry Harley, who shaved 987 men in 60 minutes with a safety razor in England.

- The biggest bubble blown with bubble gum measured 22 inches in diameter. It was created by Susan Montgomery Williams of Fresno, California on April 19, 1985.
- The tallest living animal is the giraffe.
- The most valuable animals in cash terms are race horses.

Selections from David A. Boehm, ed., *Guinness Book of World Records* (New York: Sterling Publishing Co., 1989).

D. Be prepared to discuss the following questions based on the reading. Use comparatives and contrasts.

    1. Who are the most popular singers in your country?
    2. Who is the richest person in your country?
    3. What is the longest river in your country?
    4. Which of the world records from the reading do you find the silliest? Why?
    5. Which of the world records do you find the most interesting? Why?

E. Work in groups of three to five people and reach an agreement on the answers to the following questions about your class and about life in this country. When you have finished, compare your answers with the answers of the other groups.

    1. Who tells the funniest jokes in the class?
    2. Who is the most studious student?
    3. What American food tastes the best / worst?
    4. What did you find the most difficult to get used to in this town / city?
    5. What do you like the most / least about the United States?

MODEL COMPOSITION

A Comparison of Two Cities (Shanghai and New York)

Shanghai is different from New York in many ways, but there are many things that are similar. Shanghai is one of the most populous cities in Asia, and New York is one of the most populous cities in North America. The weather in the summer is very hot in Shanghai, and it is the same in New York. Shanghai is a port and an industrial city, and New York is, too. Shanghai is a center of fashion and commerce, and so is New York. There are housing and pollution problems in Shanghai, and there are similar problems in New York. Both Shanghai and New York have serious traffic and transportation problems.

The population of Shanghai is homogeneous, but the population of New York is heterogeneous. Most of the people in Shanghai live in apartments in low buildings, while most of the people in New York live in apartments in high buildings. The housing shortage in Shanghai causes many people to live in overcrowded apartments, but the housing shortage in New York causes many people to be homeless. The traffic problem in Shanghai is caused by too many bicycles. On the other hand, the traffic problem in New York is caused by too many automobiles. While there are some differences, the major problems of big cities are almost the same everywhere in the world.

Elements of Style: Comparison and Contrast

A *comparison* tells you what is the same about two things. A *contrast* tells you what is different about two things.

The model composition uses sentences with parallel elements in order to show differences and similarities. Sentences in which parallel constructions are equal in length are called balanced sentences. They are often used to make comparisons and contrasts.

The population of Shanghai is homogeneous, but the population of New York is heterogeneous.

Shanghai is one of the most populous cities in Asia, and New York is one of the most populous cities in North America.

There are many rich people in New York, but there are many poor people, too.

F.   *Comparing and Contrasting*   Combine each pair of parallel sentences to make one balanced sentence, using the indicated connectors.

Shanghai is in Asia. New York is in North America. (but)
Shanghai is in Asia, but New York is in North America.

1. The people in Shanghai use fans to keep cool. The people in New York use air conditioning. (while)

_____

_____

2. There are many high bridges in New York. There are many deep tunnels in New York. (and)

_____

_____

3. There are many cathedrals in New York. There are many nightclubs, too. (while—start the sentence with *while*)

_____

_____

4. New York has many dirty streets. New York has many beautiful avenues. (and)

    _____

    _____

5. The people in Shanghai speak Chinese. The people in New York speak English. (but)

    _____

    _____

G.   Work with a partner and complete the following description comparing two friends. Use the correct form of the adjective or adverb.

I have two good friends named George and Kevin. George is two years _____ (old) than Kevin and is _____ (tall) and _____ (thin). He is built as _____ (straight) as an arrow, and his face is _____ (long) and _____ (angular) than Kevin's. Kevin is _____ (short) but _____ (strong) than George and has a _____ (full) and _____ (round) face. Both of my friends have gentle personalities. Kevin is _____ (quiet) than George and talks much _____ (little) than George does. When Kevin explains something, he is always as _____ (clear) as a bell, although he is often too serious. George is _____ (cheerful) than Kevin and always tells us jokes and funny stories about his life. He is _____ (experienced) in life than Kevin because he has lived a _____ (adventurous) life. This adventurous life, I feel, has made him _____ (impatient) than Kevin. George is accustomed to doing everything quickly, from working to talking. Kevin, on the other hand, speaks and works much _____ (slowly) and _____ (carefully). Both of them respect time and are usually early for appointments. I feel very fortunate to have them both as friends.

H. *Using the Superlative*   Alaska is a state that has many wonderful things. Work with a partner and complete the description of Alaska with the correct superlative form of the adjective in parentheses.

Alaska is _____ (large) state in the United States, but it is the _____ (little) populous of all the states. It is the northernmost state in the Union and the part of North America _____ (close) to Asia. Juneau, its capital, covers 3,108 square miles and is the nation's _____ (large) city in area. Mount McKinley (20,320 feet) is _____ (high) peak in the United States. Alaska has some of _____ (beautiful) scenery in the United States and _____ (active) volcanoes.

For many years, gold was _____ (important) mining product. Then, in 1968, two oil companies made one of the _____ (great) oil discoveries of all time on the Arctic North Coastal Plain. Prudhoe Bay is _____ (large) oil field in North America. Today, oil is the state's _____ (valuable) mineral product. Fish products are Alaska's _____ (important) manufacturing industry.

I. *Combining Sentences*   Work with a partner and combine each group of parallel sentences to make one balanced sentence. Use the connectors *and, but,* and *while* in sentences 1–6 and *both* in sentence 7. When you have finished, the sentences will complete a contrast paragraph in which the first sentence, or topic sentence, will be: *New York is a city of contrasts.*

   1. There are many kind and helpful people. There are many dangerous people.
   2. Many people are rich. Many people are poor.
   3. There are many old people. There are many young people.
   4. You can freeze in the winter. You can melt in the summer.
   5. There are many dirty streets. There are many beautiful avenues.
   6. There are symphony concerts. There are jazz concerts.
   7. New York is a jungle. New York is a paradise.

J. *Dictation / Dicto-Comp*   Listen to your instructor read the following paragraph. Then follow his/her directions. Note how this paragraph uses many words that are opposite or distinct in meaning in order to show contrast.

To most visitors, New York is both a fascinating and a frightening city. It is a city of great wealth and of great poverty. There are many rich people, but there are many poor people, too. There are many luxury apartment buildings, and there are many slum tenements. There is a great deal of beauty and a great deal of ugliness. The parks and the shops are beautiful, but the dirty streets and the subway stations are ugly. There are many tall skyscrapers above ground and many winding subways underground. Most things are expensive, but some things are free. The cost of entertainment is generally high, but there are usually many free lectures, concerts, and art exhibits. There is an "East Side" and a "West Side" and an "Uptown" and a "Downtown." There are people who work all day and people who work all night. The city is never asleep. New York may seem unfriendly, but it really isn't.

COMPOSITION WRITING

K. Write a composition of comparison and contrast about two cities following the model composition. First, fill in the outline with the things that you are going to compare and contrast. Use the same topic sentence with the names of the two cities you are going to write about. Be sure to use expressions indicating similarities and differences and parallel structures in your composition.

Comparison of Two Cities

    I. Similarities
       A. Main idea sentence (generalization): _____ *is different from* _____ *in many ways, but there are many things that are similar.*
          1.
          2.
          3.
          4.
   II. Differences
       A.
       B.
       C.
       D.
       E. Closing sentence (generalization)

Some things to compare: climate, people, industry, scenery, food and drink, political structure, family life, clothes, traffic, buildings, sports, transportation, and so on.

S T R U C T U R E

Comparatives of Adjectives and Adverbs

1. *Comparisons of inequality:* Adjectives and adverbs of one syllable—and of two syllables ending in *ow, y,* and *er*—form their comparatives by adding *er*. *Y* is changed to *i* before *er* is added. The word *than* is used in the second part of the comparison.

> George is two years *older* than Kevin.
> George is *happier* than Kevin.
> Alice is a *sweeter* person than Marilyn.

> *Note:* The last example sentence uses the construction *indefinite article* (**a, an**) + *comparative form of adjective* + *noun* (singular) **than.**

Adjectives and adverbs of two or more syllables form their comparatives by adding *more* before the word compared. The word *than* is used in the second part of the comparison.

> George is *more impatient* than Kevin.
> Alice is a *more patient* person than Marilyn.
> Kevin speaks *more slowly* than George.

2. *Comparisons of equality:* When two things that are the same are compared, this pattern is used: **as** + *adjective* + **as** or **as** + *adverb* + **as**.

> George is built *as straight as* an arrow.
> George isn't *as patient as* Kevin.
> My mother drives *as carefully as* my father.

3. *Irregular forms of the comparative and superlative:*

	Comparative degree	*Superlative degree*
good, well	better	best
bad, badly	worse	worst
far	further, farther	furthest, farthest
little	less	least
much, many	more	most

Superlatives of Adjectives and Adverbs

1. Adjectives and adverbs of one syllable—and of two syllables ending in *ow, y,* and *er*—add *est* to form the superlative. *Y* is changed to *i* before the ending is added. The word *the* or a possessive adjective or noun precedes the adjective or adverb.

> Mount Everest is *the highest* mountain in the world.
> The Sears Building in Chicago is *the tallest* building in the world.
> Tom is *my oldest* brother.

2. Most adjectives of two syllables and all adjectives and adverbs of three or more syllables add *the most* in front of the adjective or adverb to form the superlative.

> The president has *the most difficult* job in the United States.
> He was *the most intelligent* student in the class.

3. The expression *one of the* is used with the construction *superlative + plural noun.*

> Paris is *one of the most beautiful* cities in the world.
> Einstein was *one of the most famous* scientists in this century.

4. Note that the word *the* is not used before a superlative preceded by a possessive.

> Rhode Island is *our smallest* state.
> Susan is *her youngest* daughter.

Word Forms

Adjective	Noun
wealthy	wealth
poor	poverty
beautiful	beauty
ugly	ugliness

> *Note:* All the nouns in this list are abstract nouns. Abstract nouns are usually uncountable and in the singular form.

Is there much *beauty / ugliness / wealth / poverty* in New York?

10

The Dating and Mating Game

1. Are you a model?

2. Have you read this book?

3. Kiwi? I never had one. What does it taste like?

4. Hi!

*H*ow do you get someone of the opposite sex to talk to you in the United States? Some people go up to someone and ask for information. "Pardon me. I'm a stranger here. I'm from. . . . Can you tell me how to get to the nearest bank?" Nine times out of ten the person will try to help, and it is up to you to continue the conversation. The hardest thing to do really is to *open* the conversation. In this lesson, you will learn how people meet, date, and marry in the United States.

A.   Work with a partner of the same sex and role-play the following dialogue.

> *S1:* I'm having difficulty meeting . . . here in the United States. I don't know what to say to them. What do you say to open the conversation in your country?
> *S2:* That's easy. In . . . , I used to say ". . . ." How about you?
> *S1:* Well, in . . . , I used to say ". . . ."
> *S2:* How often were you successful?
> *S1:* Well. . . . How often did your line work?
> *S2:* . . .

B.   In the United States, many expressions are used to describe what happens in the dating and mating game. Study the accompanying nine illustrations, then read the expressions that follow them. Work with a partner and write the correct expression under each illustration. Then, find out whether your partner has ever done any of these things.

to pop the question   to carry a torch for someone
to pick someone up   to tie the knot
to break up   to feed someone a line
to have / go on a blind date   to go Dutch
to get hitched

> *S1:* Have you ever had a blind date?
> *S2:* . . . . How about you?
> *S1:* . . .

_____   _____   _____

_____   _____   _____

READING

Why I Love—and Hate Blind Dates

Into every social life, no matter how full, there must inevitably come a lonely time. You have just broken up with one person, and there is no one new on the horizon.° At times like these, there is likely to come a call from a friend, volunteering, with your okay, to fix you up.° How do you usually respond?

If you are anything like me, your first reaction is probably to say no. Also, though I know it's unreasonable, I begin to feel insulted. Has it really come to this—being fixed up with strangers?

But somewhere in there, mixed up with all the anxiety and indignation, is the burning coal of curiosity. Being fixed up is probably one of the last great adventures available to us all. It has only to be approached° in the proper spirit to yield its unusual rewards.

So why do so many blind dates go wrong? That, I believe, is chiefly the fault of the people doing the fixing. To a task requiring the utmost° concentration° and tact,° most fixers° bring the same degree of attention they devote to

(margin glosses)
point at which the earth and sky seem to meet / match you with someone on an arranged date

set about, undertaken

greatest degree of / close attention / skill in handling people / persons who arrange matters in advance putting together a sandwich. They unhesitatingly slap together° two people— two fragile and vulnerable egos—with the same abandon° they'd toss cold cuts into a hoagie.°

> put together without care / lack of control / large sandwich with a variety of fillings

Many matchmakers operate on the premise°—common among most would-be matchmakers—that any date at all is better than none, that any company whatsoever is preferable to your own. Personally, I think that's crazy—I can have a good time by myself—but most fixers, particularly if they are married, believe otherwise.

> idea on which reasoning is based; assumption

Fixees, however, can also make trouble for themselves. Some of them fail to state their non-negotiable° demands: "My date must be under 50 years old and over five feet tall." If something is truly critical, it's important to say so to the fixer. Other fixees create problems by demanding too much, by presenting a list of totally unrealistic requirements ("Al Pacino's eyes in Arnold Schwarzenegger's body"). Expect, when being fixed up, to make some sort of compromise.°

> not subject to being changed

> taking a middle course that involves making concessions

And expect, above all, to be surprised, because that seems to be, more than anything else, the greatest reason for being fixed up in the first place. Don't go into a blind date planning to meet the love of your life—chances are, you are not going to. But if you are just looking forward to meeting someone completely new, someone you would never have come across on your own, maybe even someone you would never have chosen for yourself, you can't be disappointed!

Adapted from Robert Masello, "Why I Love—and Hate Blind Dates," *Mademoiselle* (August 1982): p. 122.

C.   Be prepared to discuss the following questions based on the reading.

 1. At what age do young people in your country start dating? Where do they go on dates?
 2. How do people meet in your country?
 3. Is blind dating an acceptable custom in your country? If so, who arranges blind dates?
 4. Can a woman ask a man out in your country? Do you think it is a good idea? Why or why not?
 5. Who pays for a date in your country? Do you ever go Dutch?
 6. Have you ever had a blind date? How did it turn out?

D.   Imagine that you have played the "dating game" and are now more serious. You are looking for someone to marry. Write a short paragraph describing the person you would like to meet. Use some of the following characteristics if you like: honesty, sense of humor, tall, short, shy, talkative, older than I, younger than I, likes sports / movies / books, and so on. Begin your paragraph *I would like to meet someone who. . . .*

MODEL COMPOSITION

A Wedding

Last year, I went to my cousin's wedding when she got married in September on a lovely Sunday afternoon. My cousin, twenty-nine, and her boyfriend, thirty-one, met one morning while they were both jogging. They knew each other for two years before they decided to get married and have a big old-fashioned wedding, which both families helped pay for.

The wedding was held in a large hall with a chapel where the marriage ceremony took place. Because it was an interfaith marriage, the couple were married by a judge who was a friend of the family. The bride wore a long off-white dress and veil and carried a bouquet of flowers. Also, as is customary, she wore something old, something new, something borrowed, and something blue. The something old was her veil, which her mother and grandmother had worn at their weddings, the something new was her dress, the something borrowed was a handkerchief, and the something blue was a garter. The groom wore a tuxedo and a white boutonniere.

After the ceremony, the bride and groom and their parents stood in a receiving line, and all the guests congratulated them. Then, everyone went into the big dining hall to celebrate. First, everyone drank champagne toasts to the bride and groom and then sat down to a delicious dinner. After dinner, the orchestra began playing, and my cousin and her new husband danced while everyone applauded. Then, all two hundred guests joined in the dancing. After the wedding, the bride and groom left for their honeymoon on a Caribbean island. When they returned, they were ready to begin their new life in their new apartment.

E.   In groups of four students, study the photo of a wedding taking place in the United States. Indicate which of the following words and phrases are illustrated in the photo. Be prepared to tell the class what the other expressions mean. Later you will need the words and phrases listed here to write the composition "A Wedding," in Exercise I.

bride	to get engaged
maid / matron of honor	to get married
bridesmaids	wedding presents
bridal shower	wedding
bridal gown	wedding reception
veil	interfaith wedding
trousseau	newlyweds
groom	honeymoon
best man	
ushers	
bachelor / dinner party	
tuxedo	

F.   ***Sentence Combining***   Work with a partner and combine the following pairs of sentences, using adjective clauses. Use the second sentence in each pair as the adjective clause, which should be introduced by *who, whom, whose, which, when,* or *where.*

The bridesmaid was the next one to get married. The bridesmaid caught the bouquet.

The bridesmaid who caught the bouquet was the next one to get married.

1. The ushers were all close friends. The bridegroom chose the ushers.

_____

_____

2. The man was born in Italy. She married the man's son.

_____

_____

3. Paris is the city. They went to that city on their honeymoon.

_____

_____

4. There were many guests at the reception. The reception was held in the bride's home.

_____

_____

5. The table was decorated with flowers. They sat at the table.

_____

_____

6. The photographer asked everyone to smile. The photographer took the pictures.

_____

_____

7. The wedding took place last week. The wedding was attended by one hundred fifty guests.

_____

_____

8. The guest missed the wedding ceremony. The guest arrived late.

_____

_____

9. June is the month. Many people get married in that month.

_____

_____

G. Work with a partner and complete the following sentences with an adverbial clause of time. Remember that your clause must have a subject and a verb.

1. George dated many girls before _____

_____ .

2. George met Barbara one day when _____

_____ .

3. They saw each other whenever _____

_____ .

4. After _____ ,
   he didn't go out with anyone else.

5. They got engaged before _____

_____ .

6. They didn't want to get married until _____

_____ .

7. They both wanted a big wedding when _____

_____ .

8. At their wedding, everyone danced while _____

   _____ .

9. When _____ ,
   they went on a honeymoon.

10. They have both continued working since _____

    _____ .

H. **Dictation / Dicto-Comp**   Listen as your instructor dictates the following passage about current attitudes toward marriage. Then, follow his/her directions.

Americans seem to be going back to the marriage patterns of their great-grandparents and postponing marriage in favor of an education and a career. Back in the early 1900s, men and women married at older ages. Then, there followed a period when they married younger and younger. According to a survey taken in March 1988, the typical American male was 25.8 years old before getting married for the first time. For women, the median age was 23.6 for a first marriage. Not since 1900 had men waited that long to marry. Women hadn't delayed marriage until such a late age since the previous century.

Today, while both men and women are marrying later in life, the number of unmarried-couple households has grown almost five times since 1970. However, this still only represents less than 5 percent of all couples.

Data from the U.S. Bureau of the Census. "Marital Status and Living Arrangements: March 1988." *Current Population Reports*, Series P-20, No. 433. Washington, D.C., GPO, 1989.

COMPOSITION WRITING

I.   Describe a wedding you went to. Tell one of your classmates about it using the following questions as a guide. Then, write a composition about the wedding. Note that the questions follow the organization of the model composition. (Remember, before writing the composition, be sure you have learned the words and phrases presented in Exercise E.)

A Wedding

I. Introduction (first paragraph)
   A. Who got married? When did they get married?
   B. How old were the bride and groom?
   C. How long had they known each other before they got married?
   D. What kind of wedding did they have? Who paid for the wedding?

   II. The wedding
      A. Where did they get married? Who married them?
      B. What did the bride and groom wear?
      C. Where was the reception held?
  III. The reception and departure
      A. What happened after the wedding ceremony?
      B. How many guests attended the wedding?
      C. What did they serve at the reception?
      D. Was there any music and dancing?
      E. Where did the couple go on their honeymoon?
      F. Where did they plan to live afterward?

STRUCTURE

Adjective Clauses

Adjective clauses modify nouns or pronouns and tell you something about them. They are usually introduced by the relative pronouns *who, whom, whose, which,* and *that* and follow the noun or pronoun that they modify.

When the relative pronoun is the subject of the adjective clause, use *who* to refer to persons, *which* to refer to things, and *that* to refer to either persons or things.

> The judge *who married them* was a friend of the family.
> Everyone enjoyed the reception, *which lasted for four hours.*
> The bride wore a white dress *that was made of silk.*

When the relative pronoun is the object of the adjective clause, use *whom* to refer to persons, *which* to refer to things, and *that* to refer to persons or things.

> The man *whom you met* married my cousin.
> My sister caught the bouquet *which the bride threw.*
> The invitations *that they sent* were delivered late.

When the relative pronoun is the object of the adjective clause, it may be omitted.

> The man *you met* married my cousin.
> My sister caught the bouquet *the bride threw.*
> The invitations *they sent* were delivered late.

The relative pronoun *whose* is a possessive form. You can use *whose* to describe the subject or the object of the adjective clause. *Whose* can refer to people or things.

> She married a man *whose brother lives near me.*
> We were introduced to the man *whose son she married.*
> The church *whose walls are made of granite* is a nice place for a wedding ceremony.

Note that the words *when*, *where*, and *why* can also introduce adjective clauses.

> The church *where they got married* was in her hometown.
> I don't know the reason *why they waited so long.*
> Los Angeles is the city *where he was born.*

Adverbial Clauses of Time

An adverbial clause is a dependent clause that acts like an adverb. It can modify a verb and tell you time. Adverbial clauses of time are introduced by the words *when, whenever, while, after, before, until, since.* An adverbial clause of time can come at the end of a sentence or the beginning of a sentence. When the adverbial clause of time precedes the main clause, it is set off by a comma.

> They danced *until it was time to leave.*
> *After the ceremony ended,* there was a big reception.
> *When the orchestra started to play,* the bride and groom danced first.
> *While they were dancing,* the guests watched and applauded.
> *Before she left,* the bride threw her bouquet.
> My mother cries *whenever she goes to a wedding.*
> They have known each other *since they were children.*

11

L E S S O N

Getting Along in the United States

*W*hen we express our feelings, interests, and attitudes without words through the use of body language and gestures, we are using nonverbal language. It is estimated that when two people of the same culture speak, over half of the conversation is communicated nonverbally. When two persons of different cultures talk, nonverbal behavior becomes even more important. To get along in a country, you should know both the verbal and the nonverbal language. Are you aware of the nonverbal language in your country? Do you understand the nonverbal language in the United States?

A. Working with a partner, imagine that you need to get along in two of the situations shown in the illustrations. Use phrases from the following lists to create a short dialogue. Be prepared to role-play your dialogue in front of the class.

Party	*Bus stop*
Pardon me!	How do I get to . . . ?
I'm happy to meet you.	Is this the bus stop?
Hi. My name is. . . .	Please tell me where to get off.
How do you do?	Please speak slowly.
Are you enjoying the party?	
Store	*Restaurant*
How much is it?	Waiter! / Miss!
How much does this . . . cost?	We're ready to order now.
I'd like to buy this. . . .	I'd like. . . .
Where can I find . . . ?	Where is the men's / ladies room, please?
Where is / are . . . ?	The check, please.

B. Knowing how and when to use polite expressions is important to successfully function in a new country. Work with a partner and create a two-line exchange based on each of the ten situations described below. Use expressions from the list of polite expressions.

> You are hurrying through a crowded shopping mall and bump into a woman carrying several packages.

>> *S1:* Pardon me. I'm sorry.
>> *S2:* That's OK. No harm done.

> Your friend has just brought you a birthday present.

>> *S1:* This is a nice surprise. Thank you!
>> *S2:* You're welcome.

Polite expressions

How do you do?	Not at all.
Great! How about you?	Congratulations!
Pardon me. I'm sorry.	Don't mention it.
May I help you?	Thank you (so much).
Good-by. It was good seeing you.	Hi. How are you?
Thank you for a wonderful time!	Thanks. I'm glad you like it.

1. You are introduced to someone.
2. You meet a friend on the street.
3. Your friend does a favor for you.
4. You are a salesperson in a store. Offer assistance to a customer.
5. You are in an elevator and accidentally step on someone's toes.
6. Your friend is leaving your house after visiting you.
7. You like a friend's jacket and compliment him/her on it.
8. You thank someone as you leave for having invited you to a party.
9. It's hot, and someone has just opened a window at your request.
10. You congratulate a friend for winning a game.

Figure 1   Figure 2   Figure 3   Figure 4

READING

Getting Along Verbally and Nonverbally

When you are in another country, it is important to know the language, but it is equally important to know how to communicate nonverbally. Before saying anything, people communicate nonverbally or by making gestures.° According to a pioneer° in nonverbal communication, only 30 to 35 percent of our communication is verbal. The rest is nonverbal. When people don't know the language, the most common way to communicate is through gestures. However, many gestures have different meanings, or no meaning at all, in different parts of the world.

actions done to express a certain meaning / person who does something first and prepares the way for others

In the United States, for example, nodding your head up and down means "yes" (Figure 1). In some parts of Greece and Turkey, however, this motion can mean "no." In Southeast Asia, nodding your head is a polite way of saying "I heard you."

In ancient Rome, when the emperor wanted to spare someone's life,° he would put his thumb up. Today in the United States, when someone puts his/her thumb up, it means "Everything is all right" (Figure 2). However, in Sardinia and Greece, the gesture is insulting° and should not be used there.

let someone live who would otherwise have been killed

offensive

In the United States, raising your clasped hands above your head means "I'm the champion" or "I'm the winner" (Figure 3). It is the sign prizefighters make when they win a fight. When a leading Russian statesman made this gesture after a White House meeting, Americans misunderstood° and thought he meant he was a winner. In the Soviet Union, however, it is a sign of friendship.

didn't understand

In the United States, holding your hand up with the thumb and index finger in a circle and the other three fingers spread out means "Everything is O.K." (Figure 4) and is frequently used by astronauts and politicians. In France and Belgium, it can mean "You're worth nothing."

There are other nonverbal signals that people should be aware of when they go to another country, such as the distance to maintain between speakers. Americans usually feel comfortable when speaking with someone if the distance between them is about eighteen inches to arm's length. Anything closer makes them feel uncomfortable.

When talking to Americans, it is also important to make eye contact. If you look down when talking to an American, he/she may feel that you are embarrassed,° afraid, or trying to hide something.

feeling socially uncomfortable

In addition to knowing how to communicate nonverbally in a country, it is important to know what you can and cannot discuss. In the United States, there are certain topics to avoid° when you first meet someone. For example, don't ask people their age, weight, religion, marital status, how much money they earn, or how much something costs. You can talk about work, the weather, traffic problems, sports, food, news of the day, where one lives, consumer subjects (computers, car repairs, and so forth), and travel or vacation plans.

keep away from

These few examples illustrate that your actions can speak louder than your words. In a particular cultural context, what you say and what you don't say are equally important.

C. Be prepared to answer the following questions on the reading.

1. Do you have any difficulty understanding the nonverbal language in the United States? Which gestures have caused confusion or misunderstanding for you or people you know?
2. Have you come across any gestures that mean something different in your country and here in the United States? What are they?
3. What are some common gestures in your country, and what do they mean? Demonstrate and explain two gestures to the class.
4. Look at the four accompanying illustrations and tell the class what they mean in your country.
5. What is a comfortable distance to be maintained in your country when two people speak to each other? Do they stand closer to each other or farther apart than Americans? Do they touch each other when they speak?
6. Is it important to make eye contact in your country? Are there situations when one would not make eye contact?
7. In your country, what topics are acceptable to talk about when people first meet? What subjects are not acceptable?

D. Work in groups of three to five students. Stand up and act out the gestures you think you should make as your instructor reads the cues. Observe carefully the gestures made by others in your group.

1. You want to show that you are hungry.
2. You want to show that you are thirsty.
3. You are in a cafeteria and see something you want, but you don't know the word for it. How do you get it?
4. You want someone to come here.
5. You want the waiter to bring you the check.

E. Work with a partner and describe how to express the following situations nonverbally. Use the imperative in your descriptions.

1. You want to call a waiter.

2. Someone asks you a question and you don't know the answer.

   _____

3. Someone asks you how you are getting along. You want to say that everything is fine.

   _____

4. You want to tell someone you can't hear him/her.

   _____

5. You want to show that someone is crazy.

   _____

MODEL COMPOSITION

How to Get Along in the United States

May 21, 19___

Dear José,

   You have asked me for suggestions on how to get along in the United States. It is difficult to give advice, but I have found the following "dos" and "don'ts" helpful.

   As a rule, it isn't easy to find anyone to talk to in a big city. However, here are some suggestions. First, get or borrow a dog! Walk him several times a day! Americans love pets and usually stop to talk to anyone with a dog. Then, try to eat in a cafeteria! People generally share the same tables and will sometimes talk to you if they see that you are a stranger. Next, take your dirty clothes to a laundromat! It takes about an hour to wash and dry laundry, and many people wait in the laundromat. They often pass the time talking to the other customers. Always ask for information from a woman if you are a man, and from a man if you are a woman! It seems to get better results for a reason I can't understand. Learn the expressions *Please, Thank you,* and *You're welcome* before you come, and use them all the time! They usually work like magic.

   There are some things you shouldn't do. Don't tell the truth when people ask "How are you?"! They only expect the answer to be "Fine." Never ask people their age—men or women! Everyone wants to be young. Don't tell heavy people they are fat! Tell them they are losing weight. Everyone here is diet-conscious and wants to be thin. Don't be late for appointments! When someone says six o'clock, be sure to be there by six. Americans respect time and expect everyone to be "on time."

   Above all, don't worry! Just follow my advice and bring a lot of money and you will get along. I hope I have been of some help to you.

                                        Your friend,
                                        Miguel

Elements of Style: Writing a Process Composition

The model composition is written in the process style of composition. A process composition tells someone how to do something and very often uses the imperative form. In Lesson 7, you wrote a process composition. Reread the explanation in the "Elements of Style" section in that lesson and observe how closely the model composition "How to Get Along in the United States" follows the basic requirements listed there for writing a process composition.

F. A friend has asked you for advice on how to get along in the United States. Give him/her five points of advice using *negative imperatives*.

   give / credit card number
   Don't give anyone your credit card number.

   1. carry / cash

   _____

   2. walk / park / night

   _____

   3. put / address / key ring

   _____

   4. leave / house unlocked

   _____

   5. keep / wallet / back pocket

   _____

G. ***Using Prepositions***   The following is a letter of advice on how to get along in the United States. Working with a partner, complete the letter by writing *one* appropriate preposition in each of the blanks.

Dear Costas,

   You have asked me _____ suggestions on how to get along _____ the United States, so I am going to give you some advice.

   First, learn all _____ baseball and read the newspapers. Americans love to talk _____ sports and politics. Then, try to go _____ a baseball game. Americans like to comment _____ the game, the players, and the umpire while they are watching the game. Next, try to watch a parade. There are many parades _____ large cities. People who stand and watch the parades usually talk _____ everyone around. Then, try to stand _____ a line _____ a supermarket, _____ a movie theater, or _____ a school cafeteria. People line up everywhere and often pass the time talking _____ each other. Bring a musical

instrument _____ you or get one here. Then,

go _____ a park _____ a Saturday or a Sunday

afternoon and play it. Americans will stop and

gather _____ to listen and talk _____ you.

There are some things you shouldn't do. Don't say bad

things _____ pets. Americans love pets and won't like it if you

are unkind _____ animals. Don't get out _____ line

when you want to get _____ a bus or buy a ticket

_____ a movie. Americans are orderly about lines. Don't get

offended if people call you _____ your first name right away.

This is usual here because Americans are very informal, and they just

want to be friendly.

That is enough advice for one letter. Just come and I know you will

get along.

Your friend,

Paul

H. Class Advice   Work as a class and develop some additional suggested "dos" and "don'ts" for getting along in the United States. Select someone from the class to list them on the board. Be prepared to discuss why any suggestion is or isn't appropriate.

I. Dictation / Dicto-Comp   Listen to your instructor read the following paragraph about friendship in the United States. Then, follow his/her directions.

Making friends with an American can sometimes be a problem for people from other countries. In most cultures, a friend is someone you have known all your life and with whom you have a very close association and do many different things. While this type of friendship exists in the United States, Americans, as a rule, have many more casual friends. Because the United States has such a mobile society, Americans are constantly making new friends when they move. Though most Americans tend to have many casual friends, they don't always have a best friend. Americans usually have different circles of friends. They may have friends they work with, friends they went to school with, friends they play golf with, and so on. The friends in one group may never meet any of the friends in any of the other groups. Even though Americans tend to be outgoing and friendly toward strangers, don't wait for them to make the first move. If you want to be friends with an American, it is all right for you to start the conversation and extend an invitation.

COMPOSITION WRITING

J. Write a letter to a friend giving advice on how to get along either in the United States or in your country. Be guided by the model composition and the following outline.

    I. Introductory paragraph: state the purpose of the letter in general terms.

   II. Second paragraph: indicate specific things to do.
     A. Give three suggestions (use the imperative).
     B. Explain the reason for each suggestion.

  III. Third paragraph: indicate specific things not to do.
     A. Suggest three things not to do (use the negative imperative).
     B. Explain why they shouldn't be done.

  IV. Concluding paragraph: write a final bit of general advice and encouragement to your friend.

STRUCTURE

Imperatives

The subject of the imperative is always *you*. It is understood but not stated.

Affirmative imperative form	*Negative imperative form*
Get a dog!	Don't get a dog!
Eat in a cafeteria!	Don't eat in a cafeteria!
Open the window!	Don't open the window!
Go to a laundromat!	Don't go to a laundromat!
Be late for appointments!	Don't be late for appointments!

LESSON 12

Television Viewing

SUNDAY EVENING

	6:00	6:30	7:00	7:30	8:00	8:30	9:00	9:30	10:00	10:30	11:00	11:30
2 WCBS	★NCAA Basketball Tournament Midwestern Regional, second round (4:00)		★60 Minutes (CC)		★FILM The Wizard of Oz (1939). Judy Garland, Ray Bolger, Bert Lahr, Jack Haley, Frank Morgan, Margaret Hamilton, Billie Burke, The Singer Midgets. All aboard, all ages. (CC)				★Murder, She Wrote Jessica is arrested for murder and is put in jail (r/CC)		NEWS	CBS NEWS/ Sports Update
4 WNBC	NEWS	NBC NEWS	★Magical World of Disney "Swiss Family Robinson" (1960). John Mills, Dorothy McGuire. Tale of a shipwrecked family. (Part 2 of 2) (CC)		★Family Ties The Thompsons' home is vandalized (2 of 2) (CC)	★FILM Return of the Jedi (1983). Mark Hamill, Harrison Ford, Carrie Fisher, Billy Dee Williams, Anthony Daniels, Alec Guinness, Frank Oz. Third "Star Wars" adventure. Dazzling fun. (CC)					NEWS	Sports Machine
5 WNYW	★Columbo "Short Fuse." Columbo investigates the murder of a corporate official who was killed by an exploding cigar box (5:30)		21 Jump Street Captain Fuller's former army buddy asks Hanson and Penhall to help track down a deserter		America's Most Wanted	Married... With Children Al takes a second job as a cook (CC)	★Garry Shandling Parody of "The Fugitive" (r)	★Tracey Ullman An intimate encounter in an airplane restroom	Duet Linda plans a lavish birthday party for Amanda (r/CC)	A Current Affair Extra	NEWS	Sports Extra
7 WABC	NEWS	ABC NEWS (CC)	★Great Circuses of the World Highlights from Luxembourg, England, France, others (CC)		★Over the Edge Special about ordinary people involved in unusual situations (CC)		★The Women of Brewster Place Drama of several black women living in an inner city tenement, based on Gloria Naylor's novel; Oprah Winfrey, Jackee, Paul Winfield, Robin Givens star (Part 1 of 2) (CC)				NEWS	FILM The Defector (1966).
9 WWOR	A-Team		★FILM The Greatest Story Ever Told (1965). Max von Sydow, John Wayne. (Part 1 of 2)		Police Story				NEWS		★FILM Country (1984). Jessica Lange, Sam Shepard. Struggling Iowa farmers.	
11 WPIX	FILM The Assisi Underground (5:00)		Lifestyles of the Rich and Famous		War of the Worlds (r)		Billy Graham Crusade (CC)		INN NEWS	Paid programming	Cheers (CC)	Honeymooners
13 WNET	★Great Performances "Maria Callas: An Operatic Biography." Portrait of the opera star; performance footage; interviews (r/CC) (5:05)		★Great Performances "Toscanini: The Maestro." Profile of legendary conductor Arturo Toscanini; NBC Symphony Orchestra performances; James Levine, host and Alexander Scourby, narrator (r/CC)				★Great Performances "Bernstein at 70." Musical tribute to Leonard Bernstein; Seiji Ozawa, Michael Tilson Thomas, John Williams and John Mauceri conduct the Boston Symphony Orchestra; with Mstislav Rostropovich, Lauren Bacall, Betty Comden, Frederica von Stade, Yo-Yo Ma; Bobby McFerrin, others; Beverly Sills, host (Taped August 25, 1988) (CC) (Stereo simulcast on WNCN 104.3-FM)					★Great Performances "Maria Callas" (r/CC)
21 WLIW	★National Geographic "Grizzlies." Documentary of the endangered bear, filmed in Yellowstone Park and Alaska (r/CC)		Sneak Previews (r)	New Yankee Workshop (CC)	This Old House (CC)	Hometime (CC)	★Nature "Mozu the Snow Monkey." Documentary of female Japanese macaque born with deformed limbs (CC)		The Sandbaggers "First Principles." Drama about British secret service members; Roy Marsden stars (Two segments)			Sherlock Holmes "The Case of the Thistle Killer"
25 WNYE	Martinson Talks Books	YAI's on Our Own	Family Life Forum	Life Matters Depression	★A Conversation in Maine With Margaret Chase Smith Interview with the former senator (r)		Hanya: Portrait of a Dance Pioneer Profile of dancer Hanya Holm; rare 30's and 40's footage (r)		Anna Wyman Dance Theater		League of Their Own (r/CC)	Music of Ireland: Willie Week (r)

*I*t would be difficult to imagine a world today without television. What would we do without our favorite TV program? How could we afford to watch attractions like sports events, plays, and concerts anyplace else? Think of all the things you have seen on TV. If you were to choose the most interesting program you have ever watched on TV, what program would you pick?

A. Work with a partner. Imagine that the TV stations in your area show the programs listed on the TV schedule presented here. Ask each other what you usually watch on Sunday evenings at a certain hour. Then, exchange roles and select a different hour to talk about.

> *S1:* Do you watch TV?
> *S2:* . . .
>
> *S1:* What do you (usually) watch on Sundays?
> *S2:* . . . . How about you?
>
> *S1:* Me, too. I like that one. / I've never seen that one before. / I don't like that one. I usually watch. . . .

B. Look at the television schedule and role-play the following situation with a partner. You have only one TV set, and you both must decide what television programs you will watch tonight. You suggest a program (*Let's . . .*), and your partner disagrees (*Let's not . . .*). Be sure to give reasons for your choices. Continue suggesting programs until you can agree on what to watch. Be prepared to report back to the class on what programs you have selected and why.

R E A D I N G

How TV Americanizes Immigrants . . . for Better or Worse

Many new immigrants have an intense,° early relationship with television, the great Americanizer. It is a companion, a language lab, and food for conversation with their new countrymen. And it is a way to observe us, to see what we are like and how we are different from the people they left so far behind. — **strongly emotional**

In 1986, 601,708 legal immigrants came to the United States. After the drama, the danger of exodus,° they touched American ground at an airport. Minutes later, they were on the freeway, en route to their lives in America. For many, it was not ethnic neighborhoods or immigrant cultures that eased the transition.° To get to know America, they watched television. The television set—in color, with 24-hour programming and a dazzling° array of channels—was their first American friend. — **leaving** / **made the change easier** / **brightly shining**

Following is a newcomer's account of television's role in teaching him our language and customs.

Jack Assadourian—dark, handsome, perfectly groomed° in coat and tie, with a big moustache and designer glasses—manages a Los Angeles restaurant. — **well-dressed**

With the help of his American uncle, he got a visa and came here from Lebanon when war broke out in his country in 1975. He first worked as a foreman in a handbag factory. In the evening, he watched television at his uncle's house in New Jersey. He watched constantly, and what he saw wasn't just comedy or drama. He saw us. His own social circle was made up of other immigrants. "Television," he says frankly,° "is the only way I knew about American life. Everything I see, I see on television. How Americans relate, how they communicate." — **speaking honestly**

He saw it with a unique° eye. On "Laverne and Shirley," he saw two women working and living on their own. "In Lebanon, women don't work. Here, women are independent. It was an education for me." "Charlie's Angels" was even more of an eye-opener: "Three gorgeous women going out saving people!" But he had misgivings° about "The Bionic Woman" and "Wonder Woman" because they showed women as strong as men. Family life as he knew it was based on the strength of the man and the sensitivity,° the gentleness of the woman. "When something is wrong with one of my children, it's my wife who understands."

Still, American family life seemed very appealing° on that screen. "Happy Days," one of his early favorites, showed an open, casual household that delighted him. And "All in the Family" evoked nostalgia.° "I liked seeing the generations living together. That was like my background. Of course, Archie° and his son-in-law disagreed. Disagreement is common in families. That's part of life. But it's *all in the family.* The name is perfect."

Sometimes he wonders if there may not be too much freedom here between the sexes. But then he smiles and applies the resourcefulness° that has taken him halfway around the world. "I watch television, and I take from this culture what is good and I leave what's bad."

Adapted from Susan Littwin, "How TV Americanizes Immigrants . . . for Better or Worse," *TV Guide* (April 9, 1988): p. 4.

being the only one of its kind

feelings of doubt or distrust

awareness of other people's feelings

attractive or interesting

brought back memories
the name of the father on "All in the Family"

ability to find ways of overcoming difficulties or problems

C.   Be prepared to discuss the following questions in class.

   1.   What American television shows are popular in your country?
   2.   What did you learn about American culture from watching American television shows in your country?
   3.   Which television shows here have helped you most to understand the language and the culture?
   4.   What American television show do you find easiest to understand? Why?
   5.   How does television in your country differ from television in this country?
   6.   How does television in your country reflect your country's culture?

D.   Work in a group of three to four students and plan a television program. First, decide on the type of program you want by selecting from the following list. Then, as a group, write an outline listing the kinds of decisions you made about your program, such as the name of the program, kind of program, length, what its purpose will be, who will appear in it, and what it will be about. Share your outline with the class.

Types of television programs

game show
cartoon program
talk show
soap opera
documentary program (in-depth news story about a human or social situation)

sitcom (in which the same characters appear each week in a comic situation)
variety show (in which many different people entertain)

MODEL COMPOSITION

My Favorite Television Program

My favorite television show is "Star Trek: The Next Generation." It is on every Saturday night at 8:00 P.M. on Channel 11, and I have seen this program every week since I came here. "Star Trek: The Next Generation" is science fiction and a continuation of the original "Star Trek" series. The name of the spaceship, the *Enterprise,* is the same, but the spaceship is now bigger and better. This series takes place eighty-five years later than "Star Trek," and all the characters are new. The *Enterprise* is now under the command of Capt. Jean-Luc Picard and carries over a thousand people. As in the old "Star Trek," the ship is still chasing unfriendly aliens in space. Each week the stories introduce strange and often fascinating characters, and each episode is always packed with action. For me, the most interesting character in the series is neither the android, Data, who remembers everything, nor the half-Betazoid, Deanna Troi, who can feel emotions around her. My favorite character is the spaceship itself. I know the *Enterprise* isn't a person, but the spaceship is beautiful with so many interesting advanced technological parts.

In my country, I used to watch the original "Star Trek" all the time and became a devoted "Trekkie." I used to go to all the Trekkie conventions and buy all the Trekkie souvenir merchandise, so I know that I will watch this new series every week.

E. Retelling What You Used to Do   Think about things that you would frequently do in your country. Write five sentences describing these things and use the expression *used to.*

When I was in Mexico, I *used to* watch variety shows.

1. _____
2. _____
3. _____
4. _____
5. _____

F.   Work with a partner and complete the following sentences with the definite article *the* if necessary. If no article is necessary, put an *X* in the blank space.

1. I used to watch many programs on _____ television in my country.

2. Most people had _____ television sets, but not many had _____ VCRs.

3. Now that I am in the United States, I have _____ latest model television set and _____ VCR, and I am a regular _____ couch potato.

4. My favorite programs are _____ ones about _____ health, _____ news programs, and _____ old movies.

5. Last night, I watched a program about _____ smoking. _____ doctor on _____ program said that _____ smoking was bad for your health.

6. Next, I watched a movie about _____ World War II. (I have seen many movies about _____ Second World War.)

7. After that, I turned to _____ Channel 4 and watched _____ news.

8. Then, I fell asleep while _____ television was on.

G. The following are descriptions of two popular American television shows. Work with a partner and complete the descriptions with words from the list that precedes each paragraph. Use each word only once. When you have finished your descriptions, select which of the two programs you would like to watch, and be prepared to explain why.

"M*A*S*H": situation comedy

of	in	during	but	on
behind	the	only	through	an

This series, _____ antiwar comedy, was set

_____ wartime Korea _____ the fifties.

All the characters were members _____ the 4077th

M*A*S*H (Mobile Army Surgical Hospital) located a few miles

_____ the front lines. The series painted a picture

of _____ horror and futility of war. The conditions

were terrible, and the _____ way the doctors could keep

their sanity was _____ a sense of humor. The Korean War

lasted only three years, _____ this program went

_____ for eleven years. It is now in reruns.

"Dallas": drama

because	in	about	both	of
for	over	the	outside	to

Set _____ Texas, this series is _____

two families, the Ewings and the Barnes, who have been fighting

_____ oil rights _____ many years. Both

families have made huge fortunes in oil and live lavishly. All the Ewings

live in South Fork, _____ large family ranch

_____ Dallas, Texas. Mainly, the series is about the lives

_____ the two Ewing brothers—Bobby, the "good guy,"

and J.R., the "bad guy," whom viewers love _____ hate

_____ he is unprincipled in _____ his

personal and business affairs.

H. ***Dictation / Dicto-Comp***   Listen to your instructor read the following selection about "The Cosby Show." Then follow his/her directions.

Television shows about families are very popular in the United States, and "The Cosby Show," a weekly situation comedy about the Huxtables, has been one of the most popular. The Huxtables, an upper middle-class, black family, live in a comfortable house with their five children—four daughters and one son. When the series began, the oldest daughter was away at college, another daughter and son were teenagers, a third daughter was about nine years old, and the adorable youngest daughter was five. The father, Bill Cosby, is an obstetrician with an office in the house, so he is often home while his wife, an attorney, is out working.

The Huxtables are a happy, loving two-career family with strong family ties and the everyday little problems that parents have to deal with in rearing their children. All families can identify with the universal problems presented in the show: a son who has a messy room, a teenage daughter who wears too much make up, a child who gets bad grades in school. The parents handle all these problems firmly, calmly, and sometimes humorously, but they never get angry or place blame on any of their children. They are ideal parents bringing up their children with strong family values. It is this combination of elements—humor, family love and values—that many people feel accounts for the show's success.

I.   Write a composition about your favorite television programs, using the model composition and the following outline as guides.

My Favorite Television Programs

    I. My favorite television program in the United States
        A. What is your favorite television program in the United States?
        B. What kind of program is it?
        C. What is it about?
        D. Who is your favorite character on the program?
        E. Why do you like that character?
   II. My favorite television program in my country
        A. What program did you like to watch most in your country?
        B. What kind of program was it?
        C. How often did you use to watch it?
        D. What was it about?
        E. Why did you enjoy watching that program?

S T R U C T U R E

Used to

The expression ***used to*** + *simple verb* expresses the habitual repetition of an action in the past.

> When *did* you *use to watch* television in your country?
> I *used to watch* television every evening.

Use of the Definite Article **the**

1. *The* modifies a noun that describes a specific or unique person, place, or thing.

> *The* actor who plays J. R. Ewing on "Dallas" is Larry Hagman.
>   (describes a specific, unique person)
> There are many soap operas on television in *the* afternoon. (There is only one afternoon in a day.)

2. *The* is used to modify a noun that describes something specific, unique, or already mentioned, but the indefinite article *a* or *an* modifies a nonspecific noun.

> *A* television is a good thing to own. (nonspecific)
> *The* television I just bought is from Japan. (specific)
>
> That is *a* good idea. (nonspecific; there are many ideas)
> *The* idea you had sounds very good. (specific idea)

3. *The* always precedes an adjective in the superlative degree unless there is a possessive adjective or noun before the adjective.

> Bill Cosby is *the* funniest man on TV.
> Bill Cosby is *our* funniest man on TV.

4. *The* does not precede an uncountable noun when the noun refers to something in general. However, *the* does appear with an uncountable noun when the noun refers to something specific.

> Comedy is good for you because it makes you laugh. (comedy in general)
> *The* comedy in many sitcoms is forced. (specific)

5. *The* precedes a noun that represents the totality of a class or group: a kind of animal, a kind of flower, a kind of TV program.

> *The* turtle is a slow-moving animal.
> *The* soap opera is a popular genre in today's TV.

> *Note:* A or an, in the sense of *any,* is also used in this manner:
> **A** *program about science is always interesting.*

13

Bad Habits

$\mathcal{F}$rom time to time, we all become mildly annoyed or very irritated, by someone else's characteristic behavior pattern that we regard as a "bad" or "nasty" habit. Perhaps we dislike the fact that the person is always late or tells terrible jokes or coughs without covering his or her mouth. After all, we can't expect that others will be perfect—or that they will even agree with us about whether a particular behavior is annoying. Think about habits that you are familiar with—both your own and those of other people. What kind of habits really bother you?

A. Work with a partner and imagine that you are observing the situations shown in each of the illustrations. Role-play the following dialogue and say how you feel about what each person is doing: *Ugh! How disgusting! Yuck! How gross! Whew! How annoying! How nasty! How inconsiderate!* and so on. When you have finished, exchange roles.

> *S1:* Did you see what *the man sitting at that table* was doing?
> *S2:* No, what was *he* doing?
> *S1:* He was. . . .
> *S2:* . . .

B. Work in groups of four people and take turns talking about your own bad habits. Keep a list of other people's "bad habits" in order to report to the class after the next exercise. You may use some of the following examples or any others that you can think of.

> *S1:* Do you have any bad habits?
> *S2:* Yes, of course. No one's perfect. I. . . . How about you, (*classmate's name*)?
> *S1:* Well, I . . . .

(*Habits*) . . .

spend too much money	leave my clothes on the floor
crack my knuckles	eat too much
get impatient when I have to wait in a long line	forget people's names
	hand in assignments late
talk to myself	lose my temper in a traffic jam
smoke too much	

C. Now find out what each person in your group is going to do about stopping (kicking) one of his/her habits. Be prepared to tell the class about their plans for improvement.

> *S1:* What are you going to do about kicking your habit of. . . ?
> *S2:* Well, ...
> *S1:* That's a good idea. Good luck! What about you, (*classmate's name*)?
> *S3:* . . .

R E A D I N G

Bad Habits: Their Causes and Cures

If you dominate° every conversation, constantly forget your car keys, back-seat-drive (even in parking lots!), or never remember to return whatever you borrow, then you have one of the many types of habits that can drive friends up a wall. If you have reached the point where one of your typical behavior

take control over

patterns is even driving *you* wild, take heart°! Help is at hand.° There *are* ways of kicking those pesky habits° that annoy you and everyone around you.

gain confidence or courage / immediately available / breaking those bothersome habits

Habits are behaviors that people repeat again and again, often without even realizing it—for example, the writer who scratches his nose as he works or the student who taps her foot during an examination. Psychologists believe that people develop such habits because they have a problem or are experiencing some kind of stress.° These habits then serve to relieve the tension° that they are under.

pressure caused by difficulties in life / lessen the feeling of worry or anxiety

Many psychologists say that people will only continue to perform a habitual behavior if they get some benefit from it. Once the habit becomes unpleasant or is no longer rewarding, they may try to get rid of° it. Breaking a habit, however, is not an easy thing to do. The first step is to make up your mind that you want to eliminate the habit and convince yourself that you have enough will power° to do it.

eliminate

strength of will; determination

The following are some suggestions for how to successfully break bad habits:

1. Find out what provokes° the habit. (When do you exhibit° your habitual behavior? Where? Why?) Then, make up your mind not to behave the way you usually do under those circumstances.°

causes / show

conditions

2. Try a deep-breathing exercise. Relax and breathe in and out three or four times to help you reduce stress and as a substitute for your habit.
3. Try to imagine how good you will feel when you are free of your annoying habit. Remember that you are whatever you think you are.
4. Reward yourself for every small improvement. If you want to lose thirty pounds, for example, reward yourself for every three or five pounds that you lose. Buy yourself a record or a new item of clothing or treat yourself to a movie, play, or concert.
5. Practice self-control. Whenever you are faced with temptation,° wait ten minutes before engaging in° your habitual behavior. During those ten minutes, use daydreams or fantasies to gain control. Try not to give in to temptation. Every time you resist,° you will feel much better about yourself and have more confidence in your ability to break the habit.

something attractive / performing

fight against it

6. Finally, be realistic in the goals you set for yourself. Set small goals at first because they are easier to reach.

Some people need more than positive reinforcement (rewards) to help them break a habit; they also need negative reinforcement (punishment). If you belong in this group, try digging° your fingernails into the palm of your hand or pinching yourself every time you lose control and fall back into the habit you are trying to break.

pressing down hard

The most important thing is not to become discouraged. Remember to concentrate on your successes and not on your occasional failures. If you should slip back° into your troublesome habit, don't lose faith in yourself. Just keep your eye on your goal° and start again.

fall back

aim; purpose

D. Be prepared to discuss the following questions based on the reading.

1. Why do you think people develop habits?
2. What kind of habits do many Americans have that bother you?
3. Have you ever tried to break a habit? What did you do to overcome it? Did you succeed?

4. Do you know anyone who has successfully kicked a habit? What did he/she do to overcome it? Did he/she succeed?

5. What do you think is the best way to break a habit?

E. Write down one habit you have that you would like to get rid of. Then, write down three reasons why you would like to break this habit.

MODEL COMPOSITION

Bad Habits

Everybody has some personal habits that he or she would like to get rid of, and I am no exception. Procrastination is my number one bad habit. I do this especially whenever I have an unpleasant task to perform. This is a difficult habit to break, and as a result, I am always rushing to finish things that I have put off until the last possible moment. Twirling my hair is another irritating habit. Whenever I am nervous or uncomfortable, I fall back into this childhood pattern. I also have the bad habit of talking too much and saying foolish things whenever I am very tired. This is something I always regret the next day.

Other people have habits that I don't like either. Students who click their ballpoint pens in class drive me up a wall. People who don't move to the rear of a bus and who block the doors are two of my pet peeves. People who don't put the cap back on a tube of toothpaste are another source of irritation. I find this habit very annoying. Unfortunately, we all do things unconsciously that bother other people, but that is because nobody is perfect.

F.   *Pet Peeves*   Talk to as many classmates as possible and ask and answer each other's questions about pet peeves. Use some of the questions and habits from the lists that follow after the model.

> *S1:* What kind of people drive you up a wall?
>
> *S2:* People who (*smoke cigars*) drive me up a wall.

What kind of people {
upset you?
irritate you?
bother you?
annoy you?
drive you bananas?
}

What is one of your pet peeves?

People who . . .

don't clean up after their dogs	snore
throw cigarette ashes on the floor	use bad language
hum and whistle to themselves	gnash their teeth
laugh loudly at their own jokes	sleep diagonally in a double bed
scrape their nails on a chalkboard	pick their nose

G. What are your bad habits? Make sentences following the pattern shown in the model and using the habits listed here or other habits you may have.

>   I have the bad habit of (looking at the floor when I talk to people).

Habits

leaving my dirty dishes in the sink after a meal	glancing at a watch or clock during conversations
eating in bed	talking during movies
leaving doors or drawers open	scratching my head, nose, and so on
forgetting to mail letters	never putting anything away

H. **Using Correct Word Forms**   Complete the following sentences by using the *-ing* form (gerund) of the verbs indicated. For help in spelling these forms correctly, refer to the Handbook.

1. _____ (break) habits takes time.

2. _____ (walk) is good exercise and a way to relieve tension.

3. _____ (chew) gum is bad for your teeth.

4. Whoever is interested in _____ (be) on time needs to get better organized.

5. He is fond of _____ (sit) on his desk.

6. She is looking forward to _____ (get) rid of her bad habits.

7. The teacher is tired of _____ (tell) the students to stop _____ (eat) at their desks.

8. _____ (talk) in his sleep is his number 1 bad habit.

I. Complete the following sentences with *whenever, wherever, whichever, whatever, whoever,* or *whomever.*

1. You can either go to your room to play your radio or use earphones, _____ you please.

2. If you need help in breaking a habit, you can consult a hypnotist or a psychologist, _____ you prefer.

3. _____ told you that breaking a habit is easy was not telling the truth.

4. You should turn the lights out _____ you leave the room for more than a few minutes.

5. If you want to remember to mail your letters, you should put them _____ you will be most likely to see them when you leave the house.

6. In order to remember to do something, you can tie a string around your finger or write yourself a note, _____ you prefer.

J. Dictation Listen to your instructor dictate the following letter written to a newspaper columnist who gives advice. Then, work with a partner and write a letter telling "Annoyed" what he/she should do.

Dear Abby,

   I work in an office with many people. My problem is one coworker who constantly chews gum in a very irritating manner. This person is always popping, cracking or chewing gum loudly—and keeps this up all day without any consideration for the rest of us in the office.

   I don't object to gum chewing if it is done quietly, but this person is driving me bananas with all the noisy chewing, cracking, and popping! What can I do about it?

                                                                    Annoyed

COMPOSITION WRITING

K. Write a two-paragraph composition following the model composition about your bad habits and other people's bad habits. Before you begin, make a two-paragraph outline of the composition you are going to write.

STRUCTURE

Gerunds

Verb forms ending in *-ing* may be used as nouns. When they are used as nouns, they are called *gerunds*.

   Gerund as subject of a verb
   Talking too loud is a bad habit.
   Borrowing pens and then *forgetting* to return them is one of my irritating habits.

   Gerund as object of a preposition
   He has the annoying habit *of jingling* the change in his pocket.
   Her habit *of winking* unconsciously at the wrong time bothers me.

Whenever, wherever, whichever, whatever, whoever, whomever

whenever	on any occasion, no matter when (*adverb*)
wherever	whatever place, at those places (*adverb*)
whichever	the one which (*pronoun*)
whatever	of any sort or degree (*pronoun*)
whoever	any person who, the person who (*used as subject*)
whomever	any person whom, the person whom (*used as object*)

He has the bad habit of littering *wherever* he goes.

If you have a habit that irritates you or other people, you should try to overcome that habit, *whatever* it is.

Here is a copy of *Beating Bothersome Behavior*. Please read this book *whenever* you have the time.

L E S S O N

14

The American Way of Life

$\mathcal{T}$here are many different ways to live in the world. These different ways are neither better nor worse than your own way. They are simply different. No matter where we live, we all carry with us throughout our lives certain ways of looking at and doing things that our culture says are natural and important. This is our "cultural baggage." Look in your pockets or purse. What objects are you still carrying from your culture? Do you have any objects from the American culture with you? What are they?

A. Work with a partner and ask and answer the following questions based on the illustrations. Then, ask your partner what some of the national emblems and typical scenes are in his/her country.

> S1: Do you think the illustrations are representative of the United States?
> S2: Yes / No, because. . . .
> S1: What other emblems, images, or things do you associate with the United States?
> S2: . . .

B. Work with a partner and find out what he/she likes best about Americans and American life and what he/she likes least. Then, exchange roles.

C. It is very natural for someone to be afraid when he/she is in a new culture. Work with a partner and find out what your partner was afraid of when he/she first came to the United States. When you have finished, exchange roles. Use some of the expressions on the list or others that describe what you were afraid of.

> S1: What were you afraid of when you came to the United States for the first time?
> S2: I was afraid of. . . .

not being understood
not being able to find my way around
getting sick
not being able to eat the food

embarrassing myself
not understanding the
 language
not being able to read the signs
losing my money

READING

What Is an American?

The people of every country have their own national character. This character shows their way of thinking and reacting° to life around them. It is important to remember that a national character is a stereotype° and that not every individual in the country has the same outlook or values. Knowing the national character, however, helps a nonnative get along better in that culture. Try to imagine what kind of person you might be if you were an American.

acting in response

generalization about what
 the people of a particular
 group, country, class, race,
 sex, or religion are like

If you were a typical American, you would probably be preoccupied° with speed and efficiency.° You would often be in a hurry and at times impatient. Also, you would probably like soft drinks, hamburgers, and baseball. If you were like many American women, you would act independently and be self-reliant.°

A closer look at the average American would show other characteristics, too. If you were an American, you would value education, and you would probably trust scientific explanations. You would believe in the work ethic and think that laziness is immoral.° You would value privacy, but you would make acquaintance quickly and easily with many kinds of people, often calling them by their first names. You would value progress as one way of going forward. For you, there would be no standing still. Youth and energy would be very important to you, too. You might be a member of many groups because you would believe in volunteering° your time. You might solve many of your problems by forming committees. In business and management, you would believe in competition. The most central value in your national character would be a belief in the worth of the individual, and all your institutions would reflect this value. For example, in American family life, the relationships among family members would be democratic. It would also be easy to leave your family setting and function in the wider community as an individual.

If you were an American, you would probably be optimistic° and always believe that problems could be solved and that there would be a happy ending. However, you would feel that you had to work for this happy ending yourself and not just wait for it to happen. You would try to shape the world to your taste. You would say, "Don't just stand there—do something!" or "If you don't succeed, try again!" If someone tried to discourage you by saying "Rome wasn't built in a day," you would humorously° point out that they didn't have an American foreman° on that job.

This is how you might feel and behave if you were an American. However, if a person wants to really understand what is going on in another country, it is not enough just to study the other country. You must understand your own national character as well in order to bring about true cross-cultural communication.

Adapted from "When Americans Live Abroad . . . ," Department of State Publication 7869, Department and Foreign Service Series 129. Washington, D.C., GPO, Released May 1965.

D. Be prepared to discuss the following questions on the reading.

1. What are some of the American values discussed in the reading?
2. Does your culture have some of the same values? What are they?
3. What other values does your culture have?
4. Which American belief or practice seems very strange to you?
5. What American custom has it been the most difficult for you to get used to here? How does it differ from a similar custom in your own country?

Margin glosses:

concerned about something / working without waste

able to act without depending on others

considered bad

willingly giving one's time and effort without payment

holding the belief that things will turn out well

in a funny way

person in charge of other workers

6. What cultural traditions would you like to pass on to your children?

7. How have you changed since coming to the United States? Are you comfortable with these changes?

8. Relate a funny experience about adjusting to life in the United States.

9. Do you agree or disagree with the ideas in this reading selection? Why?

E. It is often possible to learn something about a country's values by looking at the proverbs that people in that country grow up with and learn. Here are some American proverbs and some of the values they represent:

Proverb	*Value*
Time is money.	punctuality, thriftiness
God helps those who help themselves.	self-reliance, initiative
Every cloud has a silver lining.	optimism
You've made your bed, now lie in it.	responsibility

Work with someone from your own country, if possible, and write three proverbs that illustrate the values of the people in your country. Indicate what values are represented by the proverbs and then tell the class.

MODEL COMPOSITION

The American Way of Life

The American way of life may be different from yours, and some things that seem natural and ordinary to us may puzzle you.

Americans, as a rule, are very informal and will probably call you by your first name as soon as they meet you. Although this shows a warm attitude, it does not mean that they want to begin a lifelong friendship. Americans also show their informality in their casual dress. For example, if you go to the ballet or the opera, you might see some people wearing jeans.

Most families live in individual homes in the suburbs and towns, but in the cities, most people live in apartments. Americans have few servants but many electrical appliances to help them be more efficient. The husband, wife, and children all share the domestic duties of the household because most married women work.

In their free time, Americans like to go to the movies and listen to music, do volunteer work, watch television, and read. Football, baseball, basketball, hockey, and horse racing are the major spectator sports. The most popular participant sports are swimming, bicycling, fishing, bowling, hiking, and camping. Other popular sports include tennis, golf, skiing, and jogging.

Even though the struggle for the rights of blacks, women, and homosexuals is still not complete, today, if you are divorced, a single parent, or different, it is accepted as part of the American way of life.

One thing to remember is that the United States has a history of evolutionary ideas and social changes. If you don't like the way things are now, wait a minute! You may like the new changes, despite the way things are now.

F.   Time is very important to Americans, and the language is filled with references to time. You are *on time*, you *keep time, make time, fill time, save time, use time, spend time, waste time, lose time, manage time, gain time, make up time, schedule time, kill time*, and *are given time*. Work with a partner and read the following situations. Then, answer the questions using an appropriate time expression.

1.   Tom has a lot of homework, but instead of doing it, he is listening to his records. What is he doing?

_____

2.   Richard is late for an appointment, so he is taking a taxi instead of a bus. What is he trying to do?

_____

3.   John is going to meet his friend at 3:00, but it is only 2:30 now, so he decides to take a walk. What is he doing?

_____

4.   Mary doesn't feel well and has called to see her doctor tomorrow. Her doctor says that he is very busy but that he will reschedule some appointments in order to see Mary. What will he do for Mary?

_____

5.   The audience at a rock concert are tapping their feet and clapping their hands as they listen to the music. What are they doing?

_____

G.   *Combining Sentences*   Work with a partner and combine the following pairs of sentences by using *although* or *even though*. Then, combine the same sentences by using *despite* or *in spite of*.

1.   Americans are very money-conscious. Americans do a lot of volunteer work.

_____

_____

_____

_____

2.   The pace of life is very rushed in American big cities. The pace of life is much slower in small towns.

_____

_____

_____

_____

3. Immigrants have trouble with English. Immigrants can often find good jobs.

   _____

   _____

   _____

4. Winter weather in the northern states is terrible. Americans drive in all kinds of weather.

   _____

   _____

   _____

5. Americans are friendly. Americans are hard to know intimately.

   _____

   _____

   _____

6. Americans are hospitable and generous socially. Americans are hard-driving and competitive professionally.

   _____

   _____

   _____

7. Americans take pride in their country. Americans often criticize their country's shortcomings.

   _____

   _____

   _____

8. Racial prejudice has diminished in the United States. Racial prejudice still exists.

   _____

   _____

   _____

9. The great mobility of American society makes lifelong friendship difficult. Lifelong friendships still exist.

_____

_____

_____

_____

H. *Dictation / Dicto-Comp*   Listen to your instructor read the list of what Americans do in one day, then follow his/her directions.

In one day, Americans do the following:

- Americans dream up 7 or 8 new products to sell in supermarkets or drugstores.
- Americans eat 47 million hot dogs.
- The United States government spends more than 2 billion dollars. Federal computers dole out 5.5 million of it without any human supervision.
- Almost 6,000 teenagers have sexual intercourse for the first time.
- 4,250 Americans have an abortion.
- 22,000 foreigners visit the United States.
- Americans eat 3 million gallons of ice cream and ice milk.
- Americans eat more than 400,000 bushels of bananas, the country's most popular fruit.
- 30 Americans celebrate their 100th birthday.
- 200 Americans become millionaires.
- Americans see at least 3 UFO's (Unidentified Flying Objects).
- Americans spend 3.6 million dollars on toys and accessories for their pets.
- Americans gobble up 75 acres of pizza.

Selections from Tom Parker, *In One Day* (Boston: Houghton Mifflin Company, 1984).

COMPOSITION   WRITING

I.   Write a composition about the way of life in your country. Use the model composition and the following outline as guides.

The _____*Way of Life*

  I. Introduction: general statement about the way of life in your country
 II. Informality versus formality: people's attitude
    A. How they show it
    B. Dress code

III. Living arrangements
   A. Where most people live
   B. Servants versus domestic self-sufficiency
   C. How housework gets done
IV. Free-time activities
   A. Major activities
   B. Favorite spectator sports
   C. Favorite participant sports
 V. Social attitudes
   A. Attitude toward divorce
   B. Attitude toward being a single parent
   C. Attitude toward being different
VI. Conclusion
   A. General statement about the way of life in your country
   B. Possibilities of change in your country

S T R U C T U R E

Expressing Opposition or Concession

Certain expressions can be used as transition words to introduce an opposing or contrasting statement.

1. The subordinate conjunctions *although* and *even though* have the same meaning and are used to introduce adverbial clauses of opposition or concession. The main clause to which they are linked expresses an unexpected result.

> Children usually leave their parents' home before they are married.
>   They have close family ties.
> Children usually leave their parents' home before they are married
>   *although* (*even though*) they have close family ties.
> *Although* (*Even though*) they have close family ties, children usually leave
>   their parents' home before they are married.

When the adverbial clause comes before the main clause, it is followed by a comma.

> Americans are very individualistic. They often join committees.
> *Although* (*Even though*) Americans are very individualistic, they often
>   join committees.

2. The prepositions *despite* and *in spite of* also express opposition and mean the same thing. Since both expressions are prepositions, they must be followed by an object (a noun, a pronoun, or a verbal noun). If the object of one of these prepositions is a verb, it will have to be changed to the *-ing* (gerund) form. The prepositional phrase can come at either the beginning or the end of a sentence. If the phrase comes at the beginning of the sentence, it is generally set off by a comma.

> Children usually leave their parents' home before they are married. They have close family ties.
> Children usually leave their parents' home before they are married *despite (in spite of)* having close family ties.
> *Despite (In spite of)* having close family ties, children usually leave their parents' home before they are married.

> Americans are very individualistic. They often join committees.
> Americans often join committees *despite (in spite of)* being very individualistic.
> *Despite (In spite of)* being very individualistic, Americans often join committees.

15

Birth Order

*H*ow many children do most American parents want? Do they like to have children who are close in age, or do they like to have children who are several years apart? Do Americans expect that their first-born, their second-born, and their last-born children will be different from each other or alike? These are some of the questions that you will consider in this lesson. Then, you will write about your own family and how you feel your birth-order position has affected you.

A. How would you feel if you were a child in each of the families shown? Work with a partner and find out how he/she feels about the following questions. When you have finished, exchange roles.

> *S1:* How would you feel if you were an only child?
> *S2:* . . .
> *S1:* If you were a twin, would you and your twin dress alike?
> *S2:* . . .
> *S1:* Would you like to have twins? Why or why not?
> *S2:* . . .
> *S1:* How would you tell them apart?
> *S2:* . . .

B. Now find out from your partner how many children he/she would like to have. How close in age would he/she like them to be? Why? After your partner has answered the questions, exchange roles. Be prepared to report back to the class about your partner's responses.

R E A D I N G

Birth-Order Theory

According to birth-order theory, every position in the family is special in its own way. Children in every family are treated differently and develop different personalities depending on whether they are the oldest, youngest, middle, or only child. Members of each of these groups, however, usually share similar characteristics.

First-borns

First-borns often identify with their parents' values more easily than other children. As a rule, they are more conservative° and demand more of themselves. First-borns try to excel° in everything they do and have high standards, which they apply to themselves as well as to others. As children, they are often asked to assume responsibilities beyond their age; for example, taking care of their younger siblings° while their parents are out. Their constant efforts to please Mom and Dad lead them to become high achievers and to succeed in high-pressure jobs and careers. They tend to do well in the corporate, professional, and academic fields.

It is interesting to note that more than 50 percent of all the presidents of the United States have been first-borns or first-born sons.

°liking old ways rather than change
°be outstanding

°brothers or sisters

Only Children

Only children not only have many of the same characteristics as first-borns but often carry these traits to an extreme. In contrast with first-borns, their parents' admiration and undivided attention last throughout the only children's lifetime. Their fear of disappointing their parents can become an unending effort to be perfect. As a result of their upbringing,° only children may be super-reliable,° well-organized, and sensitive to adult needs. On the other hand, their parents' overindulgence° can turn only children into dependent, spoiled,° and selfish brats.° Only children often appear to be very mature and responsible for their age. They are generally self-sufficient, enjoy privacy, and have high self-esteem.° For that reason, they may end up in similar occupations or professions as first-borns.

> **process of raising, training, and caring for a child / extremely dependable giving in to an extreme extent to someone else's desires / having lost goodness / bad-mannered children / confidence and satisfaction in oneself**

Twenty-one out of the first twenty-three U.S. astronauts were the oldest or only children in their families.

Middle Children

Middle children are different. They usually look outside of the family for approval and acceptance and are therefore more sociable and less conservative than other children. They try to obtain from their peers° the attention their older brothers and sisters received from their parents. By finding their strength outside the family, they learn valuable skills that prepare them for adult life. These might include diplomatic skills, the ability to listen and relate to others, and knowing how to compromise° and negotiate.° It is no coincidence that many middle children end up in managerial or leadership positions.

> **persons of equal rank, class, or age**

> **settle an argument by taking the middle road /try to come to an agreement**

Youngest Children

That leaves the youngest children. These, the theory goes, can become real charmers,° playful or manipulative in their desire to get attention. They develop strategies° to make their presence felt, either by behaving disagreeably or by finding creative or athletic outlets such as writing, drawing, or sports. Does baby get away with murder?° The youngest childrens' parents are often older, more tired, or more relaxed about rules that seemed important with preceding children. These children therefore grow up experiencing fewer family pressures and more independence. The result is a more creative, carefree person, which is why the youngest frequently choose careers in the arts, entertainment, or sales.

> **people who can make others like them / ways, techniques**

> **avoid getting caught or punished for misbehaving**

What does all of this mean in terms of everyday life? No one's personality fits these descriptions exactly. However, birth-order theory can help a person better understand himself or herself and can serve as a tool for self-improvement.

C.   Be prepared to discuss the following questions on the reading.

1. What is your opinion of the birth-order theory?
2. Does this reading accurately describe your characteristics according to your birth-order position? If so, in what ways is it accurate? If not, in what ways is it inaccurate?
3. Does your culture place any special significance on being the oldest or first-born?
4. Do people in your country tend to have large or small families? Why?
5. What would happen if everyone had only one child?

D.   Work with two classmates and find out how each of you feels about his/her birth-order position. First, ask what each person's birth-order position is. Then, find out what some of the advantages and disadvantages of this position were. Finally, ask each person in what birth-order position he/she would like to have been and why. Be sure to include yourself in your survey. Report to the class.

	Classmate 1	*Classmate 2*	*Myself*
1. Name?			
2. Actual birth-order position?			
3. Advantages?			
4. Disadvantages?			
5. Preferred birth-order position?			
6. Reason why?			

MODEL COMPOSITION

On Being the Youngest

The role I play in my family has definitely helped shape my personality and character. I am the only girl and the youngest in my family, coming after three boys.

As a child, my brothers always introduced me to their friends as "my little sister." I felt secure in being the youngest because I knew my brothers were always there to protect me. Sometimes, however, this sense of security over-powered me. For example, when my friends told me of their adventures abroad or at a sleepaway camp, I was afraid to try these experiences myself. I felt so loved and protected with my family that I would rather stay home than go far away and meet new people.

Being much younger than all three of my brothers does create other problems. Soon I will begin to apply to colleges, and I am already anxious about this situation. All three of my brothers attended Ivy League schools. Therefore, there is pressure on me to get into a "good" school, too.

Although it is sometimes difficult to be the youngest with three older brothers, this position has many advantages. For example, whenever I have a problem, I always have someone to turn to. This has helped make me a more understanding person and has given me a special viewpoint on life. I wouldn't trade my position as the youngest for anything in the world.

E. Sentence Combining   A reader may need to know what caused something to happen. Work with a partner and combine the following cause and result sentences using *so . . . that . . . , such a (an) . . . that . . . ,* or *such . . . that. . . .*

1. It was fun having three older brothers. I never wanted to leave home.

   _____

2. They took good care of me. I never had to do anything for myself.

   _____

3. I felt secure at home. I didn't want to travel.

   _____

4. My three brothers were good athletes. They made their school teams.

   _____

5. My brother Mark was a good actor. He was in all the school plays.

   _____

6. My brother John had a pretty girlfriend. I was jealous.

   _____

7. We were a big family. We needed a station wagon.

   _____

8. I was a naughty child. I had to be disciplined.

   _____

9. I had many toys. I couldn't play with all of them.

   _____

   _____

10. It was nice being the youngest. I never wanted to grow up.

    _____

    _____

F.   Sentence Variation   Sometimes you can use several constructions to express the same thought. Varying the construction will make your writing more interesting. Work with a partner and vary the following sentences by using the expression **would rather** + *simple verb...* than. . . .

My twin brother, Thomas, and I are very different . . .

1. I prefer to go to an Ivy League school.

   _____

2. I prefer staying home.

   _____

3. I prefer talking to my friends to studying.

   _____

4. My brother prefers watching television to listening to the radio.

   _____

5. He prefers going out to baby-sitting.

   _____

G.   Dictation / Dicto-Comp   Listen to your instructor dictate the following paragraphs. Then, follow his/her directions.

Many psychologists believe that birth order can greatly influence the way you are, the type of people you select as friends or mates, and the kind of romantic relationship or marriage you have. They recommend that people make use of birth-order theory to get to know themselves better and to better understand the personality of their husband or wife.

Opposites attract each other, say researchers, and they suggest that life is less complicated for people who marry outside their own birth order. A first-born can teach responsibility to a youngest, for example, while a youngest can help a first-born relax and be more carefree. People who have the same birth order may find that they encourage the worst characteristics of their group in each other. Two middle children could try so hard to avoid conflict that they might end up not communicating. Although good birth-order matching may help in a marriage, it is not a guarantee of happiness. Understanding and sensitivity toward your mate are also important.

COMPOSITION WRITING

H. Write a composition about your birth-order position. Follow the model composition and the outline below.

Birth Order

    I. Family
       A. General statement on the effect of birth order
       B. What is the size of your family?
       C. What is your birth-order position in the family?
   II. How your birth-order position affected you as a child
       A. What were some of the advantages of this position? Give an example.
       B. What were some of the disadvantages of this position? Give an example.
 III. How your birth-order position affected you as an adult (or a teenager)
       A. What were some of the advantages of this position? Give an example.
       B. What were some of the disadvantages of this position? Give an example.
 IV. Conclusion
       A. How do you feel about your birth-order position?
       B. Would you prefer to have had another position?

STRUCTURE

Adverbial Clauses of Result

The cause of an action can be stated in one sentence, and the result of that action can be given in another sentence. However, it is easier to understand a cause-and-effect relationship when both sentences are combined, as in the following examples:

1. **such a (an)** + *singular noun* + **that** + *result clause*

It was a big house.
All the children had to help with the housework.
It was *such a* big house *that* all the children had to help with the housework.

2. *such* + *plural noun / uncountable noun* + *that* + *result clause*

My brothers were good students.
I wasn't sure I could be as intelligent.
My brothers were *such* good students *that* I wasn't sure I could be as
    intelligent.

3. *so* + *many / much*, *adjective, or adverb* + *that* + *result clause*

My parents were busy.
They made my brothers take care of me.
My parents were *so* busy *that* they made my brothers take care of me.

Use of *would rather* and *prefer*

The expression ***would rather*** + *simple verb* means the same as *to prefer*. It
usually refers to a present or future time.

> *Note: Prefer* can be followed by either an infinitive or a gerund
> construction.

He *prefers to go* to the movies.
He *prefers going* to the movies.
He *would rather go* to the movies.

He *prefers swimming to playing* tennis.
He *would rather* swim than *play* tennis.

*I*t is usually easy to recall your first experience in a new country, in a new city, on a new job, or at a new school. You remember well what happened, what seemed strange to you, and what was just as you expected it to be. In this lesson, you will learn about other people's first-day experiences. Listen to their stories as you prepare to write about your own first-day experience somewhere.

A.   Imagine that you are in one of the situations shown in the photographs. Work with a partner and find out about his/her first impressions in the United States. When you have finished, exchange roles.

> *S1:* Do you remember your first day in the United States?
> *S2:* Yes, very well.
>
> *S1:* What are the three things you remember most clearly?
> *S2:* . . .

B.   Now think about the first time you had to use English in the United States. Work with a partner and find out when and where this occurred, what happened, and how he/she felt about it. When you have finished, exchange roles.

READING

The following narration was written by a university student about her experience while taking German for the first time. As you read, think about your reactions to your first English class in the United States.

My First Day in German Class

Beginning German class met twice a week, Mondays and Wednesdays, from 2:00 to 4:00 in the afternoon, on the sixth floor of Kirk Hall. There were about fifteen to twenty students in the class, and we were all studying German for the first time.

Our professor was an old German lady who spoke English with a very thick accent. Professor Schmidt always wore a dark skirt, a shirtwaist,° and very sensible shoes.° She was short, barely five feet tall, and plump,° but she had more energy than all of us put together.

> a woman's tailored dress /
> low, comfortable shoes /
> nicely rounded; well
> covered with flesh

On our first day of class, after a brief introduction to the course in English, she started talking in German. She was all over the room, pointing to things and holding up objects as she rattled off° strange sentences.

Several times I tried to ask her to speak more slowly, but she pretended not to see my half-raised hand. Vainly° I waited for a translation as I became more uncomfortable and unhappy. I looked around at the class and noticed that most students were eagerly listening to Professor Schmidt. They realized that our professor wanted us to listen in order to get used to the strange sounds she was uttering.°

After we had listened for a while, she held up several objects and said sentences that we all had to repeat. Listening to a strange language was hard, but pronouncing the sentences was harder still. I sat there afraid to open my mouth because I might make a mistake. I watched and listened to my classmates enviously.° They were repeating the sentences as if they had spoken German all their lives! This only made me feel more insecure.°

Soon the professor was calling on individual students. I knew she would call on me any minute. I was petrified° that if I made a mistake, the whole class would laugh at me. In my mind, I had just decided to drop° the course when the professor asked me to repeat a sentence after her. I felt everyone's eyes on me as my professor repeated the sentence and waited patiently.

My tongue felt like a whale.° I swallowed hard and repeated very slowly: *"Das ist ein Buch.°"* The professor's eyes lighted with pleasure, and she exclaimed more enthusiastically° than I deserved: *"Sehr gut, Fraulein, sehr gut!°"*

The class looked at me in admiration, and I felt I had said something really profound.° Maybe learning a foreign language is not that hard after all, I thought. With new confidence, I listened to my classmates repeat sentences and impatiently waited for my turn to recite. I gave up the idea of dropping the course and decided I would learn to speak German like a native.

Glossary:
- repeated quickly
- without result; uselessly
- saying
- wanting very much what someone else has / lacking self-confidence; uncertain
- very fearful
- get out of
- large marine mammal
- "This is a book."
- with a strong feeling of eagerness. / "Very good, Miss, very good."
- deep; full of meaning

C. Be prepared to discuss the following questions on the reading.

1. Do you remember your first day in an English class? What happened? How did you feel?
2. Were you able to understand the instructor the first day? Did he/she talk too rapidly or too slowly?
3. What is the most difficult thing for you in English—the grammar, the vocabulary, the pronunciation, or the spelling?
4. What is the best way to learn a language?

D. Evaluate your first English course. List three things you did that you found very useful and three things you would improve or eliminate. Begin your lists with the following expressions:

I especially liked. . . .
I really didn't like. . . .

MODEL COMPOSITION

My First Day in the United States

I arrived in the United States on February 6, 1988, but I remember my first day here very clearly. My friend was waiting for me when my plane landed at Kennedy Airport at three o'clock in the afternoon. The weather was very cold and it was snowing, but I was too excited to mind. From the airport, my friend and I took a taxi to my hotel. On the way, I saw the skyline of Manhattan for the first time, and I stared in astonishment at the famous skyscrapers and their manmade beauty. My friend helped me unpack at the hotel and then left me because he had to go back to work. He promised to return the next day.

Shortly after my friend had left, I went to a restaurant near the hotel to get something to eat. Because I couldn't speak a word of English, I couldn't tell the waiter what I wanted. I was very upset and started to make some gestures, but the waiter didn't understand me. Finally, I ordered the same thing the man at the next table was eating.

After dinner, I started to walk along Broadway until I came to Times Square, with its movie theaters, neon lights, and huge crowds of people. I didn't feel tired, so I continued to walk around the city. I wanted to see everything on my first day. I knew it was impossible, but I wanted to try.

When I returned to the hotel, I was exhausted, but I couldn't sleep because I kept hearing the fire and police sirens during the night. I lay awake and thought about New York. It was a very big and interesting city with many tall buildings and big cars, and full of noise and busy people. I also decided right then that I had to learn to speak English.

E. Think about the first time you held a paying job or the first time you helped someone do some work, even if it was not for pay. Answer the following questions about that experience.

1. What was your first job / work experience?
2. What was the first thing your boss asked you to do?
3. Did you understand what he/she told you to do?
4. Did you have to get help to do it?
5. If it was a paying job, how much money did you start earning? How long did you have to wait for your first raise? If it was nonpaying work, how much money do you think the job was worth? Do you think you did the work well enough to have gotten a raise if it had been a paying job?
6. Did you make new friends in your first job / work experience?
7. What kind of work will you begin looking for when you finish school?

F. Think about problems that you have adjusting to an English-speaking environment. Answer the following questions about some possible difficulties.

1. What things seem too difficult to understand right now in English?
2. What kind of situation in the United States do you hate to get yourself into (telephoning, ordering food, writing reports, and so on)?

    3. Are you ever too afraid to ask for help? Why?

    4. Is the homework in this class too difficult to do?

    5. What are you too tired to do after school?

G. Think about the first time you decided to attend a school in the United States. Then, answer the following questions using adverbial clauses beginning with the words in parentheses.

    1. Why did you decide to study in the United States? (so *or* because)

    _____

    _____

    2. When did you choose which school you would attend? (when)

    _____

    _____

    3. Why did you pick this school? (because)

    _____

    _____

    4. How long do you plan to stay here at this school? (until)

    _____

    _____

H. Complete the following narrative using the correct form of the past progressive tense.

    It was very cold and snowy my first day in New York. As I walked along, I looked at everything. Many things _____ (happen) in the city. The traffic _____ (move) along. Police officers _____ (walk) in the streets. Some people _____ (shovel) the snow. Everyone _____ (wear) heavy clothing and boots. Everyone _____ (hurry) and _____ (try) to keep warm.

I. ***Dictation / Dicto-Comp*** Listen to your instructor dictate this paragraph and then follow his/her directions.

    I arrived in the United States almost three years ago, but I remember my first days here very clearly. Nobody was waiting for me when the plane landed at the San Francisco Airport at 9:00 P.M. The weather was cool, and it was very dark outside. I was a little afraid to be in this unknown country, although I knew my uncle, who was supposed to meet me, wouldn't leave me stranded at the airport. Shortly after 10:00 P.M., my uncle finally arrived and we drove into the city.

When we arrived at his house, I greeted my aunt and cousins and told them all the news about my family back home. Then, I went to bed because I was exhausted from my long trip. The next day, I toured the city with my uncle. At first, the language wasn't a problem because my uncle was the interpreter. The week after I arrived in San Francisco, however, I decided I had to learn the language. Therefore, I worked for a few months so I could save enough money to take an English course.

COMPOSITION WRITING

J.   Write a composition about your first day in a new country, city, or school. Follow the model composition and the outline.

My First Day in a New Country / City / School

   I. Arrival
       A. When did you arrive?
       B. Where did you arrive?
       C. How did you arrive?
       D. What was the weather like?
       E. Did anyone come with you?
       F. How did you feel?
       G. Who was waiting for you?
  II. The first day
       A. What did you see?
       B. What did you do?
 III. Impressions
       A. What were your impressions of the new country / city / school?
       B. What did you decide to do?

STRUCTURE

Use of Prepositions of Place and Time

1. *In* a country:

   in the United States   in France
   in Rwanda   in the Dominican Republic

2. *In* a part of the day:

   in the afternoon   in the evening
   in the morning

3. *At* an exact time:

at three o'clock   at 6:15 P.M.
at nine-thirty

4. *At* an airport:

at Los Angeles International Airport   at Orly Airport

Use of *must* and *have to*

Must or *have to* can be used to express obligation or necessity in the present or the future.

He *must* leave now. / He *has to* leave now.
He *must* leave tomorrow. / He *has to* leave tomorrow.

Only *had to* can be used to express obligation or necessity in the past.

He *has to* go back to work now.
He *had to* go back to work on February 6, 1988.

I *must* learn English soon.
I decided that I *had to* learn English.

Use of the Infinitive and Gerund

1. Some verbs are followed by an infinitive form.

He *promised to return* the next day.
I *started to make* some gestures.
I *continued to walk* around the city.
I *wanted to see* everything.

2. Some verbs are followed by a gerund.

I *kept hearing* the waves crashing against the shore.
I *started making* some gestures.
I *continued walking* around the city.

> *Note:* The verbs *start* and *continue* may be followed by either an infinitive or a gerund.

3. Some verbs are followed by a simple infinitive (a verb without *to*).

He *helped* me *board* the bus.   He *watched* me *board* the bus.

4. The infinitive is used after *too* + *adjective*.

I was *too excited to mind.* (I didn't mind.)
He was *too tired to work.* (He couldn't work.)
She felt *too sick to go* to school. (She couldn't go to school.)
They were *too interested to leave.* (They didn't leave.)

Adverbial Clauses of Reason, Purpose, and Result

1. Adverbial clauses of reason

My friend helped me unpack at the hotel and then left me *because he had to go back to work.*
Since I couldn't speak a word of English, I couldn't tell the waiter what I wanted.

2. Adverbial clauses of purpose

I came to the United States *so that I could learn English.*
Many people came here *so that they would have better economic opportunities.*

3. Adverbial clauses of result

I wanted something to eat *so I went to a restaurant.*
It started to rain *so I took my umbrella.*

Past Progressive (Past Continuous)

The past progressive is composed of *the past tense of the auxiliary verb* **to be** + *the* **-ing** *form of the main verb.* It is used to describe a continuous or unfinished action that was going on at some time in the past.

When my plane landed, . . .	*my friends were waiting* for me.
When I left the movie theater, . . .	it *was raining.*
While my husband *was watching* TV, . . .	*I was reading.*

Note: The simple past is used to indicate a completed action in the past.

17

The Family

*M*ost Americans identify their families as one of the most important aspects of their lives. It is becoming difficult, however, to describe what a typical American family is. In the United States, families can be made up of many different types of relationships that result from such factors as divorce, remarriage, job mobility, and changing social attitudes. Look around your neighborhood and observe all the different kinds of American families. In what ways are they like, and in what ways do they differ from, the families in your country?

A.   Work with a partner to find out about his/her family. Then, exchange roles.

> *S1:* In your country, did you live in a nuclear or an extended family?
> *S2:* I lived in. . . .

If your partner lived in a nuclear family:

S1: How many brothers and sisters do you have?

S2: I have. . . .

S1: Would you want to live in an extended family?

S2: Yes / No, because. . . .

If your partner lived in an extended family:

S1: Who lived with you?

S2: . . .

S1: What was it like living in an extended family?

S2: . . .

B.   Read the following situations that might occur between a son/daughter and his/her parents in the United States. Work with a partner and role-play one of the situations. Then, be prepared to act out your situation in class.

1. A son/daughter, who has just failed an important mathematics course, must now tell his/her parents about the poor grade.
2. A son/daughter wants to borrow his/her parents' car for the evening, but the parents had already made other plans and need the car themselves.
3. A parent tries to warn a son/daughter about the dangers of his/her new habit of smoking.
4. Two parents are pressuring their son/daughter to study medicine, but he/she would rather major in music.
5. A son/daughter has announced plans to get married during his/her junior year in college. The parents try to convince the son/daughter to wait until after graduation.

READING

In this article, a well-known author talks about her own family and other families she knew as a child. The author makes the point that if you live with people who love you and whom you love, you have a family.

Free to Be—A Family

I always thought my family was different from other families.

For one thing, we lived and traveled in a house trailer° most of the winters before I was ten, so I learned to read and write from my parents and my older sister instead of going to school.

For another thing, my parents separated and divorced when I was about eleven. I don't remember feeling sad about that fact—I knew they both would

vehicle pulled by an automobile and used to live in

be happier, and I knew they loved me no matter where we lived—but movies told me you were supposed to feel bad if your parents got divorced.

Finally, my very gentle and kind mother was sick a lot of the time, so I often cooked her meals and took care of her instead of the other way around.

All of this made me feel odd.°   **strange**

So, I envied° my friend Linda who went to school like everybody else, and who lived with her mother and brother in a little apartment above a movie theater. How great to see your friends every day, and to go downstairs to a movie whenever you wanted!   **wanted the same thing someone else had**

And I envied my friend Carol who lived in a neat little row house° with her sister and brother and parents. How great to have your meals cooked for you and your clothes ironed for you, and to live in a house where you could invite your friends!   **house connected to another house by a wall**

Most of all, I envied the kids in Hollywood movies who had fresh strawberries for breakfast, clean clothes every day, birthday parties, and even horses to ride.

Years later, I talked to my now grown-up friends and realized something very interesting. Linda said she had felt funny° because her mother was a widow° and they didn't live in a real house. Carol had been a little ashamed° because her father went to work in overalls° and didn't speak English very well. Both of them had envied me because I didn't have to go to school all the time, I had traveled to lots of different places, and I made up my own rules because I was being my own mother.   **strange**   **woman whose husband has died / feeling disgraced, embarrassed, or guilty about something / loose-fitting protective clothes worn over regular clothes**

All of us felt a little bad because we didn't live the way that kids did in the movies.

Well, . . . movies and other made-up images° aren't always right or real. Neither are all of our ideas about what a "real family" is. If we feel loved and supported for being special and unique,° if we have enough food and a warm, dry place to live, if we have people we love and feel close to, then we are probably in a real family. It doesn't matter whether it is one we got born into, or one we chose, or one that chose us, or one that came together because people who already had families loved each other and decided to blend° them into one.   **pictures invented in the mind**   **the only one of its kind**   **mix together**

Of course, there will always be problems, because problems are things that make us stronger tomorrow than we were today. That's how we grow. . . .

But no one way of living can be right for everybody. How boring° the world would be if we were all alike! . . .   **uninteresting**

From Gloria Steinem, "Why You Should Buy This Book," *Free to Be . . . A Family,* Marlo Thomas & Friends (New York: Bantam Books, 1987), p. 10.

C. Be prepared to discuss the following questions on the reading in class.

    1. Do you agree with the writer about what a "real family" is? Why?

    2. How does one get a divorce in your country? Under what circumstances would you want a divorce?

    3. What is an "ideal family" in your opinion? What role would each member play in such a family?

    4. Would you bring up your children differently than you were brought up? How?

    5. Is the structure of the family unit (number of children, working women, roles of spouses) changing in your country? How?

6. Is it important for your family to eat meals together? What does your family talk about during meals or when they are together?

7. Who took care of and disciplined you when you were a child and your parents were not at home? When would your mother not be at home? And your father?

8. In your country, with whom do old people live? How do they support themselves? Do young people have respect for the aged in your country?

D. Read the statements that follow and indicate with a check mark (√) whether you agree or disagree with each of the opinions expressed. Then, in two groups—one all–male and the other all–female—discuss your opinions. Next, have one member of each group tally the results for the group. Finally, compare the two groups' results.

	Agree	Disagree
1. I wouldn't marry someone if my parents disapproved of that person.	_____	_____
2. A married woman without children shouldn't work.	_____	_____
3. A married woman with children shouldn't work.	_____	_____
4. Arranged marriages are better than letting young people choose their own mates.	_____	_____
5. Children should be physically punished if they misbehave.	_____	_____
6. The husband should be the boss in the house.	_____	_____
7. Husbands shouldn't have to help with housework.	_____	_____
8. Grown-up children should put their own needs before the needs of their parents.	_____	_____

MODEL COMPOSITION

The American Family

The most common type of family in the United States is the nuclear family, which is normally made up of two generations—parents and their still-dependent children. The typical family is middle-class, and there is generally some degree of equality between the husband and wife. Each family lives in its own separate residence, and it is not usual to share a house with one's grandparents or in-laws. American families are very mobile and are continually changing jobs and moving to other neighborhoods. It is estimated that the average American family moves about once every five years. Child care in an American family is exclusively the responsibility of the parents, and children are taught to be independent at an early age. When they become adults, most children leave their parents' house and set up their own households even though they are not married.

The American family today is undergoing real change. For example, most families have fewer children today, and some choose to have none. In addition, more than 50 percent of mothers work outside the home due to a combination of economic reasons and the changing social climate. Divorce is quite common, and one of the most significant changes is that millions of children are being brought up by only one parent, usually the mother. Nevertheless, most divorced people remarry, and many of these remarriages include at least one child from a former marriage. Therefore, many new patterns of family life are emerging in the United States.

E. Linking Words   Help your reader understand how the two sentences in each of the following pairs are related. Use appropriate connecting words to show the reader an example, a contrast, an additional detail, or a result in the second sentence. Give two examples.

1. My mother is very understanding. She always listens to whatever I have to say.

   _____

   _____

2. My father works late many nights. He still makes time to be with his family.

   _____

   _____

3. My sister Mary studies medicine. She also plays the guitar.

   _____

   _____

4. Everyone in our family works different hours. We can't always have dinner together.

   _____

   _____

5. My brother Jim is older than I. He often takes care of me.

   _____

   _____

F.   Explain how you feel about the following statement by completing each item.

> In my country today, families live differently than they did in my grandparents' generation.

For example, _____

_____

For instance, _____

_____

In spite of this, _____

_____

Nevertheless, _____

_____

However, _____

_____

On the other hand, _____

_____

Therefore, _____

_____

As a result, _____

_____

Because of this, _____

_____

G.   *Linking Words*   Work in pairs and complete the story with the appropriate linking words from the list below. Use each word only once.

and	as a result	nevertheless
for example	therefore	moreover

Mae Wong knew little English when she arrived in the United States several years ago. _____ , she decided to enroll in an English class at the local high school. At first, she found the class hard to follow. _____ , after several weeks, she was able to carry on a simple conversation in English.

_____ , Mae Wong learned more than just the language. She listened as her instructor told the class about the American way of life _____ about the changing attitudes toward women in the United States. _____ , she learned that many American women work outside the home and that

many men share in the household duties. _____ ,
Mae Wong decided that the United States was the best place for her to
live.

H. Dictation / Dicto-Comp   Listen to your instructor read the following dictation about the elderly American population. Then, follow his/her directions.

Almost a quarter of the entire U.S. population will be over sixty-five by the year 2030, according to the U.S. Census Bureau. People are living longer because of the many breakthroughs in medicine. This has led to an ever-increasing life expectancy for Americans of both sexes and has in part contributed to the "aging" of our population.

In most countries, families have traditionally taken care of older relatives. Today, in the United States, however, families often find it impossible to act as caregivers for their aging relatives. Since more than 50 percent of women have jobs outside their homes, they are consequently unable to take care of their parents. Furthermore, most people live in apartments or houses that are not large enough for an extended family. In addition, because Americans are a very mobile society, families may be spread from coast to coast. Therefore, although children might want to provide care for their parents, they cannot always do so. Another important factor is that many parents, ingrained with the American spirit of independence, do not want to live with their children.

COMPOSITION WRITING

I.   Using the model composition and the following outline as guides, write a composition about the typical family in your country. When appropriate, use transition words.

The _____ Family

  I. The family today
   A. Size and composition of the typical family
   B. Mobility of the family
   C. Relationship between husband and wife
   D. Children
    1. Position of children in the family structure
    2. Responsibility for raising the children
    3. Adult children—position and responsibilities
   E. Position and duties of elderly relatives
  II. Changes in patterns of family life
   A. Causes for the changes
   B. Effects of the changes on family life

S T R U C T U R E

Linking Words

Linking words (or transition words) are connecting words that help the reader understand how the meaning of two sentences is related. Some of the uses of linking words are as follows:

1. To give examples or illustrations—*for example, for instance.*

> The American family is undergoing real change. *For example,* most families have fewer children, and some choose to have none.
> John is a very good grandson. *For instance,* he calls his grandparents every week.

2. To show a contrast between the details in two sentences—*nevertheless, in spite of this, however, but, on the other hand.*

> Divorce is quite common. *Nevertheless,* most divorced people remarry.
> Many children would like to take care of their elderly parents. *However,* it is not always possible.
> I love my parents. *In spite of this,* I still want to live in my own apartment.

3. To show additions to details—*moreover, in addition.*

> Many families cannot take care of their parents because the majority of American women work. *Moreover,* houses and apartments are smaller than they used to be.
> My sister is a full-time student. *In addition,* she works part-time.

4. To make clear the connection between two sentences where the first sentence states a cause and the second sentence states the result or effect—*consequently, in this way, therefore, so, for this reason, because of this, as a result.*

> The majority of American women are currently working, *so* it is not always possible for them to take care of an elderly relative.
> In many American families, every member shares in the household chores. *For this reason / Because of this / Therefore / Consequently / As a result,* every member has more time for leisure activities.

18

Time Capsule

*H*ave you ever saved something from your past that was important to you? Why did you save this object? People also save articles and information about the present in order to help people living in the future understand the past. Some people put these objects in time capsules. Now think about your life today. What objects would you select to put in a time capsule that describe your life today?

A.   Work with a partner and discuss what you might find if you opened a time capsule that had been buried in 1905. Use the sketch at the start of the lesson and your imagination. Then, exchange roles.

> *S1:* Do you think time capsules are a good idea?
> *S2:* . . .
>
> *S1:* What do you think we would find in a time capsule from 1905?
> *S2:* Let's see. I think we might find. . . .

B.   Work with a partner and discuss the following situation. Your class is going to fill a time capsule. You must select one item to represent daily life today and one item to represent the English class. You must explain why you have chosen these items and be in agreement on their selection. The expressions in the following list will be useful in discussing your choices. Be prepared to list your items and explain them to the class.

To express agreement	*To express disagreement*
Fine with me.	I disagree.
I'll go along with that.	I can't agree to that.
That's O.K. with me.	I'm not so sure.

R E A D I N G

Time Capsules for Everyone

The history of time capsules goes back to ancient Babylon when people often placed objects in the cornerstones° of buildings. However, time capsules began to be popular in 1938 when a capsule was placed beneath a building at Oglethorpe University in Atlanta, Georgia. The Westinghouse Electric & Manufacturing Company first used the term "time capsule" when they buried one to celebrate the opening of the New York World's Fair of 1939. Westinghouse created the time capsule event for publicity and to help increase sales. Since then, the popularity of time capsules spread and, by the 1950s, time capsules were being buried all over the United States.*

stones set at the bottom corners of a building

*Albert Beresen, "Oh, Well," *Atlantic* v. 259 (July 1987): pp. 16, 18.

Today, there is a new twist° to time capsules. A businessman in California, Alvin Willis, Jr., has designed a time capsule for people who wish to preserve° some of their personal belongings or personal thoughts for future generations.

unexpected change or development / keep or save for a long time

Willis says the idea first came to him when he was looking for a time capsule to place in a new addition to his home as a kind of keepsake.° To his surprise, he discovered that no one was making time capsules. Suddenly, he realized that perhaps there were other people interested in buying time capsules. He soon started a business of producing time capsules and became very successful in a short time.

something, usually small, given to be kept in memory of the giver

Willis is sure that his capsules will continue to sell well because he believes that most people want to preserve some of their personal histories to pass on to their heirs.°

Many buyers want to place personal mementos° as well as family histories in their capsules. Willis recommends that they also include personal thoughts and feelings about the news of the day and predictions of the future.

persons who have the legal right to receive property from some member of the family when he or she dies / items that serve to remind or warn

He says, ". . . upon discovery, *that* sort of personal information will prove . . . meaningful and useful to the historians of tomorrow who are trying to interpret the information that they have."

Willis is hopeful that every capsule he sells is buried somewhere. Much to his surprise, however, most buyers aren't burying their time capsules. Instead, they are proudly displaying them on their shelves and coffee tables. Apparently, they are great conversation pieces.°

items that are kept in order to give people something to talk about

Adapted from Laurel Defoe, "A Novelty Designed for the Rich and Famous to Bury," *The Sacramento Business Journal* v. 4 (August 24, 1987): pp. 2, 45.

C. Be prepared to discuss the following questions based on the reading.

1. What do you think motivates individuals or towns and cities to bury time capsules?
2. Do you think that time capsules are a good way to show future generations something about people and life in the past? Why or why not?
3. Are there any time capsules in your country? If so, do you know when they were buried, where they were put, and what was put in them?
4. Do you think a personal time capsule is a good idea? Would you buy one? Why or why not?
5. What objects would you put in your personal time capsule? Why? What personal thoughts would you put in it?
6. Where would you bury your time capsule?

D. Work in groups of three to four students. Imagine that you work for an advertising agency that has just been chosen by Time Capsules, Inc., for an advertising campaign. The company wants you to write an advertisement for its time capsule that will attract many new customers. Include the following information in your advertisement.

1. slogan for the product (a slogan is an attention-getting phrase used in advertising)
2. reason why someone should buy it
3. reason why he/she should buy it now
4. explanation of what the product can do for the buyer
5. description of the capsule and its cost

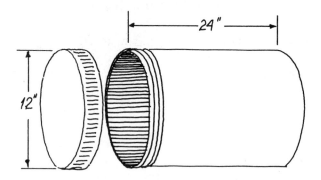

Material-Aluminum

Lightweight·Rust Resistant

MODEL COMPOSITION

What I Would Put in a Time Capsule

If I were asked to select five items to represent American life today that would be placed in a 3′ × 3′ × 3′ time capsule not to be opened until the year 5000, I would choose the following. The first item would be a pair of jogging shoes. This would represent the American people's present craze for physical fitness. Next, I would include a picture of a hamburger and of a roadside McDonald's or Burger King. Fast-food chains have spread all over the country, and the pictures would represent an American food habit. The third item would be a computer. We are living in a computer age today, and it is predicted that every child will soon become familiar with the computer in school and that every business and most homes will soon have one as well. The fourth item would be the book *How to Live to Be 100— or More* by George Burns, advertised as "the ultimate diet, sex and exercise book," and an example of the kind of book that always appears on America's best-seller lists. The last item would be a videotape of a few soap operas. On this video, one could see the clothes and homes of today as well as some of the social problems that Americans face. When they open the capsule in the year 5000, I wonder what the people of the future will think of us.

E.   Use the conditional to talk about possible results from an unreal present situation. Complete the following sentences with an appropriate ending.

    1. If I found a time capsule, _____

    _____

    2. If I were the head of my country, _____

    _____

    3. If I could live my life over again, _____

    _____

    4. If I were to start my own business, _____

    _____

    5. If everyone made love instead of war, _____

    _____

F.   Complete the following sentences by describing an unreal present situation.

    1. We might be able to provide a brighter future for our children if ____

    _____

    2. I would like to buy a time capsule if _____

    _____

    3. I would like to open a time capsule if _____

    _____

    4. I might consider visiting the moon if _____

    _____

    5. I could make my own time capsule if _____

    _____

G.   ***Using Prepositions***   Work with a partner and use the appropriate prepositions to complete the following account of a search for a time capsule.

_____ a recent trip to a small town in New Jersey, I read _____ the local newspaper that the residents _____ the town decided to open a time capsule that had been buried fifty years before.

As part _____ the town's bicentennial, the capsule was to be opened the next day _____ four young people who were not born when the capsule was buried.

However, _____ looking _____ the town's records, it was discovered that when the capsule was buried, someone forgot to indicate its location. As a result, _____ this day, no one has been able to find the time capsule.

H. Working in groups of three to four people, decide on five more items representing American life that you would put in a time capsule 3′ × 3′ × 3′. Explain why you would choose these items. Select one person to list your items and reasons for selecting them and report back to the class.

I. *Dictation / Dicto-Comp*   Listen to your instructor dictate the two paragraphs below. Then, follow his/her directions.

In 1938, Westinghouse Electric Company placed a time capsule in the ground at the site of the 1939 New York World's Fair. The contents of the capsule were chosen to indicate what life was like in the 1930s. Dozens of specialists participated in the selection. Among the items placed in the capsule was a large amount of microfilmed reading matter, including a variety of newspapers and magazines, a *World Almanac*, and a newsreel of the news events of that period. The capsule also contained many articles in common use, including a telephone, a can opener, a woman's hat, a wrist watch, a package of cigarettes, a slide rule, and a lump of coal. There were also samples of textiles, plastics, and a variety of seeds.

In 1965, Westinghouse buried another time capsule near the same site for the opening of the second New York World's Fair. Both time capsules are to be opened in the year 6939, five thousand years after the first fair closed.

From "The Story of the Westinghouse Time Capsule," the Westinghouse Historical Collection. Pittsburg, Pennsylvania.

COMPOSITION WRITING

J. Follow the model composition and the following outline to write your own one-paragraph composition on what you would choose to represent the culture of your country if you were asked to select five items to be placed in a 3′ × 3′ × 3′ time capsule. Imagine that the capsule won't be opened until the year 5000.

     A / An _____(nationality) *Time Capsule*

   A. Opening sentence
   B. Five items chosen and reasons why
   C. Concluding sentence

STRUCTURE

Use of the Conditional for Unreal or Contrary-to-Fact Conditions

When expressing a condition that is unreal or contrary to fact, use the past tense in the *if* clause, and a modal auxiliary (would, might, or could) in the main clause.

If clause	*Main clause*
If I had a time capsule, . . .	I could put personal mementos inside it.
If a time capsule were discovered in my yard, . . .	I would be very excited.
If I knew what the future would bring, . . .	I might do things differently today.
If I were an entrepreneur, . . .	I would probably have my own business.

Note: When the *if* clause includes the verb *to be,* use the form *were* for the first, second, and third persons, singular and plural.

19

Working with Tables, Charts, and Graphs

THE CAPITAL COST OF EATING

Food prices in various world capitals

	Tokyo	Paris	London	Washington	Pretoria	Brasilia	16-city average
Steak, per lb.	$24.24	$5.68	$5.86	$4.79	$2.61	$1.84	$5.96
Roast,pork, per lb.	$6.10	$3.16	$2.82	$2.59	$1.31	$1.42	$3.06
Whole chicken, per lb.	$2.61	$2.15	$1.20	$0.67	$0.85	$0.65	$1.39
Eggs, doz.	$1.08	$1.66	$1.84	$0.73	$0.82	$0.59	$1.47
Butter, lb.	$4.15	$2.42	$1.52	$1.81	$0.97	$2.35	$2.36
Cheddar cheese, per lb.	$3.96	$3.20	$2.07	$3.12	$1.67	$2.56	$3.35
Milk, per qt.	$1.32	$0.74	$0.62	$0.44	$0.43	$0.32	$0.64
Cooking oil, per qt.	$2.61	$1.45	$1.23	$1.92	$1.16	$0.47	$1.79
Potatoes, per lb.	$1.33	$0.53	$0.33	$0.47	$0.29	$0.27	$0.39
Apples, per lb.	$1.73	$0.65	$0.66	$0.84	$0.30	$0.82	$0.75
Oranges, per lb.	$1.76	$0.73	$0.73	$0.53	$0.18	$0.12	$0.59
Flour, per lb.	$0.73	$0.44	$0.21	$0.21	$0.22	$0.08	$0.33
Rice, per lb.	$1.27	$0.73	$0.63	$0.39	$0.36	$0.21	$0.64
Sugar, per lb.	$0.74	$0.50	$0.36	$0.35	$0.24	$0.20	$0.37
Coffee, per lb.	$11.07	$3.37	$5.02	$3.39	$4.90	$1.43	$4.45
TOTAL	**$64.71**	**$27.39**	**$25.11**	**$22.25**	**$16.30**	**$13.34**	**$27.53**

Note: Figures are average retail food prices for May, 1987, in U.S. dollars converted at current exchange rates. "16 -city average" is for the 16 capitals surveyed.

USN&WR—Basic data: U.S. Dept. of Agriculture

*I*n this lesson, you will read about and interpret a variety of statistical data in the form of tables, charts, and graphs. Americans are used to participating in all kinds of surveys and polls that investigate such issues as how people vote, what they think about gun control, whether they buy a certain product, what TV programs they watch, and so forth. Sometimes, the goal of such an investigation is to inform the public; at other times, the aim is to convince the public to do or to buy something. Learning to understand and work with the information presented in these visual aids is important for success in school and in daily life in the United States.

A. A collection of figures can often best be communicated by means of a table. The table shown here lists the cost of various food items in six world capitals as of May 1987 and then gives the average cost of these food items for sixteen cities. Read the list. Then, work with a partner and answer the following questions. Be prepared to discuss questions 3 and 6 in class.

   1. In what city did a pound of steak cost the most?
   2. In what city did a pound of steak cost the least?
   3. How can you explain this?
   4. In what city did a pound of rice cost the least?
   5. In what city did a pound of rice cost the most?
   6. Why do you think this was so?
   7. In what city was it the cheapest to live according to food prices in 1987?
   8. In what city was it the most expensive to live?
   9. Compare the price of a dozen eggs in Paris and in Washington, D.C.
   10. What was the average cost of a pound of potatoes in the sixteen cities?

B. Statistics that are reported in percentages are often presented in what is called a pie chart, in which the complete "pie" represents 100 percent. Read the following information and the accompanying pie charts carefully.

Foreign Student Statistics

For the fall 1987 semester, approximately 1913 students holding non-immigrant visas were enrolled at New York University in credit-bearing courses. These students represent more than 100 countries, with the largest numbers of students from the following countries:

China	190	India	100
Japan	185	Israel	79
Korea	159	Italy	74
Taiwan	116	Canada	74

The following charts depict NYU's percentages of the total non-immigrant credit-seeking students by the division in which they were enrolled and by the regions of the world they have come from.

BY REGION   BY DIVISION

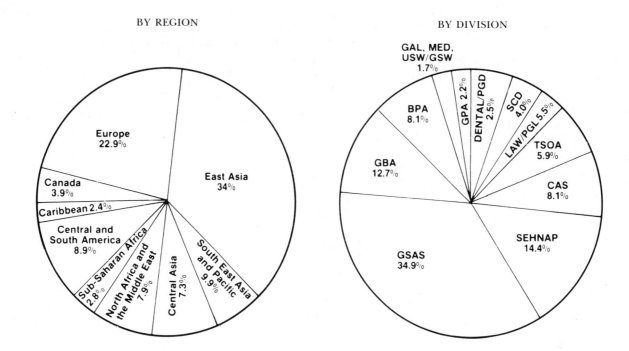

Acronyms of schools at NYU

BPA: College of Business and Public Administration
GBA: Graduate School of Business Administration
GSAS: Graduate School of Arts and Science
SEHNAP: School of Education, Health, Nursing, and Arts Profession
CAS: College of Arts and Science
TSOA: Tisch School of Arts

Now work with a partner and answer the following questions.

1. Where did the largest percentage of foreign students come from?
2. What percentage of students came from Central Asia?
3. What school had the largest percentage of foreign students?
4. What percentage of students came from Central and South America?
5. What percentage of foreign students were enrolled in the law school?
6. What percentage of foreign students were in SEHNAP?
7. What percentage of foreign students came from Europe?
8. What was the total number of foreign students enrolled in credit courses at New York University in the fall of 1987?

C. With the same partner, write five sentences based on the information in the pie charts. Be prepared to read your sentences in front of the class.

    More than 50 percent of the foreign students came from Europe and East Asia.

    There were more foreign students from East Asia than from Europe.

READING

The following article discusses and analyzes the annual census of foreign students in the United States as presented in *Open Doors,* a publication prepared by the Institute of International Education.

Enrollment Trends of Foreign Students and Scholars

TABLE 1
Foreign Students in U.S.

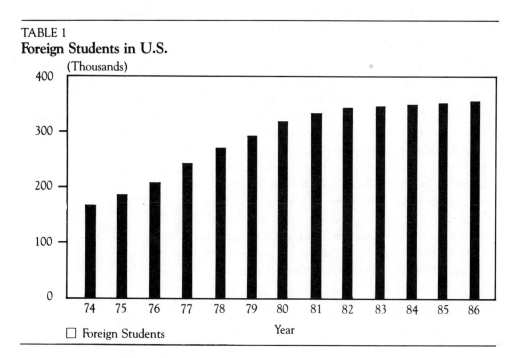

☐ Foreign Students

TABLE 2
Regions of the world, student flows to U.S., 1976–1986

Year	So./E. Asia	Middle East	Latin America	Europe	Africa
F86	170,700	47,000	43,480	36,140	31,580
F85	156,830	52,720	45,480	34,310	34,190
F84	143,680	56,580	48,560	33,350	39,520
F83	132,270	60,660	52,350	31,860	41,690
F82	119,650	67,280	56,810	31,570	42,690
F81	106,160	74,390	55,360	28,990	41,660
F80	94,640	84,710	49,810	25,330	38,180
F79	81,730	83,700	42,280	22,570	36,180
F78	76,850	70,430	41,120	21,690	33,990
F77	73,760	57,210	38,840	19,310	29,560
F76	70,020	38,490	37,240	16,700	25,860

Source: *Open Doors* (New York: Institute of International Education, 1977–1986).

What do the 1986–87 *Open Doors* data tell us about enrollment trends° affecting the ebb and flow° of foreign students and scholars to the United States? What is the significance of these data for future enrollments at U.S. universities and colleges? To be useful, data must be analyzed in relation to their context.° Our intention is to stimulate° thinking about how *Open Doors* data can be used to explain past and present student flows and plan for future foreign student enrollment in U.S. institutions.

We believe that the data must be analyzed in the general context of influences that modify° student tendencies to study in the United States, such as the strength of the dollar vis-à-vis° other currencies, the rising costs of U.S. education, governmental policies (both U.S. and international), competition from U.S. and international institutions of higher education, and political unrest in the home country. Burgess (1987) names "push" factors° that motivate° students to leave their home countries, among them being the educational philosophy in the home country. "Pull" factors that attract students to a particular country—such as linguistic accessibility,° historic links,° institutional links, cost, and financial assistance—also need to be analyzed by those responsible for marketing American institutions to the foreign student population.[1]

Clearly, enrollment variations or trends result from a great variety of causes, some of which are controlled by institutional policies but many of which are the result of domestic and/or external factors beyond institutional control.

The data have been gathered in *Open Doors,* but we must look at what is behind it as we make plans for our institutions' international educational future. The statistics alone do not tell the whole story. International educators need to be aware of the "whys," as well as the "how manys" of student flows.

[1]Burgess, Elaine. "Forecasting International Student Enrollment: How to Polish Your Crystal Ball," in *The Admission Strategist: Recruiting in the 1980s.* (New York: The College Board, 1987).

From George C. Christensen, Thomas B. Thielen, and Julie Rose, "*Open Doors* Data Portray Enrollment Trends of Foreign Students, Scholars to the United States," *NAFSA Newsletter* (November 1987): pp. 3–6.

Marginal glosses:

general directions / fall and rise

general conditions under which an event takes place / encourage activity

affect

in relation to

influences that bring about a result / provide someone with a strong reason to do something

fact that the same language is spoken / ties

D. Be prepared to discuss the following questions related to the reading.

   1. What are some of the "push" factors that made you come to the United States?

   2. What are some of the "pull" factors that made you come here?

   3. Look at the bar graphs in Table 1. Has the rate of student flow to the United States been maintained, has it increased, or has it declined?

   4. Look at Table 2. What regions showed a decline from 1985 to 1986? Why do you think this happened?

   5. What areas showed an increase from 1985 to 1986? Why do you think this happened?

E. Work in groups of three to four students from your country or region. Analyze why students from your country or region come to the United States to study. (Refer to the "push" and "pull" factors mentioned in the reading.) Make a list of the appropriate factors for students from your country or region. Then, write two or three sentences explaining what you think the trend will be in the future for students from your country or region.

MODEL COMPOSITION

Why Students from Canada Come to the United States to Study

TABLE 3
Leading countries of origin, 1978–1986

Country	F86	F85	F84	F83	F82	F81	F80	F79	F78
Taiwan	25,660	23,770	22,590	21,960	20,770	20,520	19,460	17,560	15,460
Malaysia	21,640	23,020	21,720	18,150	14,070	9,420	6,010	3,660	3,560
China	20,030	13,980	10,100	8,140	6,230	4,350	2,770	a	a
Korea	19,940	18,660	16,430	13,860	13,360	8,070	6,150	4,890	4,980
India	18,350	16,070	14,610	13,730	12,890	11,250	9,250	8,760	9,400
Canada	15,700	15,410	15,370	15,150	14,020	14,950	14,320	15,130	15,120
Japan	15,070	13,360	13,160	13,010	13,610	14,020	13,500	12,260	10,490
Iran	12,230	14,210	16,640	20,360	26,760	35,860	47,550	51,310	45,340
Nigeria	11,700	13,710	18,370	20,080	20,710	19,560	17,350	16,360	16,220
Hong Kong	11,010	10,710	10,130	9,420	8,610	8,990	9,660	9,900	10,520
Saudi Arabia	5,840	6,900	7,760	8,630	9,250	10,220	10,440	9,540	8,050
Venezuela	4,870	7,040	10,290	13,440	15,490	13,960	11,750	9,860	8,430

[a]Figures not available.
Source: *Open Doors* (New York: Institute of International Education, 1978–1986).

Table from George C. Christensen, Thomas B. Thielen, and Julie Rose, *Open Doors* Portray Enrollment Trends of Foreign Students, Scholars to the United States," *NAFSA Newsletter* (November 1987): p. 3–6.

The number of foreign students from Canada has remained fairly constant in recent years, but from 1980 to 1982, there was a slight decrease. Since 1983, however, the number of Canadian students has increased gradually every year and has held steady. There are several reasons why Canadians come to the United States to study. First, most Canadians speak English, so there is no language barrier. Second, some want to live in a country other than their own, or they want to study with a particular professor. Third, Canadians feel that the system of higher education is very flexible in the United States, and there is a perception that in the United States, they will obtain the best education in their field. And fourth, Canadians are influenced by the prestige of a degree received from an American university.

In my case, I decided to come to the United States to study because I want to be a film director. The film industry is much larger in this country than in Canada, and I knew that there were excellent film schools in the United States. In addition, I wanted the experience of living in the United States.

I believe that in the future, the trend for Canadian students coming to the United States will hold steady or, perhaps, slightly increase. We not only share a mutual boundary and language, but our cultures are not too different, and there has always been a strong bond between the two countries. Information about higher education in the United States is relatively abundant in Canada, and while the cost of living is a little higher in this country, the difference is not too great for Canadians, especially when the dollar is low.

Reasons for coming to the United States, from Marianthi Zikopoulos and Elinor G. Barber, *Choosing Schools from Afar: Selection of Colleges and Universities in the United States by Foreign Students.* (New York: Institute of International Education, 1986), p. 11.

Elements of Style: Writing Reports

Tables, charts, and graphs are often used to write reports for business, economics, the physical sciences, the social sciences, and other areas. Visual aids are essential for effective communication in reports. They present specific information that can be readily understood and remembered. They emphasize important facts and figures, present supporting data that are helpful in making analyses and drawing conclusions, and add interest to the material.

The objectives of a report are to provide information, to analyze the information, to make recommendations, and to predict future results.

The contents of the main divisions of a report are as follows:

  I. *Introduction:* This division gives the background information that the reader needs in order to understand the report and describes the research method used.

 II. *Discussion:* This division presents the results or findings and relates them by analyzing, interpreting, and discussing the data.

III. *Conclusions and/or recommendations:* This division presents the conclusions and/or recommendations.

F. Use the correct voice (active or passive) and the correct tense of the verb in each sentence.

  1. Many Iranian students _____(study) English as a second language in the United States in 1979.

  2. A new financial assistance program _____ (announce) by the university last week.

  3. In 1987, 60 percent of foreign students _____ (attract) by engineering, science, and management-related fields.

  4. Special English-language courses _____ (create) for engineering students now.

  5. A new course for foreign teaching assistants _____ (design) by the Institute for English.

  6. The number of students from Korea _____ (increase) since 1982.

G. Work with a partner and write the verb in each sentence in the correct tense using the passive voice.

1. Malaysia _____(expect) to send fewer students to the United States next year.

2. Gender _____(include) in the survey on foreign students next year.

3. Education _____(choose) by many foreign students as their major in 1987.

4. These days, employment opportunities _____ (turn down) by Asian students in order to complete their degree as soon as possible.

5. For many years, the data _____(gather) by the Institute of International Education.

6. Many Japanese _____(send) here to study English.

7. Applications for admission to the university must _____(submit) in triplicate.

8. The next freshman survey _____(take) in the coming year.

9. At present, many foreign engineers _____ (hire) by American companies.

10. The number of foreign students _____ (affect) by world events.

H. ***Dictation / Dicto-Comp***   Listen to your instructor read the paragraph below and then follow his/her directions.

  For the first time, Asian students were more than 50 percent of the U.S. foreign student enrollment, which reached 356,200 in 1987–1988, according to figures released by the Institute of International Education. Figures for the 1987–1988 academic year showed that the top five places of origin were all in Asia, led again by Taiwan with 26,700. The People's Republic of China was in second place and increasing rapidly, with 26 percent growth from 20,000 to 25,200 over the past year. India, Korea, and Malaysia completed the top five. Chinese students have been the fastest-growing group in the foreign student population for five consecutive years.

"New *Open Doors* Data Show Asians A Majority of U.S. Foreign Students," *NAFSA Newsletter* (December/January 1989): p. 3.

COMPOSITION WRITING

I. Use Table 3 from the model composition and select your country or a country from your region. Then, write a composition following the model composition and the points mentioned below.

Why Students from _____*Come to the*
United States to Study

1. Cite data from Table 3.
2. Discuss factors that influence students from your country or region to come here.
3. Discuss factors that influenced you to come here.
4. What do you think the trend will be in the future for students from your country or region coming to the United States? Why?

STRUCTURE

Active and Passive Voice

In the active voice, the subject of a verb performs the action; in the passive voice, it receives the action. Action in the past, the present, and the future can be expressed in both the active and the passive voice, as follows:

Active voice
subject + verb + object

1. Many students read the *New York Times.*
2. Many foreign students choose engineering as their field of study.
3. Fifty-one countries formed the United Nations in 1945.
4. Massachusetts is replacing Florida as the state with the fourth-largest foreign-student population.

Passive voice
*subject + auxiliary **(to be)** + past participle + agent*

1. The *New York Times* is read by many students.
2. Engineering is chosen by many foreign students as their field of study.
3. The United Nations was formed by fifty-one countries in 1945.
4. Florida is being replaced by Massachusetts as the state with the fourth-largest foreign-student population.

5. Latin American countries have restricted the amount of foreign exchange available to overseas students.
6. U.S. educators will analyze the flow of foreign students.

7. The university is going to sponsor an international conference.
8. We must examine the data on a regional and country basis.
9. We might expect the number of Indian students to increase.
10. World events can influence the flow of foreign students to the United States.

11. Foreign students had to obtain a student visa before they came here.
12. Everyone should learn a second language.

5. The amount of foreign exchange available to overseas students has been restricted by Latin American countries.
6. The flow of foreign students will be analyzed by U.S. educators.

7. An international conference is going to be sponsored by the university.
8. The data must be examined on a regional and country basis.
9. The number of Indian students might be expected to increase.
10. The flow of foreign students to the United States can be influenced by world events.

11. A student visa had to be obtained by foreign students before they came here.
12. A second language should be learned by everyone.

Note: In the passive voice, the agent (*by . . .*) may be omitted when this information is not important: *Mail is delivered once a day,* instead of, *Mail is delivered once a day* **by the post office.**

The passive voice is used when the receiver of the action is considered to be more important than the performer of the action with respect to stating the facts in the sentence.

The United Nations was started in 1945. (The emphasis is on the fact that the United Nations was started in 1945, not on who started it.)
Tom was run over by a car. (The emphasis is on the fact that Tom was run over and not on who or what did it.)

The active voice tends to make your writing more forceful, direct, and concise, the passive voice less forceful and direct and more wordy—especially if it is overused. Therefore, before you use the passive voice, think about the effect that it can have on your writing and use it only when it is the most appropriate way to express your intended meaning.

20

Compiling and Analyzing Surveys

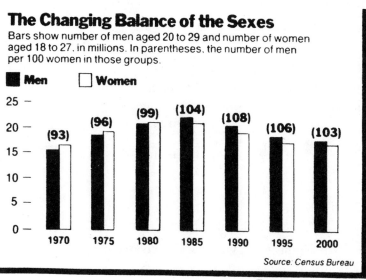

The Changing Balance of the Sexes
Bars show number of men aged 20 to 29 and number of women aged 18 to 27, in millions. In parentheses, the number of men per 100 women in those groups.

■ **Men** □ **Women**

Source: Census Bureau

The New York Times/June 5, 1988

*I*n several lessons in this text, you interviewed a partner or several classmates about their personal experiences and opinions. In other words, you conducted polls and did surveys. The United States Census Bureau conducts official surveys for the national government about many things in the United States, such as population, industrial trends, and income. The bar graph on the balance of the sexes, based on data from the United States Census Bureau, indicates changes in the male and female population in the United States from 1970 to the year 2000.

A. Read the bar graph titled "The Changing Balance of the Sexes" carefully. Work with a partner and alternate asking and answering the following questions.

   1. In what years were there fewer men aged 20 to 29 than there were women aged 18 to 27?

2. In what years were there fewer women than men?
3. Approximately how many millions of men aged 20 to 29 were there in 1975? And women aged 18 to 27?
4. In the year 2000, how many millions of men will there be? And women?
5. In the year 2000, how many men aged 20 to 29 will there be for every one hundred women aged 18 to 27?

B.   Now analyze some of the data that are shown in the bar graph titled "The Changing Balance of the Sexes." Work with a partner and compare the American male and female populations in 1970 and 1985. Do you think that life in those years was the same socially for these populations, or was it different? Be prepared to discuss this topic in class.

READING

Freshmen Found Stressing Wealth

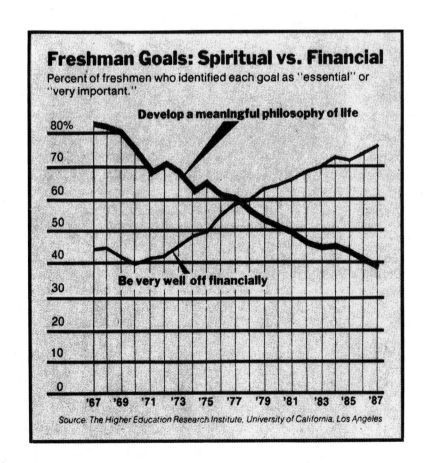

Freshman Goals: Spiritual vs. Financial
Percent of freshmen who identified each goal as "essential" or "very important."

Develop a meaningful philosophy of life

Be very well off financially

Source: The Higher Education Research Institute, University of California, Los Angeles

A record proportion of more than three-quarters of college freshmen surveyed around the country feel that being financially well off is an "essential"° or "very important" goal.* At the same time, the lowest proportion of freshmen in 20 years, only 39 percent, put great emphasis° on developing a meaningful philosophy of life.

necessary

importance

In addition, the number of freshmen saying that a key reason° for their decision to attend college was "to make more money" has reached a new high of 71 percent. Business continues to be the preferred career, as a record 25 percent of the students name it as their first choice. . . .

very important reason

These findings were drawn from questionnaires completed in the fall of 1987 by 209,627 freshmen at 390 two- and four-year institutions. . . .

Other points that emerged° from the survey were:

came out

- An increase in liberal° attitudes on many social issues, with two exceptions: a rise in freshman support for laws prohibiting homosexual relations, and a decline in the number who think marijuana should be legalized.

favoring some change, as in political or social affairs

- Despite widespread publicity about AIDS, an increase in freshmen who agree that if two people genuinely like each other, it is fine for them to have sexual relations, even if they have known each other only a short time.

- A decline in cigarette smoking.

Dr. Alexander W. Astin,** who has been conducting the study since its inception° in 1966, said the question about the importance of developing a meaningful philosophy of life was introduced a year later, after groups of students had asked that a question about values be included. That year 83 percent thought that developing a meaningful philosophy of life was an essential or very important goal. The percentage has dropped in all but two years since then, to a low of 39 percent in the latest survey.

beginning

"Students still tend to see their life being dependent on affluence° and are not inclined to be reflective,"° Dr. Astin said.

wealth

thoughtful

Freshman support for laws prohibiting homosexual relations increased in the latest survey to 53 percent, from 52 percent the previous year. Dr. Astin thinks that this reflects growing concern about AIDS. However, a record high of 52 percent of the freshmen said that it was all right for two "people"—their sex was not indicated in the question—who had known each other only a short time to have sexual relations.

Nine percent of the freshmen said they smoked cigarettes, down one percentage point from the year before. Of the women, 10.4 percent smoke, as against 7.3 percent of men.

*Being well off financially was identified as a key goal by a record 76 percent of freshmen, up from 73 percent the previous year and nearly double the level of 39 percent in 1970.

**Dr. Alexander W. Astin is the director of the 22nd annual survey of entering freshmen conducted by the American Council on Education and by the Higher Education Research Institute at the University of California at Los Angeles.

From Deirdre Carmody, "Freshmen Found Stressing Wealth," *The New York Times* (January 14, 1988): p. A14.

C. Answer the following questions based on the reading.

   1. What was your key reason for deciding to attend college?

   2. What kind of surveys of students are taken in your country?

   3. What is the preferred career choice of most college students in your country? And in the United States?

   4. What do you suppose would be the percentage of college students in your country who would think that being well off financially was very important? Explain.

   5. What do you suppose would be the percentage of college students in your country who would think that developing a meaningful philosophy of life was important? Explain.

D. ***A Class Survey*** Answer the following questions. Then, give your instructor your answer to each question as he/she makes a tally of class responses on the board. Express the results of class responses in percentages.

   1. Sex   Male _____

                             Female _____

   2. Do you smoke   Yes _____

                             No _____

   3. How important is it to you to become well off financially?   Very important _____

                             Somewhat important _____

                             Not very important _____

   4. How important is it to you to develop a meaningful philosophy of life?   Very important _____

                             Somewhat important _____

                             Not very important _____

E. Work with a partner and analyze the results of the class survey as follows.

   1. Compare the percentages of male and female students in the class who smoke with the percentages mentioned in the reading.

   2. Compare the class response to questions 3 and 4 in Exercise D with the data shown in the graph titled "Freshman Goals: Spiritual vs. Financial" accompanying the reading.

   3. Now write three sentences analyzing the data for your class compared to the data for American college freshmen in the reading and the graph.

MODEL COMPOSITION

*Analyzing the Results of a Survey on Fields of Study
Chosen by Foreign Students—1987/1988*

Foreign Students by Field of Study, 1987/88

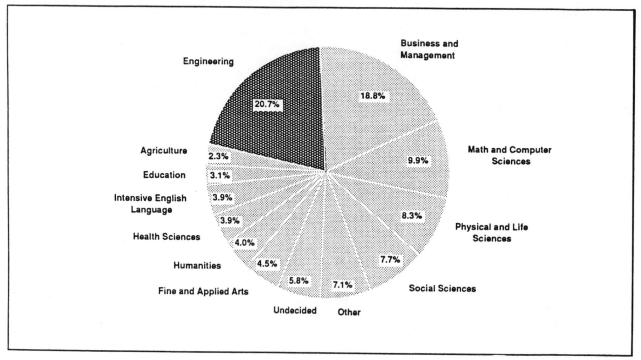

	1984/85		1987/88	
Field of Study	Foreign Students	% of Total	Foreign Students	% of Total
Agriculture	7,540	2.2	7,930	2.3
Business and Management	64,930	19.0	66,990	18.8
Education	12,140	3.6	11,140	3.1
Engineering	75,370	22.0	73,880	20.7
Fine and Applied Arts	15,900	4.7	15,860	4.5
Health Sciences	13,410	3.9	13,910	3.9
Humanities	13,030	3.8	14,250	4.0
Mathematics and Computer Sciences	35,630	10.4	35,400	9.9
Physical and Life Sciences	25,960	7.6	29,250	8.3
Social Sciences	25,000	7.3	27,650	7.7
Other	22,250	6.5	25,100	7.1
Intensive English Language	11,010	3.2	14,030	3.9
Undeclared	19,940	5.8	20,790	5.8
All Foreign Students	342,110	100.0	356,180	100.0

Since 1949 the Institute of International Education has been conducting an Annual Census of Foreign Students. In 1987/88, as in every other year since the first census was taken, engineering was the most popular field of study among international students in the United States, with 20.7% of all foreign students in that field. Business and management was the only other field of study to enroll more than 10% of the foreign students, with 18.8% of them. Math and computer sciences was third, chosen by 9.9%, followed by the physical and life sciences attracting 8.3%, and the social sciences, enrolling 7.7%.

Although the rank order of the top five field of study choices of foreign students has not changed in several years, there have been some interesting trends over the past three years. Engineering, although still the leading field, has been experiencing a slow but steady decline in its share of foreign students, dropping from 22.0% in 1984/85 to 20.7% in 1987/88. Business and management, on the other hand, has been very constant at around the 19% level over the same period. Math and computer sciences has dropped about 0.5% in the past three years, while the physical and life sciences and the other social sciences have increased by 0.7% and 0.4% respectively.

From Marianthi Zikopoulos, ed. "*Open Doors:* 1987/88 report on International Educational Exchange," (New York: Institute of International Education, 1988), pp. 24, 26.

F. You are going to participate in a survey. The class should divide itself into two groups: an all-male group and an all-female group. Then, indicate with a check mark (√) whether you agree or disagree with the following controversial statements.

	Agree	Disagree
1. The death penalty should be abolished.	_____	_____
2. Abortion should be legal.	_____	_____
3. The activities of married women are best confined to the home and to the family.	_____	_____
4. A couple should live together for some time before deciding to get married.	_____	_____
5. Women should receive the same salary as men in comparable positions.	_____	_____

Add up the responses of the members of your group and express them in percentages.

Next, make a line or bar graph to show the responses of your group. Use the vertical line to represent the percentage of students who agree with each statement and the horizontal line to represent the number of the statement.

G. *Oral Report* When you have finished the survey and the graph, prepare a group oral report on your survey. Choose someone from your group to give the oral report to the class and someone else to draw a graph on the board representing your group's responses. Be sure to take notes on each oral report. Then, prepare a combined graph that uses either two lines or pairs of bars to compare the responses of the all-male and all-female groups.

H. *Dictation / Dicto-Comp*   Listen to your instructor read the two paragraphs below and then follow his/her directions.

According to a 1989 report by the Surgeon General of the United States, smoking is responsible for more than one out of every six deaths in the United States. Smoking remains the single most important preventable cause of death in our society. The prevalence of smoking remains higher among blacks, blue-collar workers, and the less educated than among the overall population. Children, especially girls, are smoking at younger ages. Smoking among high-school seniors, after declining for years, leveled off from 1980 through 1987. One-quarter of high-school seniors who have ever smoked had their first cigarette by the sixth grade, and half by the eighth grade. There is a growing consensus that smoking-prevention education needs to begin in elementary school.

During the past twenty-five years, there have been phenomenal changes in the way Americans think about tobacco use. Nearly half of all living adults who ever smoked have quit. More people now than ever before consider smoking to be outside the social norm. Antismoking programs and policies have contributed to this change. In the 1940s and 1950s, smoking was chic; now, increasingly, it is shunned. Movie stars, sports heroes, and other celebrities used to appear in cigarette advertisements. Today, actors, athletes, public figures, and political candidates are rarely seen smoking.

Adapted from U.S. Dept. of Health and Human Services. *Reducing the Health Consequences of Smoking: 25 Years of Progress. A Report of the Surgeon General.* U.S. Dept. of Health and Human Services, Public Health Service, Centers for Disease Control, Center for Chronic Disease Prevention and Health Promotion, Office on Smoking and Health. DHHS publication No. (CDC) 89-8411; prepublication version, January 11, 1989.

COMPOSITION WRITING

I.   Write a paragraph comparing the differences in male and female responses to the survey questions in Exercise F. As a starting point, use any notes that you took on the oral reports in Exercise G. Try to follow the model composition for organization, and use the outline shown here as a guide.

   I. Background information
      A. What was the purpose of the survey?
      B. Who conducted the survey, and when was it carried out?
      C. What method was used, and how many people participated?
   II. Discussion
      What were the results of the survey, and how do they relate or how can they be interpreted?
   III. Conclusion
      Can you draw any conclusions or discuss trends and/or make recommendations based on the results of the survey?

STRUCTURE

Connecting Words and Phrases

In writing reports, the following connecting words and phrases are often used to signal the relationship between ideas.

Relationship	Connectives
Addition	and, also, too, besides, furthermore, moreover, first, second, third, one, another, finally, in conclusion
Example	for example, for instance, to illustrate
Cause and effect	because, since, thus, for this reason, therefore, consequently, accordingly
Comparison	similarly, in the same way, likewise, in a like manner
Contrast	but, however, in contrast, on the other hand, in spite of, although

Vocabulary Often Used in Reports

↑	↓	↔
rise	fall	level off
increase	decrease	maintain
	decline	stabilize
grow	shrink	constant
up from	down from	
flow	ebb	
upward	downward	
climb	dip / drop	
go up	go down	

21

LESSON

Speaking Out and Writing Opinions

*W*e use arguments and express opinions constantly when speaking and writing. Individuals, groups, and even governments must take a stand about many controversies in the world today. Some arguments are very public, like the argument over gun control and over abortion in the United States. Can you name two public arguments that are going on today in your country or in the world?

A. Imagine that you are trying to explain to a friend how you feel about one of the issues shown in the illustrations. Working with a partner, choose one of the controversies shown and role-play the following dialogue. Then, exchange roles.

> *S1:* How do you feel about . . . ?
> *S2:* Well, I think that. . . . How about you?
> *S1:* What you say is interesting, but, I believe. . . .

B. Imagine that you and a friend have read the following sentence in a newspaper: People who use drugs are as guilty as people who sell drugs and should be prosecuted accordingly. Ask your friend (a partner) what he/she thinks about this and why he/she feels that way. Agree or disagree with your friend and give your reasons.

READING

A Boy or a Girl?

If you could choose the sex of your child, would you have a boy or a girl? One of each? Would you want to make the choice yourself, or would you rather leave it up to nature? According to researchers, if parents could preselect a child's sex, more would choose boys than girls.

Since earliest times, many cultures have favored° sons. Some people say that this is due to the interest in the survival° of the family name or to the male's traditional role as a breadwinner. Others say that it is because of the dowry° expenses that parents in some cultures must pay when a daughter marries.

preferred

act of continuing to exist

property that a woman brings to her husband in marriage

Although studies show that the number of male births would increase if sex selection became possible, the long-term impact° of such a trend° is less clear. Some sociologists predict that prostitution, polyandry (having multiple husbands), and male homosexuality would increase in a society with a large majority of males. Others believe that aggressive behavior would become more prevalent° and that interest in cultural and community activities, a more traditionally female concern,° would decline.* Still other sociologists and demographers° claim that sex selection would have a beneficial effect on population control. Surveys suggest that if parents were able to choose a son or a daughter, they would have fewer children. In the United States, parents frequently choose to have one child of each sex. In any event, whether a couple had one or two children, there would be less likelihood of their continuing to have children in order to have the "missing" son or, in some cases, the "missing" daughter.

force / general direction

existing on a widespread basis in some place or time / matter of interest

people who collect and study information (statistics) about the characteristics of human populations

The issue of sex selection raises as yet unresolved° ethical° challenges. Methods involving artificial insemination° have already been used in humans to preselect a child's sex, and other methods will surely be developed in the future. Currently, however, some parents are choosing abortion after identifying a child's sex through ultrasound° or amniocentesis° if the unborn child is not the desired sex. Is one method more acceptable than another? Is any method acceptable?

Regardless of the view that one holds on the issue of sex selection, the day may be coming soon when easily applied methods will force society to face the ethical question of whether parents should be allowed to choose the sex of a child.

unanswered / having to do with the principles of morally good conduct

putting a male seed in a female by hand or an instrument

medical testing procedure that involves the use of sound above the range of normal hearing / surgical procedure that can be used to determine the sex of a child while still in the womb

*Elizabeth M. Whelan, *Boy or Girl? How to Help Choose the Sex of Your Baby* (New York: The Bobbs-Merrill Company, Inc., 1984), pp. 122–123.

C. Be prepared to discuss the following questions.

   1. Would most people in your country prefer a boy or a girl child? Why?

   2. What would the consequences be in your country if there were many more male children?

   3. Do you agree or disagree with the sociologists' predictions about a male-dominated society? Why?

   4. Would you want to be able to choose the sex of your children? What would you choose? Why?

D. Working with a partner and using the following example as a guide, list as many reasons as you can think of for wanting a son or a daughter. Then, list the reasons why you would want to have one child of each sex. Share your list and reasons with the class.

   Son

   1. A son is more responsible.
   2. Boys are more independent.

   Daughter

   1. A daughter is easier to raise.
   2. Daughters show more respect for their parents.

MODEL COMPOSITION

Choosing Sons or Daughters

I feel that whenever it becomes possible for parents to choose the sex of their child, they should be allowed to do so even though it may lead to more males than females. The first reason is that persons carrying an inherited disease that affects males would be able to choose to have a girl. The second reason is that there would be fewer deliberate abortions done because parents wanted a child of a different sex. The third reason is that unfortunately we still have wars, and more men than women are killed in wars. In addition, since women live longer than men, many widows would welcome a larger population of available males. Moreover, I don't believe the problem of more males in our society would be a permanent situation. Despite the fact that there would probably be more male children born for some time, it is likely that a shortage of women would eventually lead to an increase in the number of females born so that there would be more women available as marriage partners. After a time, the ratio of men to women would probably settle into a fairly even balance.

Elements of Style: Writing Arguments

Writing arguments or opinions means making statements and supporting them in order to convince the reader. Argument and opinion writing is used to help the reader decide between conflicting questions, to change viewpoints, and to gain practical goals. Paragraphs are developed by listing reasons to support a topic sentence. The topic sentence is often placed at the beginning of a paragraph. This sentence makes a statement (sometimes called a definition, proposition, or assertion). The rest of the composition then supports that statement by telling why and giving relevant facts. The argument or reasons point toward a final conclusion that is based on the supporting reasons.

Topic sentence *(proposition)*	Children shouldn't be allowed to watch so much violence on television.
Supporting reasons	The first reason is. . . . The second reason is. . . . The third reason is. . . .
Conclusion	In conclusion, watching violence on television has a bad effect on children, and. . . .

In writing argument and opinion compositions, the following words and phrases are often used to signal the relationship between ideas.

To show support and to give reasons and examples

first of all
for one thing
one reason that
also
in addition
moreover
next
for example
another example
for instance

To show sequence and numerical order

in the (first) place
in the next place

To show summarization

for this reason
as a result
finally
thus
in conclusion
to conclude

To show contrast

but
however
despite / in spite of
although / even though
in contrast
on the one hand / on the other hand

To show opinion

I feel
I think
I believe
it is my opinion
in my opinion

E. Complete the following assertions or propositions with the words that adequately tell how you feel about them. Then, work with someone who agrees with you and list three reasons to support your opinion. When you have finished, compare your propositions and reasons with those of a pair of classmates who disagree with your viewpoint.

    1. I think that the lyrics for rock and heavy metal music
    ————————————(should, should not) be censored.

————————————————————————————

————————————————————————————

————————————————————————————

2. I feel that the death penalty _____(should, should not) be abolished.

   _____

   _____

   _____

3. In my opinion, women in the military _____(should, should not) fight in battle.

   _____

   _____

   _____

4. I believe that drugs _____(should, should not) be legalized.

   _____

   _____

   _____

5. In my opinion, smoking _____(should, should not) be prohibited in all restaurants.

   _____

   _____

   _____

6. Parents _____(should, should not) choose a career for their children.

   _____

   _____

   _____

F. Work with a partner and answer the following questions in complete sentences using infinitives. Then add a second sentence to 1–4 supporting your opinion or giving a reason.

   1. Is it difficult to find a nonviolent program on television?

   _____

   _____

   2. In what field would you like to get a job after you finish your education?

   _____

   _____

    3. Do you think it is important to have strict nonsmoking laws in public places?

    _____

    _____

    4. In your opinion, would it be appropriate for the United States to take the first step and eliminate all its own nuclear weapons in order to encourage the Soviet Union to do so, too?

    _____

    _____

    5. What are some ways to solve the problem of homelessness in our society?

    _____

    _____

G. Complete the following sentences using adverbial clauses so that they will answer the questions in parentheses. Use different subordinate conjunctions to begin each adverbial clause.

    1. I was late _____

    _____(For what reason?)

    2. He will speak English well _____

    _____(When?)

    3. I started this course _____

    _____(When?)

    4. He came to school _____

    _____

    (Under what conditions? —use *unless*)

    5. I didn't carry an umbrella _____

    _____

    (In spite of what? —use *although* or *even though*)

    6. She needs the money _____

    _____(For what purpose?)

    7. I park my car _____

    _____(Where?)

    8. I practice my English _____

    _____(When?)

H. Work with a partner and mark the adverbial clauses used in the model composition. Then, identify their function in the sentence.

I. ***Dictation / Dicto-Comp***   Listen to your instructor read the paragraph below and then follow his/her directions.

Lotto fever has hit the United States, and more and more states are beginning to use lotteries as a means of raising revenue. While on the surface this seems an easy way to raise money, lotteries create many ethical and moral problems. For one thing, the people who play the lotto games are primarily the poor, who can least afford it. They often bet more than a dollar, and the odds against their winning are tremendous. Another objection is that the states are encouraging gambling. Some experts feel that people who bet on lotto can very easily go on to gamble on other games of chance and end up broke or in prison. A third very important argument is that the government's encouragement of gambling can have a serious effect on traditional attitudes toward work and savings. It gives people the wrong message—"You can get rich" or "Dream a little dream"—telling them, in effect, that there is an easy way to get rich without working. Schools, meanwhile, are trying to teach students that it takes hard work to achieve one's dreams.

COMPOSITION WRITING

J. Write a composition about one of the statements you made in Exercise E. Follow the model composition, the "Elements of Style" section, and the outline shown here as much as possible.

(Title)

A. *Proposition:* Firmly state your opinion or directly state a proposition.
B. *Supporting reasons:* Give three reasons in support of your opinion.
C. *Conclusion:* Make a final statement based on the points in your argument (reasons) or restate your original proposition.

STRUCTURE

Use of the Infinitive

The infinitive is used after an adjective in a sentence with a linking verb.

It will soon be possible *to choose* the sex of a child.
Women will be delighted *to see* more males.
It is reasonable *to expect* that there will soon be a balance.

The words *for* + *a noun or a pronoun* are often inserted between the adjective (+ noun) and the infinitive.

> It was a wrong thing *for the couple* to do.
> It seemed a good idea *for me* to study the alternatives.
> It isn't safe *for someone* to drink and drive.

Adverbial Clauses

Adverbial clauses act like adverbs; they are subordinate clauses that modify a verb, an adjective, or an adverb in a sentence. Adverbial clauses can start with words like *when, wherever, while, after, before, if, unless, as if, although, because, so that,* and *since.* These words that introduce adverbial clauses are called subordinate conjunctions. This means that they connect the sentence parts by joining the adverbial clause to the main clause in a dependent (or subordinate) manner.

> My doctor was happy. I continued with the treatment. (*two independent, or main, clauses*)

> He went to a disco *independent clause* { *if / when / because / so / unless* } he felt tired. *dependent clause*

1. *Adverbial clause modifying a verb*
   a. An adverbial clause can tell you *why, when,* and *how* an action is done.

> I would rather have a son *before I have a daughter.*
> My parents allowed my brother and me to watch TV *when we were young.*
> The students protested *because they believed the administration did not understand their cause.*
> *While I was still flying to the United States,* I started to practice my English.
> He got up early *so that he could jog before going to work.*

   b. When an adverbial clause begins with *if* or *unless,* it tells you under what conditions the verb in the main clause occurs.

> I usually watch television at night *unless I have a test the next day.*
> You will anger many people *if you don't put out the cigarette.*

   c. When an adverbial clause begins with *although* or *even though,* it makes an opposing or contrasting statement about the verb.

> Juan speaks English in school *although he enjoys speaking his native language, Spanish, at home.*
> They should be allowed to do so *even though it would lead to more males in our society.*

2. *Adverbial clause modifying an adjective or adverb*

a. Adverbial clauses can be used to compare adjectives and adverbs.

My friend thinks the Japanese are more industrious *than we are.*
My friend thinks the Japanese work harder *than we do.*

b. Adverbial clauses of comparison are sometimes incomplete. They are called elliptical clauses.

My friend thinks the Japanese are more industrious *than we.*
My friend thinks the Japanese work harder *than we.*

L E S S O N

Speaking Out and Writing Opinions

*I*t is difficult to express some opinions and arguments because people feel very strongly about certain issues. However, Americans expect you to express your opinions openly. When you hesitate to say how you feel about something, remember this often-quoted American expression: "It's a free country." So go ahead and say how you feel. Of course, you will also have to listen to other people and respect how they feel about the same thing.

A. Work with a partner and discuss two of the topics represented by the illustrations.

> *S1:* How do you feel about . . . ?
> *S2:* I think it's unfair. / I think it's a good idea.
> *S1:* How come?
> *S2:* What about . . . ? / I don't like. . . .

B. Work with a partner and ask how he/she feels about capital punishment. Be sure to find out why he/she feels this way. Then, exchange roles.

R E A D I N G

War Toys on the March

War toys are the leading category° of toys sold today. Since 1982 sales have increased 700%. These toys include action figures such as GI Joe, Rambo and Transformers; laser tag games; interactive toys; and an alarming increase in realistic toy guns including battery-powered Uzi submachine guns and hand grenades that really explode. Promoting these toys are a growing number of violent cartoons seen daily on television by children before and after school, and on weekends.

Parents and educators know firsthand of the problems that arise from children playing with war toys. Children often mimic° the play they see on television, therefore eliminating° the creativity and cooperation needed in children's play. They become more aggressive° in their behavior and it increases the chance they will resort to violent behavior later.

Violence in our society is at an all-time high, according to FBI statistics. Police deal daily with the question of whether a gun is real or not, sometimes with tragic outcomes. It is important for our society to work against this violence. Eliminating war toys and violent cartoons from our children's lives is a good place to start. Allowing them to have war toys and watch these cartoons implicitly ° supports violence and war as solutions to problems.

No society interested in attaining peace and justice can allow such a militarization° of the young to go unchallenged.° Any vision of a future without war and killing is impossible if the young have been raised to be passive consumers° of violence and militarism in toys, cartoons, and popular culture.

Every time we purchase a toy, we communicate our adult values to the children who receive these toys. Through play, children imitate our values. Do we want them to think that disputes° and differences are best settled by force or that the world is divided up into good guys and bad guys?

Children do need to learn how to deal with aggression, but there are more constructive ways to do this than through war toys. Fear, anger and feelings of low esteem° are often at the root of aggressive behavior, behavior that is encouraged by playing with war toys and watching violent television shows. The home and school should be places where children can build their self-esteem. Their environment should encourage communication, cooperation and the development of creative ways to solve conflicts.°

From "War Toys on the March," a brochure published by *Stop War Toys Campaign* (Norwich, Conn.: New England War Resisters League, 1988).

Margin glosses:
- one of a number of groups into which something has been divided
- copy; imitate
- removing or getting rid of
- always ready to quarrel or attack
- in a way that is understood but not plainly expressed
- process of glorifying war or the use of armed force / unopposed / not active users (choosers)
- disagreements
- opinion of oneself
- disagreements or arguments

C. Answer the following questions based on the reading.

1. Why do you think war toys are so popular among children?
2. Cite two reasons given in the reading why playing with war toys can lead to violence.
3. Are war toys popular with children in your country? What kind of war toys are popular? Do both boys and girls play with them?
4. What kind of toys did you play with as a child? Which were your favorites?

5. Do you think manufacturers should stop making and selling war toys? Why or why not?
6. What kind of television programs are popular with children in your country? Is there much violence in these programs? How do these programs compare with children's TV programs in the United States?
7. What should be the role of the parents in keeping their children from playing with war toys and watching violent television programs?

D. Work in groups of three to five people and decide on a good toy or game for children. Then, draw a diagram of the toy or game and write three sentences telling the benefits children would get from playing with it. Present your toy or game to the class.

MODEL COMPOSITION

War Toys: A Cause for Concern?

Children have been playing some form of war games throughout history, acting out the battle between the forces of Good and Evil. Today, there is an ongoing argument about whether allowing children to play with war toys leads to violent behavior. While many parents refuse to permit their children to play with guns and other war toys, some psychologists and toy-industry officials don't believe that playing with war toys leads to violent behavior in later life.

They point out that no one has been able to prove that playing with war toys is definitely linked to violent behavior in later life. Psychologists believe that children need a way to express their aggressive instincts. Playing with war toys gives children a safe way to get rid of their aggressions and anger and gives them a sense of control in their lives. They claim that the more aggressive tendencies that are discharged in play as a child, the fewer aggressive tendencies that a person will have to deal with as an adult. Other psychologists say that children see violence on television and would act out what they saw by forming a gun with their fingers even if they didn't have the toy itself. Moreover, toy manufacturers feel that playing with toy soldiers can also teach positive values such as patriotism and bravery.

Even people who are against war toys agree that in the final analysis, children learn values primarily from their parents and not from their toys.

E. Think about the topics in parentheses. Then, complete the following sentences about these topics using noun clauses.

1. (smoking) I believe _____

_____

2. (drinking and driving) I think that _____

_____

3. (the death penalty) I feel _____

_____

4. (abortion) I hope _____

_____

5. (toxic waste) I wonder _____

_____

F.   Work with a partner and identify the sentences containing a noun clause in the model composition. Then, identify the function of each noun clause in the sentence: subject, object of verb, object of preposition, or predicate noun.

G.   Indicate how you feel about the following questions.

1. Should nuclear weapons be banned?

I believe _____

_____

2. Should married women with children work?

I feel _____

_____

3. Is cheating always wrong?

In my opinion, _____

_____

4. Should a couple live together before deciding to get married?

I think _____

_____

5. Should smoking be banned from all restaurants?

In my opinion, _____

_____

6. Should animals be used in drug testing and medical research?

I feel _____

_____

7. Should all young people serve one year in national service?

I believe _____

_____

H. *Dictation / Dicto-Comp* Listen to your instructor read the paragraph below and then follow his/her directions.

     I feel that smoking should be prohibited in all public places. For one thing, smoke irritates the eyes, nose, and throat of nonsmokers. In addition, many nonsmokers don't like the smell of a lit cigarette. Another reason is that many smokers litter the environment with paper, cigarette stubs, and ashes. And still another reason is that very often, in a restaurant, smoke will spoil the taste of the food one is eating. Finally, the Surgeon General of the United States has reported that cigarette smoking is bad for the health of smokers and nonsmokers alike.

COMPOSITION WRITING

I. Write a composition about one of the statements you made in Exercise G. Follow the model composition and the outline shown here as much as possible.

(Title)

   I. *Proposition:* Firmly state your opinion or directly state a proposition.
  II. *Supporting Reasons:* Give three reasons in support of your opinion.
 III. *Conclusion:* Make a final statement based on the points in your argument (reasons) or restate your original proposition.

STRUCTURE

Noun Clauses

A noun clause is a subordinate clause that acts like a noun in a sentence. It can be used as a subject, an object of a verb or preposition, or a predicate noun. Noun clauses can begin with a word such as *who, whose, what, which, when, why, where, how, if, whether,* or *that.*

1. Noun clause as subject

   How children learn to release aggression is an important issue to study.
   What you do after school hours is your own concern.

2. *Noun clause as object of verb*

Even psychologists admit *that children don't learn values from toys.*
They continue to debate *whether playing with war toys causes violent behavior.*
They believe *that action figures like GI Joe are just modern toys.*
They don't believe *that war toys lead to violent behavior.*
He showed me *what pamphlets he had circulated to the students.*

3. *Noun clause as object of preposition*

Psychologists are interested *in how children learn aggressive behavior.*
They talked *about what the children should watch on television.*

4. *Noun clause as predicate noun*

The early years are *when children develop behavioral patterns.*
This is *where the politician will speak this evening.*

L E S S O N

Writing Letters

Institute for English

General Information

Foreign student advisor

Each student is assigned a Foreign Student Adviser to assist him or her in academic as well as personal matters.

Proficiency Examination

To evaluate your proficiency in English, all students at the Institute are required to take an examination to assess the following: grammar, listening and speaking abilities, and vocabulary. Prior to enrolling in an English course, you must take this examination. Based on the results of the examination, your advisor will help you select a course of study appropriate to your level.

How to register

You must do the following: (1) Complete the registration form; (2) Pay tuition and registration fees; (3) Obtain the signature of your advisor before enrolling in any course.

Course Information

Course Number	Course	Fee	English For Specific Purposes	Fee
20.30	Intensive course in American English M/W/Th/F 10:00–1:00; 2:00–3:00 June 16–August 18	$750.00	20.40 English for Business Students F 6:10–9:10 June 26–July 30	$175.00
20.32	Saturday Course in American English Sat. 9:00–12:00; 1:00–4:00 June 20–August 28	$250.00	20.50 English for Science Students M 1:30–4:30 June 22–July 26	$175.00
20.33	Improving Conversational Skills Tu/Th 3:30–5:30 June 19–August 10	$75.00	20.60 English for Computer Users Th 2:30–5:30 June 25–July 29	$175.00
20.35	TOEFL Preparation W 6:30–8:30 June 16–July 18	$50.00		
20.36	Beginning Accent Correction M/W 10:00–11:00; Tu/Th 9:00–10:00 June 16–August 10	$125.00		

*E*veryone has occasion to write business or personal letters at some time. Your letters represent you on paper. In order to make the best possible impression, it is important to know the forms and conventions (wordings) that one must follow in writing letters. In this lesson, you will find models of frequently used types of letters that will help you prepare your own business and personal letters.

A. Two students are waiting to register for English courses at the Institute for English. Work with a partner and role-play the following dialogue, using information from the schedule of courses. Then, reverse roles.

> *S1:* Hi! I hope we don't have a long wait. What courses are you going to take here?
>
> *S2:* My English isn't very good, so I'm going to take. . . . How about you?
>
> *S1:* I'm working now, so I'm going to take. . . . Good luck with your English!
>
> *S2:* . . .

B. After looking at the Institute for English brochure, work with a partner and answer the following questions. When you have finished, exchange roles.

> *S1:* Is there someone at the institute who can help us with course selection?
>
> *S2:* . . .
>
> *S1:* Do we have to take an entrance examination for the institute?
>
> *S2:* . . .
>
> *S1:* What's included on the examination?
>
> *S2:* . . .
>
> *S1:* How do we register for the institute?
>
> *S2:* . . .

MODEL LETTERS

Read the following letters and notice the form—the heading and inside address, the salutation, and the closing.

207 Pearl Avenue
Central, Iowa 52556
May 2, 19___

Institute for English
Central University
20 West Street
Central, Iowa 52554

Dear Sir or Madam:

I have recently arrived in this country from Korea and would like to study English full-time starting in September. I would also like to live in university housing.

Would you kindly send me the fall catalogue of English courses offered by the Institute for English and complete information about available Central University housing?

Very truly yours,
Peter Yoon

Institute for English Central University
Office of Admissions for Foreign Students
20 West Street, Central, Iowa 52554

May 26, 19__

Mr. Peter Yoon
207 Pearl Avenue
Central, Iowa 52556

Dear Mr. Yoon:

Thank you for your inquiry about Central University English programs. Enclosed is our fall catalogue containing information on courses and registration as well as housing information.

Dormitory assignments are made by the housing office one to two weeks prior to the start of the course. Off-campus apartments within walking distance of campus are also available. Apartments are unfurnished two- and three-bedroom units with kitchen, bath, and living room. There are shared laundry facilities in the basement of each apartment building.

There is a $50.00 nonrefundable deposit for all housing contracts. Prices per month vary from $200.00 to $350.00, depending on the type of accommodation. The housing office requires payment of the deposit and a full semester's rent upon assignment of housing, which is made on a first-come, first-served basis. Since both dormitory and apartment space is limited, application should be made as soon as possible.

Once again, thank you for your inquiry.

Sincerely,

Jane Smith, Housing
Coordinator

325 East 70th Street
New York, N.Y. 10021
January 10, 19__

Office of Undergraduate Foreign Admissions
New York University
22 Washington Square North
P.O. Box 909, Cooper Station
New York, N.Y. 10276

Dear Sir or Madam:

    Please send me a catalogue and an application form for admission to the College of Arts and Sciences, New York University. I have finished twelve years of school in Greece and have my transcripts with me. I arrived in this country two months ago, and I would like to enter the freshman class in September. My major field of interest is economics.

    I would appreciate any additional information you could send me about the cost of tuition and of living on campus. I also would like to know about any scholarships or other assistance available to foreign students.

    Thank you very much.

Sincerely yours,
Eleni Papadopoulos

C. Be prepared to answer the following questions.

1. Would you rather live on-campus or off-campus at a university?
2. For a foreign student, what are the advantages of living on-campus? What are the disadvantages?
3. What are the advantages of living off-campus? What are the disadvantages?
4. Would you rather have an American roommate or a roommate from your country or another country? Why?
5. Where do students live while attending a university in your country?
6. Compare the cost of housing in this city with the cost of housing in your hometown. What accounts for the difference in cost, if any?
7. Do students ever live apart from their families in their own apartments in your country? When?
8. How does the cost of tuition at a university in the United States compare with the cost in your country? Does the cost vary from one institution to another?
9. Are scholarships or loans available to students in your country? If so, are they easy to obtain?

Elements of Style: Business and Personal Letters

Business Letters

There are many different kinds of business letters. Among the most useful ones to know are the letter of request, the letter of complaint and adjustment, and the order letter.

The following is a list of things to remember when writing a business letter:

1. A business letter should always be typed, if possible. (If you must write it, use a pen and dark ink. Never write a business letter in pencil.)
2. Use plain white paper (stationery) and a matching envelope.
3. Be sure your letter is neat and attractive. Write or type on only one side of the paper. Leave at least 1½-inch margins on both sides. If you need more paper, use a second sheet.
4. State the purpose of the letter at the beginning. Be sure that the rest of your letter is related to that purpose.
5. State all the necessary information clearly and briefly without omitting important details.
6. Be courteous and friendly.
7. Be sure your return address appears on the upper left-hand corner of the envelope.
8. Proofread each business letter before you mail it, and make a copy of the letter for your own files.

Personal (Social) Letters

Personal letters (also called friendly notes or social letters) are short letters used to extend, accept, or refuse an invitation and to express thanks, get-well wishes, or congratulations. When you write such letters, be sure to sound sincere and natural.

The following is a list of things to remember when writing a personal letter:

1. Be sure that your letter is neat and attractive.
2. Use a white or light-colored sheet of paper and a matching envelope.
3. Write neatly in pen and ink. Don't use a pencil.
4. Discuss things that will interest the person to whom you are writing.
5. Be sure to include your address and the date in the letter.
6. Sign your name clearly, using your full name if the person you are writing to is not a close friend.
7. Be sure your return address appears on the upper left-hand corner of the envelope.

For a further description of business and personal letters, see the Handbook.

D. Request the booklet mentioned in the following advertisement by writing a letter to the company that placed the ad. Be sure to describe exactly what you want, and say how much money you are including with your letter to cover postage and handling. Also, say where you saw the ad, using your imagination.

Learn a foreign language in just 60 or 90 days! Send for our free booklet "Anyone Can Learn a Foreign Language." Enclose 50¢ for postage and handling. Send to:

The Language Works

31 Santa Teresa Boulevard
Los Angeles, CA 57632

E. Write a letter ordering the travel bag shown in the accompanying advertisement. Describe the travel bag carefully and include the following information:

where you saw the ad and the date   price
quantity   sales tax (if any)
model number   how you are paying for it
color   (money order, check, credit card)

TRAVEL-EASE
The Travel Bag for All Purposes

With the Travel-Ease bag, you have room for books, clothes, papers, anything! This bag is made of sturdy water-resistant canvas and comes in a choice of five exciting colors.

The bag also features large exterior pockets as well as interior storage compartments for small easy-to-lose items and sturdy shoulder-length straps.

Order your Travel-Ease bag today and enjoy the convenience of this lightweight, durable, stylish and affordable all-purpose bag.

At the low, low price of $29.95 each or $56.95 for two, the Travel-Ease bag makes a great gift for any occasion.

This offer will end soon so order today!

Send your check and order to:
Brown & Lord Luggage, P.O. Box 554, N.Y., N.Y. 10012.

Item	Color	Qty.	Total
5012	Black		
5014	Navy		
5017	Burgundy		
5020	Gray		
5021	Brown		
		Total	
Add $1.50 per pag ordered for shipping and handling. Allow 4 weeks for delivery.			
		Order Total	

Brown & Lord
Luggage since 1840

For Faster Service:
Credit Card Customer Call Toll Free:
1-800-222-2222, 24 hours, 7 days a week.

Name: _____

Address: _____

City/State/Zip _____

F. You have received the travel bag and found that it was not the color you ordered. Write a letter of complaint to the company. Tell the company that you are returning the travel bag and ask the company to send you the correct color. (See the Handbook for a discussion of complaint letters.)

G. *Dictation / Dicto-Comp*   Listen to your instructor dictate the letter below and then follow his/her directions.

> 11 Waverly Street
> Columbus, Ohio 43210
> October 20, 1990

Dear Mrs. Johnson,

It is a pleasure to write this letter because it gives me an opportunity to tell you how much I enjoyed your hospitality last weekend. It was my first visit to the home of an American family, and at first, I was very anxious about my English and my knowledge of the customs. Then, I saw you and your children waiting for me at the station, and I immediately knew that everything was going to be all right. You and your wonderful family put me at ease right away.

There are many happy memories of the weekend that I will keep with me forever. I particularly enjoyed driving through the countryside with Mr. Johnson and you and seeing the changing colors of the leaves on the trees. I liked playing baseball and Monopoly with your sons, Jimmy and Joey. They were very patient with me and full of fun. Tell them I will teach them how to play soccer on my next visit.

I am back at school now, and I am very happy because I now know a real American family. Thank you so much for a memorable day. I hope that someday you will visit my country and I can return your hospitality.

> Sincerely,
> Carlos Gómez

H.   Write a letter, choosing one of the following ideas.

1. Order something you saw advertised in a newspaper or magazine.
2. Respond to an article in a newspaper or magazine with a letter to the editor.
3. Write the telephone company and tell the company that it has charged you for long-distance calls you never made. Ask for an adjustment in the bill.
4. Thank a friend who invited you to his/her home and showed you around his/her town or city.

24

Writing with a Creative Spirit

*C*ongratulations! You have successfully written many guided compositions during this course. In the final lesson, you will have the opportunity to apply what you have learned to do some free writing using your knowledge of English and your creative ability.

Writing a Biography

Look at the photos showing scenes of John Fitzgerald Kennedy's life and then read the following fact sheet.

John Fitzgerald Kennedy (1917–1963)—Fact Sheet

I. Childhood and early years
   A. Born: Brookline, Massachusetts, in 1917.
   B. Second oldest child. Family had nine children.
   C. Father: Joseph P. Kennedy, prosperous businessman.
   D. Happy, lively family—supervised by maids and nurses—many sisters and brothers to play with.

II. Youth and early adulthood
   A. Father became ambassador to England; family went to live in London.
   B. Kennedy traveled a great deal; became interested in international affairs.
   C. Graduated from Harvard during Second World War. Then, enlisted in Navy.
   D. Served as commander of a PT boat in the Pacific. Discharged from Navy in 1945.
   E. Oldest brother, Joseph P. Kennedy, Jr., was supposed to enter politics. Joseph was killed in 1944 in the war. Result: Kennedy decided to enter politics.

III. Maturity
   A. Congressman from Massachusetts, 1946–1953. Senator from Massachusetts, 1953–1960.
   B. Elected president in 1960 at age 43. First Roman Catholic and youngest president.
   C. Inaugural address: Pledged his best efforts to help the people of the world help themselves. Told Americans "ask not what your country can do for you, ask what you can do for your country."
   D. His program—the "New Frontier"—called for:
      1. Federal aid to education
      2. Medical care for the aged
      3. Peace Corps
      4. Alliance for Progress
      5. Major legislation to secure civil rights for blacks

IV. End of life
   A. Assassinated November 22, 1963, in Dallas, Texas.
   B. Fourth American president to die by an assassin's bullet. Great loss to the country and the world; he had captured the hearts and minds of people everywhere in the world.

A.   Write a composition of four paragraphs about the life of John F. Kennedy following the outline of facts. Begin each paragraph with the phrase or clause indicated.

Paragraph 1

John Fitzgerald Kennedy was born _____

_____

_____

_____

Paragraph 2

When Kennedy was a young man, _____

_____

_____

_____

Paragraph 3

From 1946 to 1953, _____

_____

_____

_____

Paragraph 4

On November 22, 1963, _____

_____

_____

_____

B.   Now write a biography of a famous person in your country. Try to use the same four paragraph divisions used for the biography of John F. Kennedy.

   I.   Childhood and early years
  II.   Youth and early adulthood
 III.   Maturity
  IV.   End of life (if the person has already died)

Writing a College Entrance Essay

   In order to enter college, you must fill out a college application. On the application, you will be asked to write a personal-statement essay. Here are some topics that colleges have asked students to write about:

1. If you could be a talk-show host and have the opportunity to interview any three famous people, living or dead, whom would you choose, why, and what would you discuss?

2. It has been said, "In the future, everyone will be world famous for fifteen minutes." Describe your fifteen minutes.
3. Select a creative work—a novel, a film, a poem, a musical piece, a painting, or some other work of art—that has influenced the way you view the world and the way you view yourself. Discuss the work and its effects on you.
4. If you could create a public holiday, what holiday would you create?
5. What invention does the world need most?
6. Name a person who has had a significant influence on you and describe the influence.

C.   Now choose one of the preceding college entrance essay topics and write a composition on it.

Writing an Autobiographical Essay

The most commonly requested essay is the general autobiographical essay, because it allows the reader to know you as a person. The composition should include your thoughts and feelings and how you react to events in your personal life and in the world around you.

Here is an essay that worked. Do you feel you know this person from the essay? Why or why not?

Karen Duffy

Who (and Why) I Am

Slightly frizzy hair—usually in my face . . . foreign films from the fourth row of the Carolina theater (where a breeze always blows from the projector fan) . . . the lyrics of Simon and Garfunkel's "The Sound of Silence" . . . only eating plain hotdogs and pizza without pepperonis . . . pale yellow . . . my goldfish, "Aqua," who lives in a wineglass . . . a wrinkled David Bowie poster above my bed . . . Kurt Vonnegut books . . . James Dean in *Rebel Without a Cause* . . . reading "The New Yorker" for its cartoons . . . music by R.E.M. . . . crying every time Ali McGraw tells Ryan O'Neal "Love means never having to say you're sorry" . . . $F(x) = $ why? . . . jogging in the rain . . . strawberry ice cream with M&M's . . . waking up at night, inspired to write a line of poetry . . . passionate arguing over a physics problem . . . a.k.a. "Duff" . . . talking with my roommate until 3:00 AM about school, guys, and the meaning of life . . . bad taste in my mouth when saying the word "conservative" . . . intense hate of mornings and cold weather . . . what's left of John Lennon—"You may say I'm a dreamer, but I'm not the only one, I hope some day you will join us . . . and the world will live as one" . . . me.

From Boykin Curry and Brian Kasbar, eds. *Essays that Worked: 50 Essays from Successful Applications to the Nations Top Colleges* (New Haven, Conn.: Mustang Publishing Company, Inc. 1986), p. 57.

D. Now write an autobiographical composition about yourself for a college, including some of the following information asked for by some colleges.

   1. What word best describes you as a person?
   2. How would you like to be remembered?
   3. What is the most significant thing about you?
   4. Choose one extracurricular activity and describe its importance in your life.

Elements of Style: Résumé Writing

In the United States, it is very important to have a résumé when you are looking for a first job, a new job, or a change-of-career job.

The purpose of a résumé is to get you considered for a job opening that may have many applicants. The résumé is a one-page advertisement that gives information about you to prospective employers. It tells who you are, what you have done, what you do, and what you can do.

A résumé should include your experience, education and training, professional and personal skills, and personal data.

The general format of a résumé is as follows:

1. *Heading:* Your name, address, and telephone number.
2. *Work experience:* Start with your most recent job and then work backward to your previous jobs. Be sure to give beginning and ending dates for each job. Describe your duties or responsibilities in each job. List these starting with the past tense of the verbs that describe your duties and responsibilities.

   If you have had little or no work experience, start by listing your education and training in point 2 and then list your experience in point 3.
3. *Education and honors:* List the schools you attended and your degrees, if any. List dates attended, starting with the most recent and working backward. You may want to list your major and minor subjects and the skills you have acquired. List any honors or awards, starting with the most recent.
4. *Optional:* List your special interests or hobbies.
5. *Optional:* Include the statement "References will be furnished upon request."

E. Imagine that you are about to graduate from school and need to begin your job search. The office of career planning at your school has advised you to write a résumé. Follow the steps outlined in the "Elements of Style" section on résumé writing and prepare a résumé for yourself. Read the sample résumé before you begin. Share your résumé with a classmate.

F. *Class Activity* Work as a class and create a class newspaper. Be sure to choose a name for the paper, someone to be the editor, and someone to be the graphic designer. Each student will be a columnist and contribute an

MYCHELLE GARRIGAN

80 Pine Brook Rd.
Chestnut Ridge, N.Y. 10977
(419) 222-3020

EXPERIENCE

5/87–6/88; 8/88–Present	THE CENTER FOR CAREER AND LIFE PLANNING, New York, N.Y. *Administrative Assistant* • Assisted clients by administering career tests, explaining counseling options, and advising them on most compatible counselor and program. • Maintained career library, did billing, answered phones, and performed other general office duties.
9/87–6/88; 10/88–Present	NYU FOREIGN LANGUAGE DEPARTMENT, New York, N.Y. *Staff Assistant / NYU Representative* • Assisted instructors, set up audiovisual equipment, and provided information for students.
Summer '88	MCA CLASSICS/BROADWAY DIVISION, New York, N.Y. *Administrative Assistant* • Prepared promotional materials, assisted directors, operated fax machine, and answered phones.
Summer '88	TISCH SCHOOL OF THE ARTS: DANCE DEPARTMENT New York, N.Y. *Assistant to the Chair* • Assisted in the registering of students, answered phones, kept records for Summer Dance Program, and expedited mailings and special projects.
10/86–3/87	NYU GRADUATE BUSINESS LIBRARY, New York, N.Y. *Library Assistant* • Performed basic library functions, created files for resource center, and maintained circulation desk.
Summers '86, '87	SPRING VALLEY MUNICIPAL POOL, Spring Valley, N.Y. *Lifeguard*
EDUCATION	NEW YORK UNIVERSITY: COLLEGE OF ARTS & SCIENCES BA in Political Science / Minor in English— June 89 GPA 3.6
AWARDS & HONORS	NYU Trustees Scholarship 1986–1989 New York State Regents Scholarship 1986–1989 NYU Dean's List 1986–1987
INTERESTS	Calligraphy (professional), swimming, literature

article for the newspaper on a subject that interests him/her. Here are some suggestions:

1. school or class news
2. sports
3. theater, movie, play, or art reviews
4. finance
5. business
6. computers
7. human-interest stories
8. fashion
9. personal advice
10. travel
11. restaurant reviews
12. food
13. international news
14. weekend activities for the family

Your newspaper article should follow the outline below:

I. Topic sentence. (Example: "Sports build character as well as healthy bodies.")
II. Illustrative sentences with transitional words.
III. Ending sentence: the point of the article.

A Short Handbook

Symbol Chart for Correction of Compositions

The compositions you write will be marked for corrections with the symbols listed below. The errors will be underlined (or otherwise marked) in the text. The specific type of error will be indicated in the left margin of your paper. Therefore, be sure to leave a wide margin on the left side of your paper.

SYMBOLS IN THE TEXT

————————	straight underlining for all grammar errors
～～～～～～～	wavy underlining for all vocabulary and idiom errors
⌃	for any missing word
∽	for reversing two words
⟲→	for moving a whole phrase
⌐ℋ	for starting a new paragraph (indent five spaces)
no ℋ	don't start a new paragraph
ℓ	omit this punctuation mark
( )	omit this whole word or phrase

SYMBOLS IN THE LEFT MARGIN

sp.	spelling errors
punc.	punctuation errors
cap.	capitalization errors
#	errors in number (singular/plural)
det.	determiner errors (articles— *a, an, the*)
prep.	preposition errors
wd.	wrong vocabulary item or word form
t.	error in verb tense
agr.	error in subject-verb agreement
ref.	error in reference
?	something the instructor can't understand

Irregular Verbs in English

Present	Past	Past participle	Present	Past	Past participle
arise	arose	arisen	hang	hung, hanged	hung, hanged
			have, has	had	had
be (am, is, are)	was, were	been	hear	heard	heard
			hide	hid	hidden, hid
bear	bore	born, borne	hit	hit	hit
beat	beat	beat, beaten	hold	held	held
begin	began	begun	hurt	hurt	hurt
bend	bent	bent			
bet	bet	bet	keep	kept	kept
bite	bit	bit, bitten	know	knew	known
bleed	bled	bled			
blow	blew	blown	lay	laid	laid
break	broke	broken	lead	led	led
bring	brought	brought	leave	left	left
build	built	built	lend	lent	lent
burst	burst	burst	let	let	let
buy	bought	bought	lie	lay	lain
			light	lit, lighted	lit, lighted
catch	caught	caught	lose	lost	lost
choose	chose	chosen			
come	came	come	make	made	made
cost	cost	cost	mean	meant	meant
cut	cut	cut	meet	met	met
			mistake	mistook	mistaken
deal	dealt	dealt			
dig	dug	dug	pay	paid	paid
do	did	done	put	put	put
draw	drew	drawn			
drink	drank	drunk	quit	quit	quit
drive	drove	driven			
			read	read	read
eat	ate	eaten	ride	rode	ridden
			ring	rang	rung
fall	fell	fallen	rise	rose	risen
feed	fed	fed	run	ran	run
feel	felt	felt			
fight	fought	fought	say	said	said
find	found	found	see	saw	seen
flee	fled	fled	seek	sought	sought
fly	flew	flown	sell	sold	sold
forbid	forbade	forbidden	send	sent	sent
forget	forgot	forgotten	set	set	set
forgive	forgave	forgiven	sew	sewed	sewn, sewed
freeze	froze	frozen	shake	shook	shaken
			shine	shone	shone
get	got	got, gotten	shoot	shot	shot
give	gave	given	show	showed	shown, showed
go	went	gone	shut	shut	shut
grow	grew	grown	sing	sang	sung

Present	Past	Past participle	Present	Past	Past participle
sink	sank	sunk	tear	tore	torn
sit	sat	sat	tell	told	told
sleep	slept	slept	think	thought	thought
speak	spoke	spoken	throw	threw	thrown
spend	spent	spent			
spread	spread	spread	understand	understood	understood
stand	stood	stood	undertake	undertook	undertaken
steal	stole	stolen	uphold	upheld	upheld
stick	stuck	stuck	upset	upset	upset
sting	stung	stung			
swear	swore	sworn	wake	woke, waked	waked
sweep	swept	swept	wear	wore	worn
swim	swam	swum	weep	wept	wept
swing	swung	swung	win	won	won
			withdraw	withdrew	withdrawn
take	took	taken	wring	wrung	wrung
teach	taught	taught	write	wrote	written

Verb Tenses

SIMPLE PRESENT TENSE

Verb *to be*

I	}	am 'm not*	We	}	
You	}	are aren't*	You	}	are aren't*
He She It	}	is isn't*	They	)	

*Note: *I'm not* is the negative contraction for *I am not*; *isn't* is the negative contraction for *is not*; *aren't* is the negative contraction for *are not*.

Other Verbs

I	}	work don't work*	We	}	
You	}	work don't work*	You	}	work don't work*
He She It	}	works doesn't work*	They	)	

*Note: *Don't* is the negative contraction for *do not*; *doesn't* is the negative contraction for *does not*.

Use of the Simple Present Tense

1. To make a statement of fact

   Bananas grow on trees.
   Washington, D.C., is the capital of the United States.

2. To express opinions

   Richard is a good cook.
   He doesn't like spinach.

3. To express customs and habitual actions

   The English drink a lot of tea.
   My son watches television every night.

PRESENT CONTINUOUS TENSE

I	}	am studying 'm not studying	We	}	
You	}	are studying aren't studying	You	}	are studying aren't studying
He She It	}	is studying isn't studying	They	)	

Use of the Present Continuous Tense

1. To express an action that is happening at the moment of speaking or writing

   I am sitting in the library and writing you this letter.
   Many children are playing in the park.

2. To express an activity or situation that is happening over a given period of time

   She is studying French this semester.
   They are living in Chicago at present.

Note: The following are some verbs that do not usually take a continuous form. These verbs express mental states or conditions or some form of perception. Use them in the present simple tense.

Mental state			*Condition*		*Perception*
believe	like	remember	belong	owe	feel
think	love	forget	own	cost	smell
(*opinion*)	need		have	mean	taste
know	prefer		(*possess*)	resemble	hear
seem	want				see
understand	wish				

SIMPLE PAST TENSE

Verb *to be*

I } was / wasn't*   We }

You } were / weren't*   You } were / weren't*

He She It } was / wasn't*   They }

Note: Wasn't is the negative contraction for *was not*; *weren't* is the negative contraction for *were not*.

Other Verbs

I You He She It } walked / didn't walk*

We You They } walked / didn't walk*

Note: Didn't is the negative contraction for *did not*.

Use of the Simple Past

To express an action or an event in the past that is completed

My parents lived in Arizona for ten years. (They no longer live there.)
Neil Armstrong was the first man to walk on the moon.

PAST CONTINUOUS TENSE

I } was talking / wasn't talking   We }

You } were talking / weren't talking   You } were talking / weren't talking

He She It } was talking / wasn't talking   They }

Use of the Past Continuous Tense

1. To express an action that was happening at a specific moment in the past

He was doing his homework at eight o'clock last night.
They were eating dinner when the telephone rang.

2. To express two actions that were happening at the same time in the past

   The students were talking to each other while the teacher was writing on the blackboard.

PRESENT PERFECT TENSE

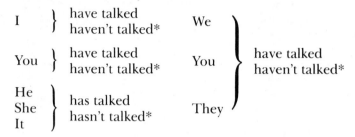

I
 { have talked
   haven't talked*

We

You
 { have talked
   haven't talked*

You
 } have talked
   haven't talked*

He
She
It
 { has talked
   hasn't talked*

They

*Note: *Haven't* is the negative contraction for *have not*; *hasn't* is the negative contraction for *has not*.

Use of the Present Perfect Tense

1. To express an action that started in the past and is still continuing

   They have been here for two hours. (They are still here.)
   She has lived in Europe since 1982. (She still lives there.)
   We have finished fifteen lessons so far. (We haven't finished the book yet.)

2. To indicate an action that happened at an unspecified time in the past. When the time is given, the simple past is used.

We have already eaten lunch.	*but*	We ate lunch at noon.
She has gone to the museum three times.	*but*	She went to the museum in July, August, and September.
I have seen that movie.	*but*	I saw that movie last week.

3. To express an action that was completed in the immediate or recent past

   They have finished their work at last.   She has recently started a new job.

   He has finally gotten a promotion.   They have just arrived.

PRESENT PERFECT CONTINUOUS

I
You
 { have been talking
   haven't been talking

We
You
 } have been talking
   haven't been talking

He
She
It
 { has been talking
   hasn't been talking

They

Use of the Present Perfect Continuous

To express the continuous nature of an activity that started in the past and is still continuing at present. It is usually used with *since* and *for*.

They have been studying in the library since three o'clock.
She has been working here for five years.

Note: The present perfect and the present perfect continuous are often interchangeable.
Verbs not used in the other continuous tenses are not used in this tense either.

PAST PERFECT TENSE

I
You
He
She
It
$\Bigg\}$ had talked
hadn't talked*

We
You
They
$\Bigg\}$ had talked
hadn't talked*

Note: Hadn't is the negative contraction for *had not.*

Use of the Past Perfect Tense

To express an action or an event in the past that happened before another action in the past

He went to bed after he had finished his work.
By two o'clock, Dr. Miller had performed three operations.
Kennedy had been president for three years when he was killed.

FUTURE TENSE

I
You
He
She
It
$\Bigg\}$ will talk
won't talk*

We
You
They
$\Bigg\}$ will talk
won't talk*

Note: Won't is the negative contraction for *will not.*

Use of the Future Tense

1. To express an action or an event that will happen after the present time

   We will play tennis tomorrow.
   She will be twenty years old next year.

2. To express a promise of action

   I will meet you after class.

Other Ways of Expressing Future Time

1. **Be going to** + *simple verb* is used to express a planned or intended action.

   We are going to have a party tomorrow.
   They are going to visit their parents next week.

Note: The use of *will* and *be going to* to express future time is often interchangeable.

2. Simple present and present continuous tenses are used with verbs that express arriving, departing, starting, and finishing.

   The train leaves at two o'clock this afternoon.
   My class starts at nine o'clock tomorrow morning.
   The plane is arriving in ten minutes.
   My parents are returning from Europe next week.

Note: A future time word is necessary when the present simple or present continuous tense is used to express future time.

Spelling

Spelling in English is difficult because English is not spelled phonetically. Many words, however, follow certain rules in their spelling.

Spelling rules	*Examples*
1. [iy]: Put an *i* before *e* except after *c* or when *e-i* sounds like *a* [e], as in **neighbor**.	grief niece } *but* { receive weight vein believe relief } *but* { deceive freight neighbor *Exceptions:* seize either neither foreign weird leisure height
2. a. Words ending in silent *e* (*like, take*) drop the *e* before adding a suffix beginning with a vowel.	take—taking ride—riding bake—baking fame—famous dance—dancing die—dying *Exceptions:* dye—dyeing canoe—canoeing shoe—shoeing hoe—hoeing
b. Words ending in *ce* or *ge* generally keep the *e* before the suffix *able* or *ous*. (The *e* is needed to keep the "soft" sound of the *c* and *g* in these words.)	change—changeable service—serviceable outrage—outrageous
3. Words ending in silent *e* (like *base*) keep the *e* before adding a suffix beginning with a consonant. *Note:* The words *judgement* and *judgment* are both correct. The same is true of *acknowledgement* and *acknowledgment*.	base—basement safe—safety, safely amuse—amusement nice—nicely *Exceptions:* argue—argument whole—wholly true—truly
4. Words ending in *y* preceded by a consonant change the *y* to *i* before adding a suffix that does not begin with *i*.	marry—married, marriage } *but* { marrying carry—carried, carriage } *but* { carrying angry—angrily
5. a. Words of one syllable ending in a single consonant preceded by a single vowel double the consonant before adding a suffix beginning with a vowel.	run—runner, running fat—fatter sit—sitter, sitting
b. Don't double the final consonant when there are two final consonants.	test—testing, tested lock—locked, locking
c. Don't double the final consonant when two vowels precede the final consonant.	look—looking heat—heating, heated break—breaking
6. a. When a word is accented on the last syllable and ends in a single consonant preceded by a single vowel (like **begin**), double the final consonant before adding a suffix beginning with a vowel.	refer—referred, referring begin—beginning transfer—transferred, transferring admit—admitted, admitting
b. Don't double the final consonant when the accent is on the first syllable.	travel—traveled, traveling
c. Don't double the final consonant when two consonants come at the end of the word.	resist—resisted, resisting

Plurals of Nouns

Rules for plurals of nouns	Examples
1. Most nouns form their plural by adding *s* to the singular form.	door—doors table—tables boy—boys desk—desks
2. Nouns ending in *s, ss, sh, ch, x,* or *z* form their plural by adding *es*.	dish—dishes box—boxes kiss—kisses watch—watches fizz—fizzes atlas—atlases church—churches Jones—Joneses
3. a. Nouns ending in *y* preceded by a consonant are made plural by changing the *y* to *i* and adding *es*. b. Nouns ending in *y* preceded by a vowel are made plural by adding *s* only.	lady—ladies try—tries sky—skies family—families baby—babies ally—allies *Exception:* the names of people Kelly—the Kellys boy—boys play—plays key—keys
4. Many nouns ending in *f* or *fe* change the *f* to *v* and add *es*.	wife—wives life—lives thief—thieves shelf—shelves leaf—leaves calf—calves *Exceptions:* chief—chiefs chef—chefs handkerchief—handkerchiefs roof—roofs belief—beliefs cliff—cliffs
5. a. Nouns ending in *o* preceded by a vowel add *s* to the singular. b. Nouns ending in *o* preceded by a consonant usually add *es* to the singular.	rodeo—rodeos patio—patios zoo—zoos shampoo—shampoos audio—audios tomato—tomatoes hero—heroes Negro—Negroes echo—echoes *Exceptions:* banjo—banjos piano—pianos auto—autos solo—solos
6. Some nouns form their plural irregularly.	child—children tooth—teeth mouse—mice man—men foot—feet louse—lice woman—women goose—geese ox—oxen
7. Some nouns have the same form in the singular and the plural.	sheep—sheep fowl—fowl Swiss—Swiss deer—deer Chinese—Chinese fish—fish Japanese—Japanese
8. Compound nouns are usually made plural by adding *s* to the important word. *Note:* When a compound word is written as one word, the plural *s* is added to the whole word.	son-in-law—sons-in-law passer-by—passers-by high school—high schools court martial—courts martial spoonful—spoonfuls mouthful—mouthfuls cupful—cupfuls
9. Some nouns ending in *s* are usually singular. They have no plural form.	mumps economics mathematics measles politics news
10. Some nouns ending in *s* are always plural. They have no singular form.	scissors pliers pants clothes trousers spectacles (*glasses*)
11. Letters, numbers, and signs usually add *'s* to form the plural.	+'s His *1*'s look like my *7*'s. −'s He minds his *p*'s and *q*'s. He never remembers to cross his *t*'s.

Capitalization

Rules for capitalization	*Examples*
1. Capitalizing first words:	
a. Capitalize the first word of every sentence.	Where are you going? How cold I am! My name is Anna.
b. Capitalize the first word of a direct quotation.	"Why were you late?" asked the teacher. The student answered, "My car broke down."
c. Capitalize the first word of a line of poetry.	'Tis said that absence conquers love; But oh believe it not!
d. Capitalize the first word and all following nouns in the greeting of a letter.	Dear Mrs. Brown Dear Sir
e. Capitalize the first word in the complimentary closing of a letter.	Sincerely yours, Yours truly, Very truly yours,
2. Capitalizing names of persons:	
a. Capitalize a person's given name or names and his or her family name.	Mary Brown John Doe Igor Bilbinski
b. Capitalize all abbreviations used with a person's name, including his or her initials.	Prof. Susan Watson Mr. James A. Smith, Jr. Dr. Freud Gen. D. D. Eisenhower
c. Capitalize titles of respect when they are used before a person's name.	President Johnson Sir Winston Churchill Queen Victoria Father O'Mally
d. Capitalize words that show relationship, such as *mother* and *father,* when they are used in place of a person's name.	No, Dad, I didn't take your newspaper. Yes, Mother, I'll be home by twelve. We visited Grandma last Sunday.
e. Don't capitalize a noun that shows relationship when there is a possessive pronoun before it unless it is used with a person's name.	I wish my mother and father were with me now. I saw my uncle last night. *but* My Uncle Willie travels a great deal.
f. The pronoun *I* is always capitalized.	John and I are studying Spanish.
3. Capitalizing place names:	
a. Capitalize the names of definite geographic areas or divisions of the earth's surface.	Orient West Coast Arctic Circle Temperate Zone
b. The words *north, south, east,* and *west* are capitalized when they indicate parts of the world or parts of the country. When they indicate a simple direction, they are not capitalized.	Park Avenue is east of Broadway. We spent our vacation in the West.
c. Capitalize the names of rivers, oceans, lakes, islands, and mountains.	Staten Island Mt. Whitney Lake Como Atlantic Ocean Amazon River Andes
d. Capitalize the names of countries, states, cities, towns, streets, and rural routes.	England Route 1 Wall Street Maine Las Vegas Fifth Avenue
e. Capitalize the names of parks, buildings, and stations.	Grand Central Station Chrysler Building Empire State Building Central Park

Rules for capitalization	Examples
4. Capitalizing titles:	
a. Capitalize the first word and each important word in the titles of books, magazines, newspapers, stories, articles, poems, and chapters of books.	*The New York Times* *The Old Man and the Sea* Chapter 2: "The Rules of Grammar" "How to Build a Bookcase"
Note: The articles (*a, an, the*), the conjunctions (*and, but, or*), and short prepositions (*at, on, by, to,* etc.) are not capitalized unless used as the first word of a name or title.	
b. Capitalize the first word and each important word in the titles of plays, motion pictures, and radio and television programs.	*Death of a Salesman* "Dallas" *My Fair Lady* "Mission Impossible" *Tarzan of the Apes*
c. Capitalize each important word in the titles of famous documents.	Magna Carta Declaration of Independence Constitution of the United States
5. Capitalizing religious terms:	
a. Capitalize all names referring to God.	Allah Zeus Our Heavenly Father Buddha Jehovah Jesus Christ the Lord
b. The pronouns *he, his, him, thou, they,* and *thine* are capitalized when they refer to the Deity.	Trust in God, for He will lead you.
c. Capitalize all names for the Bible, its books and divisions, and names of other sacred books.	Koran Book of Genesis Good Book Talmud Old Testament
d. Capitalize the names of religious bodies and their place of worship.	Christian Jewish St. Patrick's Cathedral Buddhist Moslem First Presbyterian Church
6. Capitalizing expressions of time:	
a. Capitalize the names of the days of the week and the names of the months of the year.	Saturday Sunday Monday June July November
b. Don't capitalize the names of the seasons.	spring fall (autumn) winter summer
c. Capitalize the names of holidays and the names of special occasions.	Independence Day Labor Day Christmas Ramadan
d. Capitalize the names of historical periods and events.	Renaissance War of the Roses Dark Ages First Crusade
7. Capitalizing names of racial groups, nationalities, and languages:	
a. Capitalize the names of racial groups.	Black Caucasian Asian
b. Capitalize the names of nationalities.	Spanish Australian Swiss French Lebanese Swedish
c. Capitalize the names of languages.	Italian Turkish English Chinese Russian Quechuan
d. Capitalize adjectives derived from the names of racial groups, nationalities, and languages.	a Japanese camera a Thai silk an English terrier a French cook

Rules for capitalization	*Examples*
8. Capitalizing trade names, names of organizations, and transportation:	
a. Capitalize the names of organizations and clubs.	Girl Scouts International Student Association
b. Capitalize the names of business firms and the trade names of their products.	Ford Motor Company General Motors Pepperidge Farm Bread Beechnut Gum Cadillac Kleenex
c. Capitalize the names of schools and other institutions.	Boston University Memorial Hospital American Language Institute
d. Capitalize the names of departments and agencies of the federal government and of state governments.	Department of State Bureau of Motor Vehicles Department of Health and Human Services
e. Capitalize the names of political parties. (But don't capitalize the word *party.*)	Republican party Socialist party Democratic party
f. Capitalize the names of particular ships, trains, and airplanes.	*Chicago Limited* *Olympia* *Orient Express* *Eagle*
9. Additional rules of capitalization: School subjects are not capitalized unless they are names of languages or of specific numbered courses.	She is studying Spanish and chemistry this term. Mr. Welles is teaching Chemistry I this term.

Punctuation

It is important to use the correct punctuation marks in order to make your writing easy to understand. The correct use of punctuation marks helps make the written language clear and precise.

Punctuation mark and use	Examples
1. The period (.): a. Use a period after a declarative or an imperative sentence.	I often watch television in the evening. Give me the past tense of *speak*.
Note: A period coming at the end of a quotation is placed inside the quotation marks.	The teacher said, "I want you to come early to class."
b. Use a period after most abbreviations.	Mrs. Mr. U.S.A. etc. Ave. St.
Note: Periods are not used after the letters that represent longer names of trade organizations, government agencies, or international bodies.	YMCA UNICEF UN NATO
c. Use a period after an initial in a name.	H.G. Wells Mrs. P.L. Maguire John F. Kennedy
d. Use a period between dollars and cents when the dollar sign is used.	$4.87 $.99 $123.45
e. Use a period before decimals or between the whole number and the decimal.	.74 .003 1.2 22.66 4.75
2. The question mark (?): Use a question mark at the end of a direct question. *Note:* Question marks come only at the end of a sentence in English.	How do you feel today? Where are you going? The child asked his mother, "What time is Father coming home?"
3. The exclamation point (!): a. Use an exclamation point after an exclamatory sentence.	What a beautiful baby you have! How nice of you to invite me!
b. Use an exclamation point after a word, a phrase, or sentence when you want to be very emphatic.	Hey! Look out! There's a car coming. Ouch! You hurt my finger. Why don't you keep quiet!
4. The comma (,): a. Use a comma after an introductory adverbial clause or verbal phrase.	If I don't learn English this semester, I will be very unhappy. (adverbial clause) To learn a language, you must practice. (verbal phrase)
Note: When the adverbial clause is short and closely related to the main clause, the comma may be omitted.	When we met we shook hands. If I see Mary I will give her your message.
b. Use a comma before a coordinate conjunction that joins the clauses of a compound sentence. The coordinate conjunctions are *and, but, or, nor, for, yet,* and *so.*	Your answers are correct, but you did the wrong exercise. My alarm clock didn't ring this morning, and I was two hours late for work.
Note: When the two parts of a compound sentence are short, the comma may be omitted.	Jane danced and Robert sang.

Punctuation mark and use	Examples
c. Use a comma to set off parenthetical and interrupting expressions.	Yes, Virginia, there is a Santa Claus. Picasso's paintings are strange, aren't they?
d. A conjunctive adverb is often set off by a comma when it stands first in the clause.	Furthermore, I don't have enough money for the trip. Accordingly, you will have to report to Dean Smith.
e. Use a comma to set off a noun of address.	"Hugo, what time is it, please?" "I'm sorry, Mr. Gómez, but Dr. Jones isn't in right now."
f. Use a comma to set off an appositive.	Our new teacher, Mr. Green, comes from Illinois. Miss Lark, our English teacher, comes from Maine.

Note: When one word or a group of words is added to another word as an explanation, it is called an appositive.

g. Use a comma to set off the second and all following items in a date or an address.	On January 1, 1863, Lincoln issued the Emancipation Proclamation. The building at 33 West Street, Buffalo, New York, has been sold.
h. Use a comma to separate items in a series.	My favorite sports are swimming, tennis, and skiing. Tom eats breakfast at eight, lunch at noon, and dinner at seven.

Note: When three adjectives are equal modifiers of a noun, such as *day* in the example, they are separated by commas. When the last adjective in a series is thought of as part of the noun, no comma is used before it.

It was a warm, sunny, pleasant day.
It was a warm spring day.

i. Use a comma to set off nonrestrictive phrases and clauses. Nonrestrictive modifiers are not essential for the basic meaning of the sentence. They add details, helping to explain, illustrate, or describe; but the basic meaning of the sentence would be clear without them. They are always set off by commas.	The woman in the pink dress, who comes from Iowa, is a little hard of hearing. (nonrestrictive adjective clause) The tiger, driven mad by hunger, killed the sheep. (nonrestrictive participial phrase) The students, under great pressure, took the examination. (nonrestrictive prepositional phrase)
j. Use a comma to set off a speaker's directly quoted words from the rest of the sentence.	Frank said, "I'll see you later." Or, "I'll see you later," Frank said, "back at the house."
k. Use a comma for emphasis and contrast.	I want coffee, not tea. It wasn't the children, but the adults, who were making all the noise.
l. Use a comma to set off each group of three figures in a number over 999.	12,444 3,480,753 1,000
m. Use a comma to set off degrees and titles.	Jane Kilroy, M.D. John D. Rockefeller, Sr.
5. Quotation marks (" "):	
a. Use quotation marks to enclose the exact words of a speaker.	The doctor said, "Bobby has a high temperature." "I have just arrived," William said, "and I don't know anyone here."
b. With direct quotations, marks of ending punctuation are usually placed inside the quotation marks.	"Where are you going?" I asked my brother.
c. Use quotation marks for titles of stories, articles, chapters, songs, radio and television programs, and short poems.	The poem "Trees" was written by Joyce Kilmer. Somerset Maugham wrote "A String of Beads." We saw "Star Trek" on Channel 68.

Punctuation mark and use	Examples
d. Quotation marks can be used to call attention to words that the writer is defining or explaining, and to special or technical terms that may be new to the reader.	It is customary to say "You're welcome" whenever anyone says "Thank you." A "mugwump" is a political independent.
6. The colon (:):	
a. Use a colon after the salutation in a business letter.	Dear Ms. Smith: Dear Sir:
b. In writing time, use a colon between the figure designating the hour and the figures designating the minutes.	I usually get up at 7:15 A.M.
c. Use a colon after a statement that uses the expression *as follows* or *the following* to introduce a list.	The following are the official languages of the United Nations: English, French, Russian, Spanish, Chinese, and Arabic.
7. The semicolon (;):	
a. Use a semicolon between the two parts of a compound sentence if they are not joined by a coordinate conjunction.	The girls met in the auditorium; the boys met in the gymnasium. Everyone laughed at his ideas; nevertheless, he kept on working.
b. Use a semicolon to separate items in a series if the items contain commas.	My classmates include Pierre, a Frenchman; Klaus, a German; and Yasuo, a Japanese.
8. The hyphen (-) and the dash (—):	
a. Use a hyphen at the end of a line to indicate a divided word (one that is broken into syllables).	Are you going to the reception tomor- row night?
b. Use a hyphen to connect compound numerals and fractions when they are written as words.	two-thirds twenty-one forty-second
c. Use a hyphen to separate two numbers referring to pages in a reference.	Garner, Helen, *Art through the Ages*, pages 94–96.
d. Use a dash to indicate a sudden change of thought.	I am going shopping today—but perhaps I will go tomorrow instead.
9. The apostrophe ('):	
a. Use an apostrophe in a contraction to show the omission of one or more letters.	I won't go. Where there's a will, there's a way.
b. Use an apostrophe to form the possessive case of a noun.	the girl's book the students' desks
c. Use an apostrophe to form the plurals of letters, numbers, and symbols.	2's x's 7's #'s
10. Underlining (___):	
a. Use underlining to indicate the titles of books, magazines, newspapers, plays, and motion pictures.	I read *The Grapes of Wrath* a long time ago. I buy the *New Yorker* every week. I saw that old movie *Perils of Pauline*.
b. Use underlining for the names of a particular airplane, ship, or train.	The name of Lindbergh's plane was the *Spirit of St. Louis*. I read about the sinking of the *Titanic*.
c. Use underlining for words, letters, or numbers, used as words.	Be careful not to reverse the e and the i in friend.

Punctuation mark and use	*Examples*
11. Parentheses ( ): a. Use parentheses to enclose numbers or letters that mark the items in a series.	Before you mail the letter, be sure that you (a) seal the envelope, (b) put a stamp on the envelope, and (c) write your return address on the envelope.
b. Use parentheses to put a side remark or a few extra words in a sentence that you think the reader will find helpful or interesting.	Ellen (standing in the corner with Bob) is the sister of my best friend.

Division of Words

In English, if you have to divide a word between two lines, you must break it between syllables and put a hyphen at the end of the first line. When you are not sure how to divide a word, look it up in a dictionary. English syllables are difficult to determine, but they usually follow pronunciation.

Here are some general rules that you can use:

1. Words of one syllable are never divided.
2. A word should never be divided so that a syllable of one letter stands alone.
3. Words that are spelled with a hyphen should be divided only at the point of the hyphen.

A Good Rule to Follow

Try *not* to divide words between two lines when you write a composition.

Numbers

Rules for writing numbers	*Examples*
1. Numbers that can be expressed in one or two words are generally spelled out in ordinary writing; other numbers are usually written in figures.	There were twenty-one people in the room. Only two students came to class yesterday. We passed 245 cars on the road yesterday. Mr. Smith worked 160 hours last month.
The form in which numbers are written should be consistent. If one of two or more numbers in a sentence cannot be expressed in two words or less, figures are used for all.	There were 18 Frenchmen, 192 Americans, and 3 Chinese on the boat to Valparaiso.
2. In business writing, figures are generally used since they usually express dimensions, weights, money, measure, totals, distances, etc., and it is easier to read figures.	18 yards 3 by 5 inches 4 tons 5,000 miles 80% $8.92
3. When a number occurs at the beginning of a sentence, it should be written out.	Fifty dollars isn't much to pay for that coat. Ten percent of the people here speak Spanish.
4. Figures are used for dates (except in very formal writing).	October 4, 1900 January 1
5. Figures are used for the time when A.M. or P.M. is used.	4 P.M. *but* four o'clock
6. Figures are used for street numbers (with no comma in numbers larger than 999).	185 West End Avenue 1600 Broadway
7. Figures are used for pages and other references.	p. 89 pp. 46-52 Chapter 14 *or* Chapter XIV
8. Figures are used for sums of money, except sums in round numbers or, in formal style, sums that can be written in two or three words.	$5.33 $.88 88¢ a million dollars *or* $1,000,000

The Sentence and Its Parts

A sentence is a group of words with a subject and a predicate that expresses a complete thought. The four kinds of sentences are shown in the following table.

Type of sentence	Examples
Simple—has one independent clause.	The man is drinking coffee.
Compound—has two or more independent clauses.	The man is drinking coffee, and the woman is drinking tea.
Complex—has an independent clause (also called the main clause) and at least one dependent clause (also called the subordinate clause).	The man who is drinking coffee is my uncle.
Compound-complex—has two or more independent clauses and one or more dependent clauses.	The man who is drinking coffee is my uncle, and the woman who is drinking tea is my cousin.

PARTS OF SPEECH

Part of speech and function	Examples
1. Noun—the name of a person, place, thing, action, or abstract quality.	
a. Subject of verb.	The *boy* went home.
b. Object of verb.	She ate the *apple*.
c. Object of preposition.	The girl came from *France*.
2. Pronoun—word that takes the place of a noun and has the same functions.	
a. Subject of verb.	*He* went home.
b. Object of verb.	I love *him*.
c. Object of preposition.	I spoke to *them*.
3. Verb—predicate word that shows action, state, or being.	
a. Shows action.	She *wrote* a letter.
b. Shows state or being. This type of verb is called a linking verb because it links the subject to the predicate noun or adjective. Linking verbs include: *seem, become, appear, be, grow, remain, stay, get, act, look, smell, taste, feel*.	They *seem* happy. He *became* a doctor. It *smells* delicious.
Note: Some verbs can be either action or linking verbs.	
4. Adjective—word that describes a noun. Tells you about a noun.	They are *good* students.
5. Adverb—word that modifies a verb, an adjective, or another adverb. Tells you about a verb, an adjective, or another adverb.	He spoke *rapidly*. (modifies the verb *spoke*) She is a *very* good student. (modifies the adjective *good*) He walked *too* slowly. (modifies the adverb *slowly*)

Part of speech and function	Examples
6. Preposition—word that indicates the relationship between a noun or a pronoun and some other part of the sentence. Shows the relationship between a noun or a pronoun and some other part of the sentence. A preposition will always be followed by a noun, pronoun, or noun equivalent (gerund).	I walked home *with* him. She comes *from* Bolivia. He is tired *of* studying.
7. Conjunction—word that connects words, phrases, and clauses. Connects words, phrases, and clauses. Correlative conjunctions (*either . . . or . . .* ; *neither . . . nor . . .* ; *both . . . and . . .* ; *not only . . . but also . . .*) are used in pairs to connect two parallel sentence elements. (See Lesson 5.)	Mary *and* John come to school by bus *or* by subway. *Neither* Juan *nor* Chantal knows what the assignment is.
8. Interjection—word or phrase used as an exclamation without any connection to other grammatical elements. Serves as an exclamation but is independent of other grammatical elements.	Yuck! Nuts! Oh boy! Sorry! Excuse me!

VERBALS

A verbal is a word that looks like a verb but is not used like a verb. A verbal can be used as a noun, an adjective, or an adverb, as shown in the following table.

Type of verbal and function	Examples

1. Infinitive phrase—consists of *to* + name of verb.
  a. Noun.
    (1) Subject of verb.
    (2) Predicate word.
    (3) Object of verb.
  b. Adjective—modifying a noun.
  c. Adverb.
    (1) Modifying a verb.
    (2) Modifying an adjective.
    (3) Modifying an adverb.
	
	To learn a language well takes hard work.
	He is *to become* president next year.
	I want *to see* the movie.
	This is the best place *to be*.
	
	He went *to see* the dentist.
	I was happy *to see* him.
	He came too late *to take* the test.

2. Gerund—a verbal noun that always ends with -*ing*.
  a. Subject of verb.
  b. Predicate word.
  c. Object of verb.
  d. Object of preposition.
	
	Swimming is my favorite sport.
	My favorite sport is *swimming*.
	He enjoys *playing* tennis.
	I am fond of *swimming*.

3. Participle—starts with present participle or past participle of verb. Present participle—always ends in -*ing*. Past participle (sometimes called the third form). *Note:* Participial phrases act like adjectives and often follow the noun that they modify.	 I saw the movie *playing in that theater*. I read the book *written by Mailer*.

PHRASES

A phrase is a group of two or more words that does not contain either a subject or a verb. A phrase can start with a verbal (infinitive, participle, or gerund) or a preposition, and it can act like a noun, an adjective, or an adverb.

He comes *from Japan.* (prepositional phrase)
Fishing in the ocean, John caught a tuna. (participial adjective phrase)
Fishing for tuna is his favorite sport. (gerund phrase as subject)
He wanted *to live near the school.* (infinitive phrase as object of verb)

CLAUSES

A clause is a group of words with a subject and a verb. There are two kinds of clauses: main clauses (also called independent or principal clauses) and subordinate clauses (also called dependent clauses), as shown in the following table.

Type of clause and function	*Examples*
1. Main clause Has a subject and a verb and expresses a complete thought. It does not act as a subject, modifier, or complement in a sentence, and it can stand alone. *Note:* All sentences are main clauses.	The boy gave the girl the book.

2. Subordinate clause
Has a subject and a verb but does not express a complete thought. It is not a sentence and cannot stand alone.
  a. Noun clause—has a subject and a verb and acts like a noun. (See Lesson 22.)
    (1) Subject of verb.
    (2) Predicate word.
    (3) Direct object.
    (4) Object of preposition.
 	
  b. Adjective clause—acts like an adjective and describes a noun. It follows the noun that it modifies. (See Lesson 10.)
  c. Adverbial clause—acts like an adverb and tells you when, where, why, how, to what extent, and under what conditions. (See Lessons 10, 15, and 21.)
	
	Whoever called you didn't leave a message.
	Watergate is *what brought Nixon down.*
	I told him *what he had to study.*
	People sometimes get upset by *what they read in a newspaper.*
	I am reading the book *that I borrowed from John.*
	The girl *who came to the party with me* is my cousin.
	
	While I was watching television, the phone rang.
	I studied *until the library closed.*

LINKING WORDS OR PHRASES

Linking words or phrases are used to show the relationship between different parts of a sentence or between sentences. These are sometimes called transitional or connecting words or phrases. (See Lessons 2, 14, 17, and 20.)

Linking words or phrases and function	Examples
1. To show addition *also, and, in addition, besides, furthermore, likewise, moreover, too*	*In addition* to French, John is studying Spanish. *Besides* a writing class in the morning, I have an oral class in the afternoon.
2. To show contrast *although, even though, but, on the contrary, however, nevertheless, on the other hand, yet, while, despite, in spite of*	The doctor was very busy; *nevertheless*, she made time to see me. *In spite of* feeling sick, Mary came to class.
3. To show similarity *in like manner, likewise, in the same way, similarly*	Children should be polite to adults. *In like manner*, adults should be polite to children. Akira does his homework every day. You should do *likewise*.
4. To show result *accordingly, as a result, because of, consequently, for this / that reason, therefore, since*	Jane didn't have a clock. *Accordingly*, she was always late. Tom was absent a lot. *Because of* that, he failed the course.
5. To show condition *if, unless, provided (that)*	I will be there *unless* it rains. We will have a picnic *provided that* it doesn't rain.

Paragraphs and Compositions

This section summarizes what you have put into practice in the first part of the book in your compositions.

PARAGRAPHS

A paragraph is a group of sentences that talks about only one idea. We call this one idea the *topic* of the paragraph.

A paragraph is a convenient way of presenting the writer's thoughts in an organized form.

Characteristics of a Paragraph

1. A paragraph develops just one topic.
2. Every sentence in a paragraph says something about the topic of the paragraph.
3. The first line of every paragraph is indented. This means that the first line begins a little farther to the right than the other lines in the paragraph.
4. There is no set rule for the length of a paragraph. It can consist of one sentence or of many sentences. It should be long enough to make its topic clear to the reader. As a general rule, your paragraphs for the lessons in this book will be about five sentences long.

The Topic Sentence

Many paragraphs are built around a *topic sentence*. A topic sentence states in general terms the main thought of the paragraph. The other sentences in the paragraph explain, discuss, or illustrate the idea stated in the topic sentence. The topic sentence is usually the first sentence in a paragraph. Sometimes, however, it appears in the middle or at the end of the paragraph.

A paragraph doesn't need to have a topic sentence. If a paragraph doesn't have a topic sentence, all the sentences in the paragraph still express one central idea.

Essentials of a Good Paragraph

1. A good paragraph is *adequately developed*. This means that you must tell enough about the central idea to make it clear to the reader.
2. A good paragraph has *unity*. This means that all the sentences in the paragraph talk about the central idea (or topic).
3. A good paragraph has *coherence*. This means that the sentences in the paragraph are arranged in a logical order. Coherence also means that all the sentences are linked together so that the reader can follow the thoughts as they move from one sentence to another.

Organization of a Good Paragraph

There are different ways of arranging the details of a paragraph.

1. *Using chronological (or time) order:* If you are telling a story or giving directions, the order will usually be chronological. This refers to the order in which the details happened, were done, or should be done. (See "You Are What You Eat" Lesson 5; "The Heimlich Maneuver" Lesson 7; and "A Typical Day in My Life" Lesson 8.)
2. *Using topic statement order:* If you use a topic sentence that makes a general statement, you can then follow it up by adding details, giving examples, or explaining the topic statement. (See "Bad Habits" Lesson 13; "The American Family" Lesson 17; and "Choosing Sons or Daughters" Lesson 21.)
3. *Using comparison-and-contrast order:* This order is used to describe two persons or things. You can present all the details about the first and then follow with details about the other. Or, you can take up the differences and similarities one at a time and show how the two are alike or different. (See "A Comparison of Two Cities" Lesson 9.)
4. *Using problem-solution order:* If you are using a problem-solution order in writing your composition, you will first tell what the problem is and, where applicable, give the causes of the problem. Then, you will suggest solutions to the problem and explain why you chose these solutions. (See "What I Would Put in a Time Capsule" Lesson 18.)

Sentence Variety

A paragraph composed of sentences that are all of the same structure or the same length can be very dull. In order to make your paragraph more interesting and alive, it is a good idea to use sentence variety. One way to do this is to vary the length of your sentences. Another way is to vary the word order of the sentences. (See "A Letter to a Friend" Lesson 3.)

COMPOSITIONS

A composition is a piece of writing made up of one or more paragraphs. A composition has a subject (or theme) that can be broken down into a number of topics. Each topic in a composition should have its own paragraph.

A new paragraph generally follows a change in thought from one part of a topic to another or from the general idea to a specific case. A new paragraph is a signal for these changes of thought. For example, if you were writing a composition on "The United States," this would be the subject of the composition. This could then be broken down into two paragraphs with the following topics:

I. Physical characteristics
II. People

If you were writing a composition on the "Life of John F. Kennedy," this would be the theme. This could then be broken down chronologically into the following four paragraphs.

I. Childhood years
II. Youth and early adulthood
III. Maturity
IV. End of life

Each paragraph in a composition is a part of the subject of the whole composition. The topic of each paragraph depends on the paragraph that comes before it and the paragraph that follows it.

Essentials of a Good Composition

1. A good composition limits the content of the composition to one subject (or theme).
2. A good composition presents and develops the subject matter in an orderly manner.
3. A good composition sticks to its subject.
4. A good composition shows continuity from one paragraph to the next in the same way that sentences do within a paragraph.

Organization of the Composition

Many compositions can be arranged basically as follows:

1. *Introduction:* Usually tells the reader what the composition is about (generalization).
2. *Body:* Tells the story or explains the facts.
3. *Conclusion:* Ends the composition. It is usually a short summary of your ideas or the last details of a story (generalization).

These three divisions do not tell exactly where each topic idea goes. In order to write a well-planned composition, it is necessary to decide where each topic should be. One way to do this is to organize the details of a composition through the use of an *outline*—that is, a detailed plan of your composition.

Purpose of an Outline

1. An outline tells you what to write.
2. An outline sets out the order in which your thoughts should be written.
3. An outline tells you how to paragraph your composition.
4. An outline helps you stick to the subject of the composition from the beginning to the end.

Preparing an Outline

When you write an outline, you list very briefly and in the proper order the ideas you wish to include in your composition. Then, you write the composition following the outline. If your outline is well arranged, your composition will be well arranged.

For paragraph divisions, use Roman numerals (*I, II, III,* and so forth). For subdividing a paragraph, use capital letters (*A, B, C,* and so forth), indenting them evenly. If you want to subdivide still more, use Arabic numerals (*1, 2, 3,* and so forth) and indent again. For even more subdivision, indent again and use lower-case letters (*a, b, c,* and so forth). Place a period after each number or letter.

The form for a topic or sentence outline is as follows:

I. _____
    A. _____
        1. _____
            a. _____
            b. _____
        2. _____
    B. _____
        1. _____
        2. _____
            a. _____
            b. _____
        3. _____
II. _____
    A. _____
    B. _____
    C. _____

Two Different Kinds of Outlines

1. *Topic outline:* This is the most common form of outline. The topics and subtopics are noted in brief phrases or single words and are numbered and lettered consistently. No punctuation is needed after the topics in a topic outline.

The _____ Family

  I. The family today
    A. Size and composition of the typical family
    B. Mobility of the family
    C. Relationship between husband and wife
    D. Children
        1. Position of children in the family structure
        2. Responsibility for raising the children
        3. Adult children—position and responsibilities
    E. Position and duties of elderly relatives
 II. Changes in patterns of family life
    A. Causes for the changes
    B. Effects of the changes on family life

2. *Sentence outline:* In this outline, each head or subhead is a complete sentence. Each sentence in a sentence outline must end with a period or a question mark.

My Favorite Television Program

  I. My favorite television program in the United States
    A. What is your favorite television program in the United States?
    B. What kind of program is it?
    C. What is it about?
    D. Who is your favorite character on the program?
    E. Why do you like that character?

II. My favorite television program in my country
   A. What program did you like to watch most in your country?
   B. What kind of program was it?
   C. How often did you use to watch it?
   D. What was it about?
   E. Why did you enjoy watching that program?

The Different Types of Compositions

Description

The descriptive composition describes something or someone. It tells how a person, place, or thing appealed to the senses—that is, how he, she, or it looked, sounded, smelled, tasted, or felt.

There are two different kinds of description:

1. *Description to give information:* When writing a description to give information, be sure to include enough details for clarity and to arrange your details in an orderly way so that it is easy for the reader to understand. (See Lesson 3, "Describing What Is Happening Around Us," and Lesson 6, "Life in the Twenty-first Century.")
2. *Description of animals or persons:* When writing a description of people, carefully select the outstanding features or traits that distinguish them from other people. Also, describe what the people do as well as how they act. (See Lesson 9, "Comparing and Contrasting People and Places.")

Narration

A composition in narrative style tells a story. It tells what a person or thing did during a particular period of time. The span of time can be of short duration, or it can cover a long period. In narrative writing, events are described in the order of their happening. This type of composition is presented in a chronological (or time) order, with one action following another as it happened in the original experience.

When writing a narrative composition, be sure that you create interest through movement of actions in the story and that you include enough details for clarity. (See Lesson 8, "A Typical Day," and Lesson 10, "The Dating and Mating Game.")

Exposition

All expository writing deals with facts and ideas in order to give the reader information.

The subject matter of an expository composition may:

1. *Present factual information:* When writing an exposition to present factual information, be sure your facts are correct and clearly expressed. Also, make certain that the facts are arranged in a logical order and that there is a single central theme. (See Lesson 4, "In the United States," and Lesson 17, "The Family.")
2. *Explain a process:* When writing an exposition to explain something, (a) divide your explanation into steps, (b) arrange the steps in the order in which they should be performed, (c) include all the necessary information, and (d) use words that give the exact information. (See Lesson 7, "Giving and Following Directions," and Lesson 11, "Getting Along in the United States.")

Linking Sentences

In order for the reader to be able to move from one sentence to another easily, the sentences must be tied together in some way. Sometimes, the best way to link sentences is to use connecting words that show how one sentence is related to another.

For example, we said that in narrative writing, it is important to show time relationship between sentences. Adverbial linking expressions like the following help you do this:

First . . .	Finally . . .	After dinner . . .
Then . . .	As soon as I arrived home . . .	The next morning . . .
After that . . .	Before eating dinner . . .	

When writing descriptive paragraphs, it is very important to use direct linking expressions. The reader must not only see the details but also know how they are related to one another. The following linking expressions help show how the details are related:

To the right . . .	Directly in front of . . .	As you turn left . . .
In the center . . .	At the top . . .	On the opposite side . . .
In the corner . . .	Under the windows . . .	

When writing an expository paragraph explaining how to make or do something, linking expressions like those shown below help the reader follow the steps of the process smoothly:

First . . .	After that . . .	After adding the lemon . . .
Next . . .	Then . . .	Before turning on the oven . . .

When writing a paragraph of comparison or contrast, you can emphasize the contrast with linking words like the following:

On the one hand . . .	But . . .	However . . .
On the other hand . . .	Yesterday . . .	Nevertheless . . .
In spite of . . .	Today . . .	

When you want to make clear the connection between two sentences where the first sentence states a cause and the second states a result or effect, you can tie the sentences together with one of the following linking words or expressions:

Therefore . . .	For this reason . . .	As a result . . .
So . . .	Consequently . . .	Because of this . . .

Business and Personal (Social) Letters

BUSINESS LETTERS

Parts of a Business Letter

There are six parts of a business letter: heading, inside address, salutation, body of the letter, complimentary closing, and signature.

Form of a Business Letter

Heading: _____
                                                    _____
                                                    _____

Inside   _____
address: _____
                                 _____

Salutation: _____
Body (message):   _____
                                 _____
                                 _____
                                 _____

Complimentary closing: _____
Signature: _____

Heading

The heading of a business letter consists of the complete address of the sender and the date of the letter. The heading is usually written with no punctuation at the end of each line.

Inside Address

When you write to a company, put the complete name and address of the company above the salutation. When you write to an individual, make sure to include his or her full name and title as well as his or her address.

Salutations for a Business Letter

Company	Dear Sir or Madam:
Man	Dear Sir: Dear Mr. Smith:
Single woman	Dear Miss / Ms. Jones:
Married woman	Dear Mrs. / Ms. Brown:
Marital status unknown	Dear Ms. Richards:

Place a colon (:) after the salutation.

Body of the Letter

The body of the letter is the main part of the message and states the purpose of writing the letter.

Complimentary Closing

In business letters, there are a number of different closings you may use:

Very formal	Respectfully yours,	Yours respectfully,
Formal	Yours truly,	Very truly yours,
Informal	Sincerely yours,	Yours sincerely,
Friendly	Cordially yours,	Cordially,
		Sincerely,

Place a comma after the complimentary closing.

Signature

The signature is the name of the person who wrote or dictated the letter. It should always be written by hand. When signing a business letter, always write your full name.

Man	John W. Smith	Mr. John W. Smith
Single woman	Mary L. Brown	Miss / Ms. Mary L. Brown
Married woman	Helen Smith	
	Helen Smith (Mrs. John W. Smith)	
	Mrs. / Ms. Helen Smith	

If you have an official position, you should write your title after or under your signature:

Martin F. Stone, Director	Helen W. Smith
Stanley L. Brown	Assistant Professor
Executive Secretary	

Addressing an Envelope

Write your own name and address in the upper-left-hand corner of the envelope.

Write the complete name and address of the firm near the center of the envelope. When writing to an individual, include the person's full name and title and the name and address of the company for which he or she works.

Be sure to include the Zip Code, both in your own address and in the address to which the letter is sent.

Types of Business Letters

Letters of Request

1. Requests for booklets, catalogues, samples, and so forth

This is one of the most commonly used types of business letters. You must state in your letter exactly what you want. If you want a booklet or a catalogue, give the exact title. If you saw something advertised in a newspaper, in addition to an exact description of the item, give the date and the name of the newspaper where you saw the item.

Letters of request for pamphlets or other items offered publicly need only identify the request and give adequate information for its delivery. (See Peter Yoon's letter to Institute for English asking for a catalogue in Lesson 23.)

2. Requests for information

A letter requesting information should be courteous, as brief as possible, and clear. The best way to be courteous is to use words and phrases like *please* and *I would appreciate.*

(Letter to a book club asking for information)

> 6802 Parkview Road
> Sarasota, FL 34236
> June 26, 19___

History Book Club
Camp Hill, Pennsylvania 17012–8805

Dear Sir or Madam:

Would you kindly send me complete information about your History Book Club.

I have been a history buff for a long time and am interested in becoming a member.

Thanking you, I am

> Very truly yours,
> Max Green

Letters of Complaint and Adjustment

Letters of complaint and adjustment are sent when some error has occurred in the course of a business transaction. The customer should assume that the mistake was not committed intentionally and that the company will be glad to adjust the matter once it understands the circumstances. Therefore, a first letter of complaint should be calm, courteous, and tactful.

A letter of complaint and adjustment should include the following information:

1. Begin your letter by stating the circumstances of the transaction.
2. Give all the necessary details, explaining simply and courteously what is wrong.
3. Explain the adjustment you want made.

(Letter of complaint and adjustment)

> 70 Park Terrace West
> San Jose, CA 95128
> November 21, 19___

Macy's Order Dept.
Box 1280
San Francisco, CA 94132

Dear Sir or Madam:

On November 14, I ordered by phone one pair of women's black, cashmere-lined Italian leather gloves, size 6½, at $32.00 a pair. When they were delivered yesterday, I found that you had sent size 8 instead of the size requested.

Would you please send the correct order as soon as possible and arrange to pick up the package you sent by mistake.

> Very truly yours,
> Gladys L. Rowen
> (Mrs. Frank Rowen)

Order Letters

An order letter must be very clear and complete. The letter should describe the articles wanted and include all the necessary details such as item number, size, color, style, quantity wanted, and price. If necessary, include the shipping instructions. Also, mention how you want to pay for the merchandise. If you saw the article advertised in a newspaper or a magazine, be sure to mention which publication and the date of the advertisement.

(Order letter)

> 520 Ninth Avenue
> Belmar, N.J. 07719
> November 21, 19___

Wallachs
32–36 Forty-seventh Avenue
Long Island City, N.Y. 11101

Dear Sir or Madam:

Please send me the following article, advertised in the November 20 *New York Times:*

1	#3L, Men's Racquet Club Shetland wool crewneck sweater from the Shetland Isles of Scotland, size—large, color—yellow	$45.00
	Handling charge	1.95
	TOTAL	$46.95

I am enclosing a check in the amount of $46.95 to cover the cost of the sweater plus the handling charge.

> Very truly yours,
> Joseph Argan

PERSONAL (SOCIAL) LETTERS

Parts of a Personal (Social) Letter

There are five parts of a personal letter: heading, salutation, body of the letter, complimentary closing, and signature.

Form of a Personal (Social) Letter

Heading: _____

_____

_____

Salutation: _____

Body (message): _____

_____

_____

_____

_____

Complimentary closing: _____

Signature: _____

Heading

The heading of a social letter should include your complete address and the date of the letter. (If you are writing to someone who knows you well, such as a close friend or relative, you do not need to include your address.) The heading is usually written with no punctuation at the end of each line. Write the name of the month of the year in full.

Salutations for a Social Letter

Friend	Dear Betty, Dear Harold,
Man	Dear Mr. Edwards,
Single woman	Dear Miss / Ms. Seymour,
Married woman	Dear Mrs. / Ms. Jones,
Marital status unknown	Dear Ms. Taylor,

Place a comma after the salutation.
Note: Instead of "Dear Mr. Edwards," you can say "My dear Mr. Edwards," when you write to someone whom you do not know very well.

Body of the Letter

The body of the letter is the main part of the message and states the purpose of writing the letter.

Complimentary Closing

In a friendly letter, you may use the following endings:

Formal	*For people you don't know well or haven't seen for some time*	*Very friendly*
Sincerely yours,	As always,	Affectionately,
Sincerely,	As ever,	Fondly,
Very sincerely,		Love,
Very sincerely yours,		

Signature

If you are writing to someone who knows you well, such as a close friend or relative, sign your first name only:

> Tom   Roberta   Jerry

If you are writing to a friend who doesn't know you too well, or if your first name will not identify you clearly, write your full name.

> John W. Smith   Jennie I. Jones

If a woman is married, she should always write her own first name in her signature. She may add her married name on the following line, if necessary.

> Janet Roberts   (Mrs. William Roberts)

Addressing an Envelope

Write your own name and address in the upper-left-hand corner of the envelope.

Write the complete name and address of your friend near the center of the envelope.

Be sure to include the Zip Code, both in your own address and in the address to which the letter is sent.

Types of Personal (Social) Letters

Informal Invitations

A letter of invitation should sound sincere and cordial. Be definite in giving the time and place of the affair and indicate whether it is going to be formal or informal.

(Letter of invitation)

> 110 Wilson Road
> Bedford, MA 01730
> February 21, 19___

Dear Mr. Howard,

My husband and I would be very happy if you could come to dinner on Friday night, March 3, at seven o'clock. We are having a small informal party afterward. We do hope you can join us.

> Sincerely yours,
> Mrs. Janet Roberts

Note of Acceptance

Acknowledge invitations promptly and express your appreciation for an invitation sincerely. To avoid confusion, repeat the time, place, and date of the affair you have been invited to.

(Note of acceptance)

> 17 Shade Street
> Lexington, MA 02173
> February 24, 19___

Dear Mrs. Roberts,

I will be very glad to dine with you and your husband on Friday, March 3, at seven o'clock and to attend the party afterward. It was very nice of you to ask me.

> Yours sincerely,
> Richard Howard

Note of Refusal

A letter of regret is written when you cannot accept an invitation to an affair. Be sure to acknowledge the invitation promptly. Express pleasure that you were invited and tell why you cannot accept the invitation.

(Note of refusal)

> 17 Shade Street
> Lexington, MA 02173
> February 24, 19___

Dear Mrs. Roberts,

I am very sorry that I will not be able to dine with you and your husband on Friday, March 3. Unfortunately, I expect to be in Chicago on that day.

Thank you for asking me, and I hope you will give me the opportunity to say "yes" some other time.

> Sincerely yours,
> Richard Howard

Bread-and-Butter Letter

A bread-and-butter letter is a letter of thanks written after you have been entertained by someone overnight or longer. You should mention something noteworthy about the event in your letter. It doesn't have to be a long letter, but it should be written naturally and sincerely. It should express the appreciation of the writer for the hospitality that he or she has received. The outline presented below is useful to follow when writing this kind of letter. An example of a bread-and-butter letter appears as a dictation in Lesson 23.

Bread-and-Butter Letter

I. Arrival at host's or hostess' home
   A. Topic sentence: thank the host or hostess for the hospitality
   B. The journey to the host's or hostess' home
      1. How you felt during the trip
      2. Anything that happened on the way
   C. Arrival at the host's or hostess' home
      1. How you felt when you got there
      2. People waiting for you
II. Hospitality
   A. General statement about the good time you had there
   B. Details about anything you especially enjoyed and why
      1. What you enjoyed doing and seeing
      2. Any particular food or custom that was new to you
III. Return
   A. Where you are now and what you are doing
   B. How you feel now and what you think of the stay in your host's or hostess' home
   C. Concluding sentence: general statement of thanks and so forth

Get-Well Note

A get-well note is a letter sent to a friend who is sick or hurt to cheer the friend up and let him or her know that you are concerned about the illness or injury.

(Get-well note)

66 West Spring Street
Kansas City, Mo. 64111
October 29, 19___

Dear José,

Miss Brown, our English teacher, has just told us that you were in the hospital for an appendectomy. I hope that you are feeling better now and that you will soon be completely recovered. Everyone in the class misses your good-natured personality and sense of humor. Besides, I have nobody to help me with my homework when you are away. We are all looking forward to your quick return. Please get well soon.

With kindest regards and best wishes for your good health, I am

Your classmate,

Yasua

_____

QUIZ: LESSON *1*

Fill in the blank spaces with the correct form of the verb *to be*.

The Weather in Boston

There _____ four seasons in Boston: winter, spring, summer, and autumn. In the winter it _____ often very cold and windy, and in the summer it _____ sometimes very hot and humid. The weather in the spring and autumn, however, _____ usually very pleasant. For many people, these _____ the two best seasons of the year because they _____ the only times the climate is comfortable. Boston _____ a city where the weather often changes every few hours during the whole year. People like to say, "If you don't like the weather now, wait a while." There _____ one thing that is certain about Boston weather. It seldom stays the same.

QUIZ: LESSON 2

QUIZ A

Rewrite the composition above the printed lines and change the subject pronoun to *He*. Make all other necessary changes. All the italicized words require changes. Follow the example in the first sentence.

What Am I?

     <u>*Mr. Dodd usually goes to work by limousine or taxi. He starts*</u>
     I usually *go* to work by limousine or taxi.   *I start*

_____

work at different times, and *I* sometimes *have* to work nights,

_____

holidays, and weekends. *I* never *start* and *finish my* work in

_____

the same place unless *I am* on a shuttle run. Before *I go* to

_____

work, *I put* on *my* uniform. If *I go* overseas, *I* usually *take* a

_____

small bag with *me* because *I have* a twenty-four- to thirty-hour

_____

layover before *my* return flight. Then *I am* off for a few

_____

days.

_____

     My work is usually pleasant and sometimes exciting because it

_____

takes *me* all over the world. *I meet* all kinds of people and

_____

talk to everyone. *I try* to make everyone comfortable and *give*

_____

special attention to elderly and handicapped passengers and to

_____

children traveling alone. *I know* how to give first aid and

_____

what to do in case of a hijacking, bomb threat, or forced

_____

landing. *I* also *show* people what to do in case of an

emergency. During mealtimes, *I serve* the passengers food, and

I always *ask,* "Coffee or tea?" When the plane lands, *I assist*

passengers as they leave the plane.

QUIZ: LESSON 2

QUIZ B

Fill in the blanks with the appropriate preposition.

What Am I?

I usually go to work _____ limousine or taxi. I start work _____ different times, and I sometimes have to work nights, holidays, and weekends. I never start and finish my work _____ the same place unless I am _____ a shuttle run. Before I go to work, I put _____ my uniform. If I go overseas, I usually take a small bag _____ me because I have a twenty-four- _____ thirty-hour layover _____ my return flight. Then I am _____ for a few days.

My work is usually pleasant and sometimes exciting because it takes me all _____ the world. I meet all kinds _____ people and talk _____ everyone. I try to make everyone comfortable and give special attention _____ elderly and handicapped passengers and _____ children traveling alone. I know how to give first aid and what to do _____ case _____ a hijacking, bomb threat, or forced landing. I also show people what to do _____ case _____ an emergency. During mealtimes, I serve the passengers food, and I always ask, "Coffee _____ tea?" When the plane lands, I assist passengers as they leave the plane.

QUIZ: LESSON 3

Fill in the blank spaces with the correct form of the verb in parentheses.

A Letter to a Friend

Dear Carla,

It _____ (be) three o'clock in the afternoon now, and

I _____ (sit) in the library and _____ (write) you

this letter. It _____ (be) a lovely spring day outside, but it

_____ (be) almost time for final exams, so there

_____ (be) a lot of students studying in the library today.

The library _____ (be) open until 2:00 A.M., and you can find

many students studying here until very late. Right now, there

_____ (be) three students sitting opposite me. One

_____ (read) a philosophy book, another _____

(study) mathematics, and the other _____ (look) at art pictures.

On one side of the room, there _____ (be) five students

working out problems on computers. On the other side of the room, there

are two students who _____ (wear) earphones and

_____ (listen) to music while they _____

(study). I wish I could listen to music and study at the same time. Most of the

students _____ (be) American, but there _____

(be) lots of foreign students here, too. Some of the American students

_____ (lean) back in their chairs, with their feet up on the

table. (This isn't usual in our country, but it isn't unusual here.)

There _____ (be) lots of good-looking fellows in the library

today, and I _____ (be) very busy people-watching.

This _____ (be) one of my favorite pastimes.

It _____ (be) more interesting than doing homework.

Well, I really must say "Good-by" now and get back to my work. Wish me

luck on my exams! I hope all _____ (go) well with you. I miss

you, so please write soon.

Fondly,

María

QUIZ: LESSON 4

QUIZ A

Fill in the blanks with the definite article, if necessary. If no article is necessary, put an X in the blank space.

The United States

_____ United States is a very large country. From _____ Atlantic Ocean on _____ East Coast to _____ Pacific Ocean on _____ West Coast, it is about three thousand miles wide. _____ Canada is the country to the north of _____ United States, and _____ Mexico is the country to the south. _____ Rio Grande is the boundary between _____ Mexico and _____ United States. The country is a composite of different geographic formations—high mountains and deep canyons, great river systems and landlocked lakes, rolling plains, forests and rocky coasts, sandy beaches, and even deserts. The major mountain ranges are _____ Appalachian Mountains in _____ East and _____ Rocky Mountains in _____ West. The most important rivers are _____ Mississippi and _____ Missouri rivers in _____ central part of the country and _____ Colorado and _____ Columbia rivers in _____ West. There are fifty states in _____ Union today. The two newest states, _____ Hawaii and _____ Alaska, are geographically separated from the other forty-eight states.

_____ United States has a heterogeneous population. The American people are of almost every creed and every ethnic background. This mix of many kinds of people is the result of the great immigration from abroad throughout American history. The population is now over 240 million people, including 1.5 million Native Americans. _____ English is the common language.

QUIZ: LESSON 5

Fill in the blanks with the correct preposition.

You Are What You Eat

John Smith, Mr. Average American, is a family man _____ two school-age children and a wife who works part-time. Let's look _____ his eating habits during a typical week.

Mr. Smith has either a small breakfast _____ juice, toast, and coffee or a big breakfast _____ ham or bacon and eggs, toast, and coffee. _____ weekends, Mrs. Smith tries to find time to make him waffles, pancakes, or French toast _____ both butter and maple syrup.

Mr. Smith works _____ a large office _____ 9:00 _____ 5:00. _____ 10:30 every morning, he has a doughnut or a Danish and coffee _____ the fifteen-minute "coffee break." He usually takes an hour _____ lunch _____ noon or 1:00 P.M. _____ lunch, he goes _____ a coffee shop and has soup and a ham and cheese or roast beef sandwich _____ lettuce and tomatoes, and some coffee. Sometimes, he has a hamburger and French fries and a soda.

Mr. Smith tries to be home _____ 6:00 or 6:30 every evening so that he can have dinner _____ his wife and children. His wife serves not only a full meal _____ chicken, meat, or fish, a salad, and vegetables but also a dessert _____ pie or cake. The parents have coffee, and the children drink milk. _____ about ten o'clock, while watching television, Mr. Smith has a snack _____ either some ice cream or another piece _____ pie.

Once a week, Mr. Smith goes out _____ his wife _____ a restaurant _____ dinner. They usually go _____ a Chinese, Italian, or Mexican restaurant because they like to try different international cuisine. _____ Saturday or Sunday afternoon, the whole family eats out _____ a fast-food place because that is what the children prefer.

Mr. Smith is gaining too much weight, and Mrs. Smith is very worried _____ him. She often says _____ him, "You should go _____ a diet." He usually answers, "I know. I'll start tomorrow—or the day _____ ."

QUIZ: LESSON 6

Fill in the blanks with the correct form of the verb in parentheses.

My Life in the Year 2001

In the year 2001, I _____ (be) thirty-one years old, and
I _____ (think) my life _____ (be) very different then from my life today. I _____ (plan) to be a famous
photographer, and I _____ (hope) to have a good job
and make enough money to live comfortably. I _____
(want) to live in a small, quiet suburb near a big city, with a loving wife and
two or three children. I would like to have two sons and a daughter. My
family and I _____ (live) in a house made of a tough new
plastic material. A new form of strong zippers and Velcro _____
(hold) the house together, so it _____ (be) very easy to change
the design and add new rooms and parts whenever we _____
(want) to. A few days each week, I _____ (commute) to the city
in my autoplane with my personal robot, EZ. This car _____
(be) crashproof and _____ (run) on a computer, so
I _____ (have-neg) to drive it. I will be able to watch
television, read the paper, or do other things in my car while
I _____ (ride) to work. If there _____ (be)
too much traffic on the road, my autoplane _____ just
_____ (fly) over the other cars and continue on its way. At
work, I _____ (program) my robot to take all my photos at the
right speed, distance, and light when I _____ (push) its
buttons from a remote control. I _____ (expect) to earn good
money at my job, but I _____ (use-*negative*) money. Instead,
everyone _____ (use) credit cards to buy everything.
I _____ (think) my life _____ (be) much easier in
the year 2001. I can't wait.

QUIZ: LESSON 7

Fill in the blanks with the correct preposition.

The Heimlich Maneuver

You are _____ the cafeteria _____ three friends when a student _____ the table next to yours begins to choke, apparently _____ a piece of food. It becomes obvious that she cannot breathe or speak, and then her face starts to turn slightly blue. Something must be done quickly! What should you do to help?

Fortunately, there *is* something you can do, and it doesn't require a lot _____ first-aid training. _____ the contrary, the technique _____ helping a choking victim is easy both to learn and to perform, and is very often effective. This technique, called the Heimlich maneuver, has been approved _____ the American Heart Association. Here is how to perform the Heimlich maneuver.

_____ the victim standing _____ front _____ you, start _____ putting your arms _____ his or her waist _____ behind. Make a fist _____ one hand and grasp the fist _____ the other hand. Then, place the fist _____ the victim's abdomen. The thumb side _____ your fist must be facing the victim's abdomen, and the fist should be positioned just _____ his or her waist or navel and _____ his or her ribs. Next, compress the victim's abdomen _____ using your other hand to pull your fist in and up in one rapid motion. (Be sure your fist is positioned low enough so that you do not compress the victim's rib cage when you do the Heimlich maneuver, because such pressure may break some of the victim's ribs.) If the victim is still choking _____ you have compressed his or her abdomen, then repeat the abdominal-compression step, pulling your fist rapidly in and up. It may take several repetitions _____ this step before you can dislodge whatever the victim is choking _____ .

You can also perform the Heimlich maneuver as described _____ on a victim who is sitting _____ as long as the back _____ the victim's chair is not thick enough to prevent you _____ grasping him or her _____ the waist when you stand _____ the chair.

QUIZ: LESSON 8

QUIZ A

Rewrite the composition above the printed lines, and change the subject pronoun to *he*. Make all other necessary changes. All the italicized words require changes. Follow the example in the first sentence.

A Typical Day in My Life

> *His alarm clock rings at seven o'clock every morning, and John usually gets up at once.*

    My alarm clock rings at seven o'clock every morning, and I usually get up at once.

_____

I jump out of bed and *do* physical exercises for ten minutes. Then *I am* ready

_____

either to get back into bed or to take a quick cold shower. After *my* shower, *I*

_____

plug in *my* electric razor and *shave*. Then, *I plug* in *my* electric toothbrush and

_____

brush my teeth. Next, *I comb my* hair, *wash my* face again, and *put on* after-shave

_____

lotion. After that, *I pick out my* clothes for the day and *get* dressed. *I prepare my*

_____

own breakfast, which is usually grapefruit juice, scrambled eggs, toast, and

_____

coffee. *I* always *listen* to the news and weather report on the radio while *I eat*

_____

breakfast. By 8:00 A.M., *I am* ready to put on *my* coat and leave for school. *I*

_____

generally *go* to school by subway, but the subway is always crowded, so *I don't*

_____

often get a seat. In the subway, on *my* way to school, *I look* at the signs on the

_____

walls of the car, *watch* the faces of other passengers, and *read* the newspaper

_____

headlines over someone's shoulder. It takes *me* about half an hour to get to

_____

school. When *I get* to school, *I* usually *have* time to talk to *my* classmates for a

_____

few minutes before class starts. *My* first class begins at nine o'clock, and *my* last class ends at three. After school hours, *I* sometimes *go* to the Student Center

or to a coffee house with *my* friends for an hour or so. Afterward, *I go* home.

As soon as *I get* home from school, *I do my* homework and *study my* lessons for

the next day. At seven o'clock, *I eat* dinner with *my* brother. After dinner, *I*

relax. Some nights, *my* brother and *I* watch television for an hour or two

together. *I* really *enjoy* some of the sports programs because they are easy to

understand. Other nights, *I listen* to *my* jazz records or *work* on *my* stamp

collection, or *write* letters. *My* favorite nights are when *I take* a walk in the

evening, *visit* a friend, or *go* out on a date. *I try* to get home by midnight,

because by twelve o'clock *I am* generally rather tired. *I take* off *my* clothes, *get*

into bed, and *fall* asleep immediately. *I sleep* until the alarm goes off again the

next morning.

QUIZ: LESSON 8

QUIZ B

Fill in the blanks with the correct preposition.

A Typical Day in My Life

    My alarm clock rings _____ seven o'clock every morning, and I
usually get _____ at once. I jump _____ of bed and do physical
exercises _____ ten minutes. Then I am ready either to get back
_____ bed or to take a quick cold shower. _____ my shower, I
plug _____ my electric razor and shave. Then, I plug _____ my
electric toothbrush and brush my teeth. Next, I comb my hair, wash my face
again, and put _____ after-shave lotion. _____ that, I pick _____
my clothes _____ the day and get dressed. I prepare my own breakfast,
which is usually grapefruit juice, scrambled eggs, toast, and coffee. I always
listen _____ the news and weather report _____ the radio while I eat
breakfast. _____ 8:00 A.M., I am ready to put _____ my coat and leave
_____ school.

    I generally go _____ school _____ subway, but the subway is
always crowded, so I don't often get a seat. _____ the subway, _____
my way _____ school, I look _____ the signs _____ the walls
_____ the car, watch the faces _____ other passengers, and read the
newspaper headlines _____ someone's shoulder. It takes me _____
half an hour to get _____ school. When I get to school, I usually have
time to talk _____ my classmates _____ a few minutes _____ class
starts. My first class begins _____ nine o'clock, and my last class ends
_____ three. _____ school hours, I sometimes go _____ the
Student Center or _____ a coffee house _____ my friends _____
an hour or so. _____ , I go home.

    As soon _____ I get home _____ school, I do my homework and
study my lessons _____ the next day. _____ seven o'clock, I eat dinner
_____ my brother. _____ dinner, I relax. Some nights, my brother
and I watch television _____ an hour or two together. I really enjoy some

_____ the sports programs because they are easy to understand. Other nights, I listen _____ my jazz records, work _____ my stamp collection, or write letters. My favorite nights are when I take a walk _____ the evening, visit a friend, or go out _____ a date. I try to get home _____ midnight, because _____ twelve o'clock I am generally rather tired. I take _____ my clothes, get _____ bed, and fall asleep immediately. I sleep _____ the alarm goes _____ again the next morning.

QUIZ: LESSON 9

Fill in the blanks with the correct preposition.

A Comparison of Two Cities (Shanghai and New York)

Shanghai is different _____ New York _____ many ways, but
there are many things that are similar. Shanghai is one _____ the most
populous cities in Asia, and New York is one of the most populous cities
_____ North America. The weather _____ the summer is very hot
_____ Shanghai, and it is the same _____ New York. Shanghai is a
port and an industrial city, and New York is, too. Shanghai is a center
_____ fashion and commerce, and so is New York. There are housing and
pollution problems _____ Shanghai, and there are similar problems
_____ New York. Both Shanghai and New York have serious traffic and
transportation problems.

The population _____ Shanghai is homogeneous, but the population
_____ New York is heterogeneous. Most _____ the people _____
Shanghai live _____ apartments _____ low buildings, while most
_____ the people _____ New York live _____ apartments
_____ high buildings. The housing shortage _____ Shanghai
causes many people to live _____ overcrowded apartments, but the
housing shortage _____ New York causes many people to be homeless.
The traffic problem _____ Shanghai is caused _____ too many
bicycles. _____ the other hand, the traffic problem _____ New
York is caused _____ too many automobiles. While there are some
differences, the major problems _____ big cities are almost the same
everywhere _____ the world.

QUIZ: LESSON *10*

Fill in the blanks with the correct form of the verb in parentheses.

A Wedding

Last year, I _____ (go) to my cousin's wedding when she _____ (get) married in September on a lovely Sunday afternoon. My cousin, twenty-nine, and her boyfriend, thirty-one, _____ (meet) one morning while they _____ both _____ (jog). They _____ (know) each other for two years before they _____ (decide) to get married and have a big old-fashioned wedding, which both families _____ (help) pay for.

The wedding was held in a large hall with a chapel where the marriage ceremony _____ (take) place. Because it _____ (be) an interfaith marriage, the couple were married by a judge who _____ (be) a friend of the family. The bride _____ (wear) a long off-white dress and veil and _____ (carry) a bouquet of flowers. Also, as _____ (be) customary, she _____ (wear) something old, something new, something borrowed, and something blue. The something old _____ (be) her veil, which her mother and grandmother _____ (wear) at their weddings, the something new _____ (be) her dress, the something borrowed _____ (be) a handkerchief, and the something blue _____ (be) a garter. The groom _____ (wear) a tuxedo and a white boutonniere.

After the ceremony, the bride and groom and their parents _____ (stand) in a receiving line, and all the guests _____ (congratulate) them. Then, everyone _____ (go) into the big dining hall to celebrate. First, everyone _____ (drink) champagne toasts to the bride and groom and then _____ (sit down) to a delicious dinner. After dinner, the orchestra _____ (begin) playing, and my cousin and her new husband _____ (dance) while everyone _____ (applaud). Then, all two hundred guests _____ (join) in the dancing. After the wedding, the bride and groom _____ (leave) for their honeymoon on a Caribbean island. When they _____ (return), they _____ (be) ready _____ (begin) their new life in their new apartment.

QUIZ: LESSON *11*

Fill in the blanks with the correct preposition.

How to Get Along in the United States

May 21, 19___

Dear José,

You have asked me _____ suggestions on how to get along _____ the United States. It is difficult to give advice, but I have found the following "dos" and "don'ts" helpful.

_____ a rule, it isn't easy to find anyone to talk to _____ a big city. However, here are some suggestions. First, get or borrow a dog! Walk him several times a day! Americans love pets and usually stop to talk _____ anyone _____ a dog. Then, try to eat _____ a cafeteria! People generally share the same tables and will sometimes talk to you if they see that you are a stranger. Next, take your dirty clothes to a laundromat! It takes about an hour to wash and dry laundry, and many people wait in the laundromat. They often pass the time talking _____ the other customers. Always ask _____ information _____ a woman if you are a man, and _____ a man if you are a woman! It seems to get better results _____ a reason I can't understand. Learn the expressions "Please," "Thank you," and "You're welcome" before you come, and use them all the time! They usually work _____ magic.

There are some things you shouldn't do. Don't tell the truth when people ask "How are you?"! They only expect the answer to be "Fine." Never ask people their age—men or women! Everyone wants to be young. Don't tell heavy people they are fat! Tell them they are losing weight. Everyone here is diet-conscious and wants to be thin. Don't be late _____ appointments! When someone says six o'clock, be sure to be there _____ six. Americans respect time and expect everyone to be " _____ time."

_____ all, don't worry! Just follow my advice and bring a lot _____ money and you will get along. I hope I have been _____ some help _____ you.

Your friend,

Miguel

QUIZ: LESSON *12*

Fill in the blanks with the correct preposition.

My Favorite Television Program

My favorite television show is "Star Trek: The Next Generation." It
is _____ every Saturday night at 8:00 P.M. _____ Channel 11, and I
have seen this program every week since I came here. "Star Trek: The Next
Generation" is science fiction and a continuation _____ the original "Star
Trek" series. The name _____ the spaceship, the *Enterprise,* is the same,
but the spaceship is now bigger and better. This series takes place eighty-five
years later than "Star Trek," and all the characters are new. The *Enterprise* is
now _____ the command _____ Capt. Jean-Luc Picard and carries
_____ a thousand people. As in the old "Star Trek," the ship is still
chasing unfriendly aliens _____ space. Each week the stories introduce
strange and often fascinating characters, and each episode is always packed
_____ action. _____ me, the most interesting character _____ the
series is neither the android, Data, who remembers everything, nor the half-
Betazoid, Deanna Troi, who can feel emotions _____ her. My favorite
character is the spaceship itself. I know the *Enterprise* isn't a person, but the
spaceship is beautiful _____ so many interesting advanced technological
parts.

_____ my country, I used to watch the original "Star Trek" all the
time and became a devoted "Trekkie." I used to go _____ all the Trekkie
conventions and buy all the Trekkie souvenir merchandise, so I know that I
will watch this new series every week.

QUIZ: LESSON *13*

There are fourteen words missing from the composition. Read the word choices for each space. Then circle the word that fits best and write it in the space.

Bad Habits

Everybody has some (1) _____ habits that he or she would like to get (2) _____ of, and I am no exception. Procrastination is my number one bad habit. I do this especially (3) _____ I have an unpleasant task to perform. This is a (4) _____ habit to break, and as a (5) _____ , I am always rushing to finish things that I have put (6) _____ until the last possible moment. Twirling my hair is another (7) _____ habit. Whenever I am nervous or uncomfortable, I fall (8) _____ into this childhood pattern. I also have the bad habit of talking too much and saying foolish things whenever I am very tired. This is something I always (9) _____ the next day.

Other people have habits that I don't like (10) _____ . Students who click their ballpoint pens in class drive me up a (11) _____ . People who don't move to the rear of a bus and who (12) _____ the doors are two of my pet (13) _____ . People who don't put the cap back on a tube of toothpaste are another source of irritation. I find this habit very annoying. Unfortunately, we all do things unconsciously that bother other people, but that is because (14) _____ is perfect.

1. private	popular	personal
2. kick	break	rid
3. whenever	wherever	whatever
4. average	normal	difficult
5. final	result	end
6. on	off	in
7. procrastinating	irritating	curling
8. forward	down	back
9. regret	redeem	refer
10. too	neither	either
11. banana	wall	peeve
12. black	block	close
13. dogs	cats	peeves
14. everybody	somebody	nobody

_____

QUIZ: LESSON *14*

Fill in the blanks with the correct tense of the verb in parentheses.

The American Way of Life

The American way of life may _____ (be) different from
yours, and some things that _____ (seem) natural and ordinary
to us may _____ (puzzle) you.

Americans, as a rule, _____ (be) very informal and
_____ probably _____ (call) you by your first
name as soon as they _____ (meet) you. Although this shows a
warm attitude, it _____ (mean-*negative*) that they want
_____ (begin) a lifelong friendship. Americans
also _____ (show) their informality in their casual dress. For
example, if you _____ (go) to the ballet or the opera, you
_____ (see) some people wearing jeans.

Most families _____ (live) in individual homes in the
suburbs and towns, but in the cities, most people _____ (live) in
apartments. Americans _____ (have) few servants but many
electrical appliances to help them be more efficient. The husband, wife, and
children all _____ (share) the domestic duties of the household
because most married women _____ (work).

In their free time, Americans _____ (like) to go to the
movies and listen to music, do volunteer work, watch television, and read.
Football, baseball, basketball, hockey, and horse racing _____
(be) the major spectator sports. The most popular participant sports
_____ (be) swimming, bicycling, fishing, bowling, hiking, and
camping. Other popular sports include tennis, golf, skiing, and jogging.

Even though the struggle for the rights of blacks, women, and
homosexuals _____ (be) still not complete, today, if you
_____ (be) divorced, a single parent, or different, it
_____ (be) accepted as part of the American way of life.

One thing to remember is that the United States _____
(have) a history of evolutionary ideas and social changes. If you

_____ (like-*negative*) the way things are now,

_____ (wait) a minute! You may like the new changes, despite

the way things _____ (be) now.

QUIZ: LESSON *15*

Fill in the blanks with the correct preposition.

On Being the Youngest

The role I play _____ my family has definitely helped shape my personality and character. I am the only girl and the youngest _____ my family, coming _____ three boys.

As a child, my brothers always introduced me _____ their friends as "my little sister." I felt secure _____ being the youngest because I knew my brothers were always there to protect me. Sometimes, however, this sense _____ security overpowered me. _____ example, when my friends told me of their adventures abroad or _____ a sleepaway camp, I was afraid to try these experiences myself. I felt so loved and protected _____ my family that I would rather stay home than go far away and meet new people.

Being much younger than all three _____ my brothers does create other problems. Soon I will begin to apply _____ colleges, and I am already anxious _____ this situation. All three _____ my brothers attended Ivy League schools. Therefore, there is pressure _____ me to get _____ a "good" school, too.

Although it is sometimes difficult to be the youngest _____ three older brothers, this position has many advantages. _____ example, whenever I have a problem, I always have someone to turn to. This has helped make me a more understanding person and has given me a special viewpoint _____ life. I wouldn't trade my position as the youngest _____ anything _____ the world.

QUIZ: LESSON 16

QUIZ A

Fill in the blanks with the correct tense of the verb in parentheses.

My First Day in the United States

I _____ (arrive) in the United States on February 6, 1988, but I _____ (remember) my first day here very clearly. My friend _____ (wait) for me when my plane _____ (land) at Kennedy Airport at three o'clock in the afternoon. The weather _____ (be) very cold and it _____ (snow), but I _____ (be) too excited to mind. From the airport, my friend and I _____(take) a taxi to my hotel. On the way, I _____ (see) the skyline of Manhattan for the first time, and I _____ (stare) in astonishment at the famous skyscrapers and their manmade beauty. My friend _____ (help) me unpack at the hotel and then _____ (leave) me because he _____ (have to) go back to work. He _____ (promise) to return the next day.

Shortly after my friend _____ (leave), I _____ (go) to a restaurant near the hotel to get something to eat. Because I couldn't _____ (speak) a word of English, I couldn't tell the waiter what I _____ (want). I _____ (be) very upset and _____ (start) to make some gestures, but the waiter _____ (understand—*negative*) me. Finally, I _____ (order) the same thing the man at the next table _____ (eat).

After dinner, I _____ (start) to walk along Broadway until I _____ (come) to Times Square, with its movie theaters, neon lights, and huge crowds of people. I _____ (feel—*negative*) tired, so I _____ (continue) to walk around the city. I _____ (want) to see everything on my first day. I _____ (know) it _____ (be)

impossible, but I _____ (want) to try.

    When I _____ (return) to the hotel, I

_____(be) exhausted, but I couldn't sleep because

I _____ (keep) hearing the fire and police sirens during

the night. I _____ (lie) awake and

_____ (think) about New York. It

_____ (be) a very big and interesting city with many tall

buildings and big cars, and full of noise and busy people. I also

_____ (decide) right then that I

_____ (have to) learn to speak English.

QUIZ: LESSON 16

QUIZ B

Fill in the blanks with the correct prepositions.

My First Day in the United States

I arrived _____ the United States _____ February 6, 1988, but I remember my first day here very clearly. My friend was waiting _____ me when my plane landed _____ Kennedy Airport _____ three o'clock _____ the afternoon. The weather was very cold and it was snowing, but I was too excited to mind. _____ the airport, my friend and I took a taxi _____ my hotel. _____ the way, I saw the skyline _____ Manhattan _____ the first time, and I stared _____ astonishment _____ the famous skyscrapers and their manmade beauty. My friend helped me unpack _____ the hotel and then left me because he had to go back _____ work. He promised to return the next day.

Shortly _____ my friend had left, I went _____ a restaurant _____ the hotel to get something to eat. Because I couldn't speak a word _____ English, I couldn't tell the waiter what I wanted. I was very upset and started to make some gestures, but the waiter didn't understand me. Finally, I ordered the same thing the man _____ the next table was eating.

_____ dinner, I started to walk _____ Broadway until I came _____ Times Square, _____ its movie theaters, neon lights, and huge crowds _____ people. I didn't feel tired, so I continued to walk _____ the city. I wanted to see everything on my first day. I knew it was impossible, but I wanted to try.

When I returned _____ the hotel, I was exhausted, but I couldn't sleep because I kept hearing the fire and police sirens _____ the night. I lay awake and thought _____ New York. It was a very big and interesting city _____ many tall buildings and big cars, and full _____ noise and busy people. I also decided right then that I had to learn to speak English.

QUIZ: LESSON *17*

Fill in the blanks with the correct preposition.

The American Family

The most common type _____ family _____ the United States is
the nuclear family, which is normally made up _____ two generations—
parents and their still-dependent children. The typical family is middle-class,
and there is generally some degree of equality _____ the husband and
wife. Each family lives _____ its own separate residence, and it is not
usual to share a house _____ one's grandparents or in-laws. American
families are very mobile and are continually changing jobs and moving
_____ other neighborhoods. It is estimated that the average American
family moves _____ once every five years. Child care _____ an
American family is exclusively the responsibility _____ the parents, and
children are taught to be independent _____ an early age. When they
become adults, most children leave their parents' house and set up their own
households even though they are not married.

The American family today is undergoing real change. For example,
most families have fewer children today, and some choose to have none.
_____ addition, more than 50 percent of mothers work _____ the
home due _____ a combination _____ economic reasons and the
changing social climate. Divorce is quite common, and one _____ the
most significant changes is that millions _____ children are being
brought _____ by only one parent, usually the mother. Nevertheless, most
divorced people remarry, and many _____ these remarriages include
_____ least one child _____ a former marriage. Therefore, many new
patterns _____ family life are emerging _____ the United States.

QUIZ: LESSON *18*

Fill in the blanks with the correct preposition.

What I Would Put in a Time Capsule

If I were asked to select five items to represent American life today that would be placed _____ a 3′ × 3′ × 3′ time capsule not to be opened _____ the year 5000, I would choose the following. The first item would be a pair _____ jogging shoes. This would represent the American people's craze _____ physical fitness. Next, I would include a picture _____ a hamburger and _____ a roadside McDonald's or Burger King. Fast-food chains have spread all _____ the country, and the pictures would represent an American food habit. The third item would be a computer. We are living _____ a computer age today, and it is predicted that every child will soon become familiar _____ the computer _____ school and that every business and most homes will soon have one as well. The fourth item would be the book *How to Live to be 100—or More,* by George Burns, advertised as "the ultimate diet, sex, and exercise book," and an example of the kind of book that always appears on America's best-seller lists. The last item would be a videotape _____ a few soap operas. On this video, one could see the clothes and homes _____ today as well as some _____ the social problems that Americans face. When they open the capsule in the year 5000, I wonder what the people of the future will think _____ us.

QUIZ: LESSON *21*

Fill in the blanks with the correct preposition.

Choosing Sons or Daughters

    I feel that whenever it becomes possible _____ parents to choose the sex _____ their child, they should be allowed to do so even though it may lead _____ more males than females. The first reason is that persons carrying an inherited disease that affects males would be able to choose to have a girl. The second reason is that there would be fewer deliberate abortions done because parents wanted a child _____ a different sex. The third reason is that unfortunately we still have wars, and more men than women are killed _____ wars. _____ addition, since women live longer than men, many widows would welcome a larger population _____ available males. Moreover, I don't believe the problem _____ more males _____ our society would be a permanent situation. _____ the fact that there would probably be more male children born _____ some time, it is likely that a shortage _____ women would eventually lead _____ an increase in the number of females born so that there would be more women available _____ marriage partners. _____ a time, the ratio _____ men _____ women would probably settle _____ a fairly even balance.

QUIZ: LESSON 22

Fill in the blanks with the correct preposition.

War Toys: A Cause for Concern?

Children have been playing some form _____ war games _____ history, acting _____ the battle _____ the forces _____ Good and Evil. Today, there is an ongoing argument _____ whether allowing children to play _____ war toys leads _____ violent behavior. While many parents refuse to permit their children to play _____ guns and other war toys, some psychologists and toy-industry officials don't believe that playing _____ war toys leads _____ violent behavior in later life.

They point _____ that no one has been able to prove that playing _____ war toys is definitely linked _____ violent behavior _____ later life. Psychologists believe that children need a way to express their aggressive instincts. Playing _____ war toys gives children a safe way to get rid _____ their aggressions and anger and gives them a sense _____ control _____ their lives. They claim that the more aggressive tendencies that are discharged _____ play as a child, the fewer aggressive tendencies that a person will have to deal _____ as an adult. Other psychologists say that children see violence _____ television and would act _____ what they saw _____ forming a gun _____ their fingers even if they didn't have the toy itself. Moreover, toy manufacturers feel that playing _____ toy soldiers can also teach positive values such _____ patriotism and bravery.

Even people who are _____ war toys agree that _____ the final analysis, children learn values primarily _____ their parents and not _____ their toys.

Sources

Lesson 1

"Angry, Sad, Happy? Blame the Weather," *U.S. News and World Report, Inc.* (August 1, 1983): p. 52+. Interview w/ psychologist James Rotton.

Levine, Beth. "Can the Weather Affect Your Mood?" *Seventeen* (September 1987): p.166+.

Saline, Carol. "Cold Comfort," *Philadelphia Magazine* v. 80 (February 1989): p. 33+.

Lesson 4

Pena, Federico. "The Challenge of Immigration," *USA Today* (January 1987): p. 61+.

Greenhouse, Linda. "Redefining the Boundaries: Who May Come In; Immigration Bill: Looking for Skills and Good English," *New York Times* v. 137, section 4, col 1 (April 10, 1988): p. E5 (n), p. E5 (L).

Wormwood, Lisa. "While Immigration Reform Waits, Lottery Fills the Void," *Christian Science Monitor* (April 13, 1989): p. 7.

World Book Encyclopedia (Chicago: World Book, Inc., 1989), v. X, pp. 874–875 and v. XVIII, pp. 82–83.

Lesson 11

Ekman, Paul. "The International Language of Gestures," *Psychology Today* (May 1984): p. 64+.

Friedman, Roberta. "Hand Jive," *Psychology Today* v. 22 (June 1988): p.10.

"Gestures; are they saying more than you mean?" *Teen Magazine* v. 29 (October 1985): p. 70+.

Davis, Flora. "How to Read Men Better," *Woman's Day* (November 15, 1983): p. 96+.

Lesson 13

Convey, Kevin R and Pippin Ross. "Nasty Habits and How to Shed Them," *Boston Magazine* v. 90 (January 1988): p. 98+.

Steacy, Anne. "Kicking a Habit," *Maclean's* v. 100 (June 22, 1987): p. 29.

"How to Kick Your Bad Habits," *Ebony* v. 41 (September 1986): p. 86+.

Lesson 14

"When Americans Live Abroad . . . ," Dept. of State Publication 7869, Dept. and Foreign Service Series 129. Washington, D.C., GPO, Released May 1965.

"American Way of Life," *USA Travel Information,* US. Travel Service, U.S. Dept. of Commerce, p. 5.

U.S. Bureau of the Census. "Statistical Abstract of the United States: 1989 (109th edition)." Washington, D.C., GPO, 1989.

Lesson 15

Baxendale, Ted. "Birth Order: How It Affects Your Love Life," *Cosmopolitan* v. 199 (November 1985): p. 154+.

Hanauer, Cathi. "Oldest, Youngest, Middle, or Only: What Your Birth Order Says About You," *Seventeen* v. 46 (January 1987): p. 106+.

Leman, Kevin. "Were You Born for Each Other (Birth Order Personalities)," *Redbook* v. 167 (August 1986): p 96+.

Lesson 17

U.S. Dept. of Commerce, Bureau of the Census. "Population Profile of the U.S.: 1984/85." *Current Population Reports,* Series P-23, No. 150. Washington, D.C., GPO, April 1987.

U.S. Dept. of Commerce, Bureau of the Census. "Social Indicators III. Selected Data on Social Conditions and Trends in the U.S." Washington, D.C., GPO, December 1980.

U.S. Dept. of Labor. "Time of Change." *1983 Handbook on Women Workers.* Bulletin 298. Washington, D.C., GPO.

Lesson 21

Elizabeth M. Whelan. *Boy or Girl? How to Help Choose the Sex of Your Baby* (New York: Bobbs-
    Merrill Company, Inc., 1984), p. 122 + .

Hrdy, Sarah Blaffer. "Daughters or Sons," *Natural History* (April 1988): p. 63 + . (Special
    Report)

Hillard, Paula Adams. *Parents Magazine* v. 63 (April 1988): p. 170 + .

Lesson 22

"War Toys on the March," a brochure published by *Stop War Toys Campaign* (Norwich, Conn.:
    New England War Resisters League, 1988).

"Do Toy Guns Fan Violence? Debate Flares," *The New York Times* v. 137, col. 5 (June 16,
    1988): p. 17 (n) p. C1 (L).

Klaven, Ellen. "Bam, Bam, You're Dead!" *American Baby* v. 50 (September 1988): p. 84 + .

Lesson 24

"Kennedy, John F.," *Academic American Encyclopedia* v. 12, p. 42 + .

Leuchtenburg, W.E. "John F. Kennedy, twenty years later." *American Heritage* (December
    1983): p. 50 + .

Manchester, William. *One brief shining moment: remembering Kennedy.* (Boston: Little Brown,
    1983).

Credits

Credits continued from p. ii.

"A Novelty Designed for the Rich and Famous to Bury," by Laurel Defoe, *The Sacramento
Business Journal* v. 4 (August 24, 1987): pp. 2 + . Reprinted by permission of *The Sacramento
Business Journal.*

"The Story of the Westinghouse Time Capsule," courtesy of the Westinghouse Historical
Collection, Pittsburg, Pennsylvania.

"Open Doors Data Portray Enrollment Trends of Foreign Students, Scholars to the United
States," by George C. Christensen, Thomas B. Thielen and Julie Rose, *NAFSA Newsletter*
(November 1987): pp. 3–6. Reprinted by permission.

*"Choosing Schools from Afar; the Selection of Colleges and Universities in the United States by Foreign
Students,"* by Marianthi Zikopoulos & Elinor G. Barber (Institute of International Education,
1986), p. 3 + . Reprinted by permission.

"New 'Open Doors' Data Show Asians A Majority of U.S. Foreign Students," *NAFSA
Newsletter* (December/January 1989): p. 3. Reprinted by permission.

"Freshmen Found Stressing Wealth," by Deirdre Carmody, *The New York Times* (January 14,
1988): p. A14. Copyright © 1988 by The New York Times Company. Reprinted by
permission.

"Open Doors: 1987/88 Report on International Educational Exchange," by Marianthi
Zikopoulos, ed. (Institute of International Education) p. 24 + . Reprinted by permission.

"War Toys on the March," from the Stop War Toys Campaign's brochure (War Resisters
League,1988). Reprinted by permission.

"Who (and Why) am I," by Karen Duffy in *Essays that Worked: 50 Essays from Successful
Applications to the Nations Top Colleges* by Curry, Boykin and Brian Kasbar (New Haven, Conn.,
Mustang Publishing Co., Inc., 1986), p. 57.

Black and White Photographs
Page 1 State University of New York at Albany, Joseph Schuyler/Stock, Boston; *48* NASA
(National Aeronautics and Space Administration); *84* Katrina Thomas/Photo Researchers,
Inc.; *112* Statue of Liberty, Rafael Macia/Photo Researchers, Inc.; *112* baseball scene, Alan
Carey/The Image Works; *112* Lincoln Memorial, Mark Antman/ The Image Works; *112*
Pizza Hut scene, Reproduced with permission, © PepsiCo Inc. 1986; *121* single child family,
Jerry Howard/ Positive Images; *121* twins, Barbara Rios/Photo Researchers, Inc.; *129*

highway, Mark Antman/Stock, Boston; *129* supermarket, Robert A. Issacs/Photo Researchers, Inc.; *129* money machine, Mark Antman/The Image Works; *129* parade, Barbara Alper Stock, Boston; *137* nuclear family, Hella Hammid/Photo Researchers, Inc.; *137* extended family, Jerry Howard/Positive Images; *194* JFK as boy, John F. Kennedy Library; *194* JFK in PT boat, UPI/Bettmann Newsphotos; *194* JFK campaigning, Bruce Roberts/Photo Researchers, Inc.; *194* JFK with Jackie, John F. Kennedy Library.

Art

Drawings by George M. Ulrich and Glenna Lang.

Realia

Pie charts of "The Making of Americans," from *The New York Times*, April 10, 1988. Copyright © 1988 by The New York Times Company. Reprinted by permission.

Map of New York University. Reprinted by permission of New York University.

TV Schedule in *The New York Times* Television Guide for March 19–25, 1989. Copyright © 1989 by The New York Times Company. Reprinted by permission.

Tables of "Foreign Students in U.S.," "Regions of the world, student flows to U.S., 1976–1986" and "Leading countries of origin, 1978–1986." by George C. Christensen, Thomas B. Thielen and Julie Rose, *NAFSA Newsletter* (November 1987): pp. 3–6. Reprinted by permission.

Table of "Capital Cost of Eating." Copyright, September 21, 1987, *U.S. News & World Report.*

Pie charts of "Foreign Students Statistics," from NYU's *International Newsletter,* Spring 1988, v.4, No.2, p.2. Reprinted by permission.

Graph of "Freshman Goals: Spiritual vs. Financial," in "Freshmen Found Stressing Wealth," by Deirdre Carmody, *The New York Times* (January 14, 1988): p. A14. Copyright © 1988 by The New York Times Company. Reprinted by permission.

Pie chart of "Foreign Students by Field of Study, 1987/88" and Table of "Foreign Students by Field of Study, Selected Years, 1954/55–1987/88," in *"Open Doors: 1987/88* Report on International Educational Exchange," by Marianthi Zikopoulos, ed. (Institute of International Education), p. 24 +. Reprinted by permission.

Graph of "The Changing Balance of the Sexes," in "Coming Soon: More Men Than Women," by Jib Fowler, *The New York Times* (June 5, 1988). Copyright © 1988 by The New York Times Company. Reprinted by permission.